WITHDRAWN

WITH DEAREST LOVE TO ALL

WITH DEAREST LOVE TO ALL

*The Life and Letters
of Lady Jebb*

by

MARY REED
BOBBITT

CHICAGO

HENRY REGNERY COMPANY

With this book the author
pays tribute to Vassar College
on the occasion of its centennial

TO BOB

'As with novels, so with letters; women write better letters than men. They put in what we want to know, how people felt about things, how they lived, what they ate and wore, what they worried about—all those immediacies which make the life of an epoch live again.

'History should be written more from letters. Who cares about the Battle of Crécy, dates, places and all that we are crammed with in the name of history? What had they to do with it? History is from day to day; and it is not events, it is sociology; it is the progress of thought.'

from Alfred North Whitehead's
DIALOGUES

ILLUSTRATIONS

Richard Claverhouse Jebb, August, 1882

Maud DuPuy

George Darwin

Maud and George Darwin with Ella DuPuy holding her 'guitar', Newnham Grange. Photographed by Dew Smith

Portrait of Caroline Jebb by Sir William Blake Richmond, about 1888. Owned by the author

At the Cambridge boat races, June, 1887? Nellie DuPuy, centre top, in leg-o'-mutton sleeves. Carrie DuPuy is seated at her feet and to her right

Richard C. Jebb, M.P., 1895

PREFACE

————⟨⟩————

During childhood I was occasionally aware of some shoe-boxes full of letters from my great-aunt Cara Jebb which my mother, Emma DuPuy Reed of New York City, had inherited from her mother, Ellen Reynolds DuPuy, to whom they had been written. I am very grateful for my mother's vigilance in preserving them from the ravages of fifty years of house-cleaning, and for her imagination in feeling that there was 'a book there some place' if only it could be sought and found. When I finally decided to look through them, I saw that the first job lay in arranging them chronologically, since none of the letters was dated by year, and some of them not by month. Fortunately a few were still in their envelopes. Many of the letters were cross-written to save paper weight. The real task, however, was the selection of the letters that best presented the long past Civil War days, and her life in Victorian England thereafter.

I especially want to thank my English cousin Margaret (Lady Keynes) also a great-niece of Lady Jebb, who gave me endless encouragement and advice, and whose notes about many people mentioned in the letters make this book much more interesting than it might otherwise have been.

And much gratitude goes to a great-nephew of Lady Jebb, Herbert Spencer, of Erie, Pennsylvania, who kept her precious file of letters received from interesting correspondents, along with other papers. Not only did he send me these, but also her journal of Civil War times, her diary at Jebb's death, and several pictures and pertinent clippings.

Albion, Michigan   M. R. B.
U.S.A.

13

CHAPTER I

In *The Times* of July 24th, 1930, there appeared a letter entitled LADY JEBB, from 'a Cambridge friend', which read:

'Many who would have grieved deeply at the news of Lady Jebb's death (recorded in *The Times* earlier this month) are now no longer here to describe, as they would have done, a most brilliant and remarkable personality. Yet not a few remain on whom she made an ineffaceable impression. . . .

'It was not only that she possessed a Titianesque beauty of eyes, dark auburn hair, and rich colouring, but there was colour also and beauty in the tones of the voice which reminded one of Ellen Terry. . . . Lady Jebb had not only beauty but a fine mental equipment; and her literary capacity showed itself when she came to write the memoir of her husband. . . .

'Perhaps what was chiefly remarkable about her was her unusual vitality, a vitality of the mind as well as of the body. She was immensely interested in life, whether it was the life of nations and the achievements of statesmen, or the personal fortunes of her own friends, their hopes or disappointments, the mysteries of their successes or failures. . . .'

Who was this woman who provoked such feelings in the breasts of Englishmen? Caroline (or Carrie) Lane Reynolds was born to Eleanor and John Reynolds, rector of St. James Episcopal Church, Evansburg, Pennsylvania, on December 26th, 1840, their fourth and youngest child.

Her father John had emigrated to the United States and first married Ann Kettlewell in South Carolina, where they lived **and** had six children. When Ann died, he travelled north taking first one parish, then another, until he came to Evansburg or Perkiomen, where he met and married Carrie's mother, Eleanor Evans, in 1832.

Eleanor Evans was the youngest daughter of Owen Evans, 'a large landowner in Montgomery County, and a man of unusual ability and force of character. "Squire" Evans owned jointly with his cousin Oliver Evans the first steam-mill built in America at Pittsburgh, Pennsylvania. Moved by patriotism he also built a factory in his village of Evansburg for the manufacture of muskets, when the war with Great Britain began in 1812. He married his first cousin Eleanor Lane.'[1]

Another member of the Evans family was Carrie's cousin, Dr. John Evans, who was instrumental in the founding of Northwestern University, and who selected for its site the suburb of Chicago, which was afterwards named Evanston in his honour.[2]

After Carrie's father and mother were married, Eleanor soon found that the Reverend John Reynolds was not only an eccentric but an extremely selfish husband. One of the many stories of his high-handedness that survived was that on their wedding night he said to her, 'I always sleep in the middle of the bed, but you may take either side you wish.' And although it may have been an English custom, Eleanor could never understand why having used *her* money to buy their wedding silver, he had had *his* initials engraved on it.

Although John was selfish, he was original and amusing, while the rather humourless Eleanor may not have understood that facet of his character. His keen sense of humour, which was passed on to all his children, often saved him in disastrous situations. In later life he wore a bright red wig and thick glasses. Sometimes he would fall when outdoors, and sitting calmly on the sidewalk, he would say, 'No, I need no assistance. Pray, just hand me my glasses, and then I can find my wig and arise by myself.'

In later years Eleanor was asked why she had ever married such

[1] Caroline Jebb, *The Life and Letters of Sir R. C. Jebb*, Cambridge University Press, 1907, pp. 177–8.
[2] Charles Meredith DuPuy, *A Genealogical History of the DuPuy Family*, Phila, J. B. Lippincott, 1910, p. 91.

a difficult man, to which she replied it was because he had such beautiful pink cheeks. All the children inherited his clear complexion, in fact his daughters had such pretty colouring that they were often suspected of wearing rouge.

Carrie later wrote to her sister Ellen about her relationship with her mother. 'She and I always understood each other,' she wrote, 'and in my childish troubles, without either of us saying anything, I knew I had her sympathy. . . . Do you know I cannot recall the slightest occasion when in word or deed she deviated from the strictest truth? If she told stories of her youth, they were as exact as photographs. She was really a rare and remarkable character, as wise as she was good.

'When you think that she had no home teaching and only six months of school, her mastery of figures, her memory of the rules of grammar, etc., show what a fine intellect she had. She had a brave, strong spirit; and though her life was full of disappointment, she was really on the whole happy. She was always interested in everything which is a great point in happiness.'

Not much is known about Carrie's childhood. She used to say that her happiest days were spent in Kent, Connecticut, where her father had a church for a short while. She and her brother John played together constantly, and one winter they went coasting against their mother's orders. They met with an accident, the sled overturning in such a way that Carrie's arm was badly hurt, in fact a bone was broken. She was determined, however, that her mother should not know of their disobedience and never told her of the pain. Her arm finally mended, but was always shorter than her other one.

In the mid-century, Carrie's father was in charge of St. Barnabas' parish in Burlington, New Jersey, and the three girls were sent to St. Mary's Hall, a school still flourishing there today. The eldest daughter, Ellen, graduated at thirteen, then taught in her father's school, connected with his church in Hoboken, and at sixteen was teaching mathematics and classics at St. Mary's Hall, many of her pupils being older than she was. The other two girls graduated at early ages, too, for their father had taught all of them Latin and Greek before they went to school.

When Ellen was twenty she married Charles M. DuPuy, civil

engineer and inventor, of Philadelphia. Carrie, then only thirteen, had already begun to attract admirers, too. She received her first marriage proposal at the age of fourteen. (She later could account for thirty-seven such proposals, the last when she was seventy-seven.) Her parents had an uneasy time while she went dancing and riding with her many friends in Burlington, Perkiomen, Norristown and Philadelphia.

In the mid-1850's Carrie began to take special interest in an Army officer, eleven years older than she. Lieutenant Adam Jacoby Slemmer, originally from Norristown, had graduated from West Point Military Academy in 1850 with honour, ranking twelfth in a class of more than one hundred cadets. He had been stationed in Florida, where he took an active part in the war against the Seminole Indians and had been promoted for gallant conduct. After serving in California and elsewhere, he became an assistant professor of ethics and mathematics at West Point.

Carrie seems to have been swept off her feet by Addy, attracted, perhaps, by his handsome uniform, and the thought of an Army life of travel and adventure. The Reynolds were more than glad to have her settle down, and it was with a sigh of relief that they gave consent to the marriage of their sixteen-year-old daughter to Addy Slemmer in August, 1856.

The next year the Slemmers' baby, named Bertie, was born. Some time after this they were moved to Fort Moultrie, South Carolina, where Carrie wrote the first of her existing letters to her older sisters, Ellen and Polly, probably written in 1858 or 1859. This and all later letters beginning 'My dear Sister', were meant for Ellen DuPuy.

'My dear Sister,

Why shouldn't I be more punctilious about writing letters? I've been ten times busier, for the last few weeks, my dear, than kind fortune has ever compelled you to be. We made no less than two moves since we were cast on these hospitable shores, or rather sand banks. First, down into our own quarters, as soon as our goods came, and afterwards, into Captain Doubleday's end of the garrison. He and his wife have both gone East on a two months' leave, with the prospect of having it extended at the end of that time;

and so we thought we might as well be as comfortable as we could, and moved over into their rooms, which, by the way, are elegant. My parlour and bedroom are both twenty feet square besides the embrasures of the windows, all of which, and there are four to each room, open down to the floor, and have outside Venetian doors.

'I ought to have written you immediately, on my arrival, and then I could have given you accurate descriptions of all my surroundings while the impressions were still fresh. But now everything here seems so much like an old story that my pen can hardly be persuaded to write about anything so stale. I suppose you even yet remain in ignorance of the names of the "Defenders of their country" who are so fortunate, so the South Carolinians think, as to be stationed here? Each officer has some individual characteristic to distinguish him from the common herd.

'First in height, decidedly first in weight, first in years, and first in rank, stands Captain Abner Doubleday of the 1st Artillery, U.S. (very disrespectfully called "Old Forty-eight hours" by those who have no veneration for a man's patronymic). He is remarkable for being a thorough, simon pure, decided spiritualist, and for nothing else. Oh, I beg his pardon, he does tell anecdotes most amusingly. He had the misfortune to be in Mexico during the latter part of the war and you can't tell what a misfortune it is for other people. Lieut. Davis says that Capt. Doubleday was not within ten miles of a single battle, but of his own presence a man himself is the best judge, and Captain has told me, once a day, ever since I came here, that he participated in the battle of Monterey, always accompanying the information with a full, true and very particular account of the whole, from the moment they opened their eyes in the morning, up to the end of the third day, when they were allowed to close them again.

'He has gone out to Bloomington, Illinois, to see his mother, and he told me that if he had time he meant to call upon you, if he stopped in Chicago on his way back. If he does, just start him on Mexico, and if he gets talking about some of the eccentric officers he was thrown with there, you will pass a delightful evening. He is one of the most amusing men on a first acquaintance that I ever met. His only fault is that he is an extremely small pamphlet, and when you get to the end, as there are only five books in our library, one has to commence all over again.

'By far the most agreeable, and gentlemanly officer here is Lieut. Talbot, who was originally from Washington, and whose peculiarity is a devotion to the Roman Catholic religion, and to the fair sex, also. Lieut. Davis, who ranks next to him, isn't worth much, and is *only* remarkable for the extreme smallness and whiteness of his hands. Indeed, there is a suspicion extant that he rubs them with tallow every night, on retiring, and then covers them up with kid gloves.[1]

'Lieut. Tillinghast, our Regimental Quartermaster, has taken for Mrs. Tillinghast, Belle Wyman's sister, a woman I can't bear, although I have had the discretion not to inform her of the fact. I have seldom seen a woman moving in good society with so little of the real lady about her. She has only been married a year, but her army experiences extend back a much longer time. Her father, the theater manager, informed her once, after a quarrel still more violent than the ones they usually indulged in, that he wished she were dead, and that the sooner she left his house the better. So she thought she would go and keep house for her brother Lieut. Powell Wyman who was then stationed with Captain Brannen in Florida. Thereby hangs a tale.

'Do you remember reading about a year ago of the sudden disappearance of Mrs. Captain Brannen, daughter of Col. Crane, and sister of Surgeon Crane? Well, she and Wyman were in Florida together, and it came about that after a time, they were considerably too much together so that Captain Brannen was compelled to forbid Wyman the house, and also to forbid her to see him there, or elsewhere. One day when Captain Doubleday was walking on his porch he heard an awful scream which came from the garden, and almost in the same breath, he heard Brannen say, "For God's sake, Doubleday, Tillinghast, come here!"

'Captain Doubleday says he rushed down to the garden immediately, and there saw Wyman holding Captain Brannen with one hand, and trying to draw a pistol with the other. Before anyone

[1] All of these officers were later helpful to Major Anderson when they left Moultrie and went across by night to Fort Sumter, December, 1860.

could prevent it, he fired one barrel, without effect, and was trying to fire the other barrel, when he was seized and prevented. Mrs. Brannen was standing by with her hair all disarranged, and just as the officers came up, she screamed, and fell over in violent hysterics.

'Soon after that her husband sent her home to her relations, but her influence over him was still so great that she was able to persuade him to hush the matter up, and for the sake of her reputation, not to pursue Wyman with the law. He was transferred at once to another company, and Miss Wyman came with him. Wyman is now in Europe on a year's leave, with the intention of resigning, when his leave is up. His position in the army is very unpleasant, as he is now almost universally cut by all the officers. He is an exceedingly intelligent and gentlemanly officer.

'We have been having a great deal of gaiety at this post lately, owing to the presence of ten strange officers who were ordered here on Court Martial to try Lieut. Tillinghast for insubordination and conduct not becoming an officer and a gentleman. He was pronounced guilty, but as there were many extenuating circumstances, his punishment was simply a reprimand.

'Our Charleston society is very pleasant, and some of the first people there have given me cordial invitations to visit. This Sullivan's Island, where we are situated, is their summer resort from the yellow fever, you know. Please give my love to Charlie and the little ones, and believe me,

Your affectionate sister,

CARRIE'

In the spring of 1860 the Slemmers were sent from Moultrie to Barrancas Barracks, about eight miles from Pensacola, Florida, in the north-west part of the state. Nearby was the Federal Navy-yard, at Warrington, a small village, with Commodore Armstrong in command. Heavy frigate-like warships were built there, and the gulf fleet was stationed there a great part of the time. Brigs, schooners and full-rigged ships loading cotton, some for Massachusetts, and some for England, made Pensacola a humming metropolis.

Carrie wrote again to Ellen, April 29th, 1860.

'Please ma'am, don't be thinking dreadful things of me because of my not writing sooner. . . . Guess where I am? Not on that Paradise, just three miles long called Sullivan's Island, where the sullen ocean regardless of your mood persists in its monotonous music, all the year round. Nor yet resting in that charming spot, familiarly called Norristown. . . . Any letters addressed to me at Warrington, Florida, will be pretty sure of reaching my hands. On consideration, I'm not so sure of that either. If the letters have to travel the same circuitous and disagreeable route which I "just managed to survive", the chances are ten to one that they will be tired out before they get half through, and give it up in despair. The route to this place is a hard road to travel, and its conclusion is not quite like the other side of Jordan, at least so I thought when I first came here.

'Now the Gulf, so blue with its white borders of sand, the magnolia blossoms so beautiful, and the China trees so fragrant with their loads of flowers compel me almost against my will to acknowledge that "all save the spirit of man is divine". By the "spirit of man" I mean society, of course. I came here with the intention of finding fault with everything and everybody, and one does not like to be "baulked of one's intentions" by not discovering any fault to find.

'I was so sorry to leave Charleston where I had for the first time in my life been perfectly contented, that I think in my mind an Eden would suffer in comparison with my darling little sand bank of an island. Just think how much it means to be perfectly contented for six months with all your surroundings and all your associates so as never to desire a change. I never expect to have it happen to me again. If we were to be sent back to the same place next year, it would not be the same as it was, for some of the people would be changed, and even if that were not so, as somebody says with truth, "we never take up a friendship where we lay it down."

'The friend whose attention and friendship tended more than any other to make me happy is slowly dying of consumption, and I cannot hope ever to see him again. You cannot tell the misery of saying goodbye to a friend whom you love with the certain knowledge that not only time and distance, but very soon death will separate you beyond the hope of remedy. Man, I think, was meant to do great things in the world, and that is the reason we find it so hard to realize that there are barriers we *cannot* overcome, try as hard as we may. I cannot hope ever to be so completely happy again.

'There, I think I have wearied you sufficiently with my regrets now. I will take up a book, and see if an hour's reading will not restore some tone to my spirits. If I can only persevere, it will have some effect, but generally after ten minutes, my book falls into my lap, my eyes fix themselves dreamily on the blue water, and my thoughts go back with an unutterable longing to my last home. There are other things besides hope deferred which make the heart sick. I have had in my mind all day long one text of scripture, which I cannot banish, "Verily the heart knoweth its own bitterness and the stranger intermeddleth not with its joy."

'Now here comes an interruption in good earnest. Two Navy officers who do me the honor of thinking me very pretty and agreeable, are coming for me to walk and as any company is better than my own, I will not say them nay. Au revoir.

'My walk is over, Sunday is gone, and on Monday morning I resume this letter in, I hope, a somewhat more cheerful strain. I thought at first I would tell you the reason of this transfer, but it is a very long story, and so I think I will leave it until a more convenient season. There is another reason, to tell it will certainly make me feel badly as thinking about it always does, and I am learning to be very careful of my feelings, and to banish as well as I may all thoughts which tend to make me unhappy.

'Everybody says my arrival here is a great success. You know, we have a Navy-yard within a mile of us, where a number of officers are constantly stationed, which together with the Man-of-Wars, which are always coming and going, make up quite a pleasant little society. Although I have been here not quite two weeks almost everybody has called on me, and a day seldom goes by without some of the officers come here to call for me to go walk. Night before last, I had an escort of four, besides my husband. I am grown more talkative and gayer than ever, now my heart is not in it, and every day I hear remarks made about my youth and freshness and charming naïveté, and I wonder to

23

myself if people ever have heard of whited sepulchres, outside fair and beautiful, but inside full of dead men's bones.

'Most of the Navy officers here just now are married, but that makes them none the less gallant, as they say if they were to give up all society on their wives' account and shut themselves up in their ships, they would be worse off than the single officers who can always, while on shore, solace themselves with society. The Winder family and ourselves were invited to go on board the *Savannah* a couple of days ago, and I was very much pleased with the inspection. Lieut. Cunard, my escort, after talking very pleasantly to me for ten minutes, turned round abruptly and to my utter astonishment ordered all the officers under him officially not to answer any more of Mrs. Slemmer's questions, for she asked too many; it was his opinion she intended to write a book. This was done so seriously, that for a moment I thought he was in earnest.

'After we left the ship, the officers in solemn conclave discussing the subject of our visit, Resolved: First, if it was the first Man-of-War Mrs. Slemmer had ever visited, then she did not see anything, as she talked too much to do two things well at once, and, Secondly, that this opinion be conveyed to Mrs. Slemmer as tenderly as possible by her warm friend and admirer, Lieut. Worden, and, Resolved: That she be invited to visit the ship again as soon as possible to remedy her fault. Lieut. Cunard told Addy that the next time I was to come without him, and they would immediately put out to sea and relieve him of a wife who must drive him half distracted.

'We are boarding now as our house is not quite ready for us yet, and you cannot tell how happy I shall be to go to housekeeping again. It is so awkward not to be able to ask gentlemen in to tea after walking that I should rejoice on this account solely, if there were no other reasons. I have made very good friends already of Colonel Winder's family, but I have not room to tell you anything about them in this letter. . . .[1]

'With dearest love to all. . . .'

[1] John H. Winder, Captain of Company G., 1st U.S. Artillery, at Barrancas Barracks, later became a brigadier general in the Confederate Army, and was widely known for his cruelty in connection with the military prisons in the

It has been said that at one time the Slemmers had to transfer to another post because Carrie and another officer were becoming too enamoured of each other. When she realized how seriously they were beginning to feel, she went immediately to her husband, told him the situation, and thereupon they both agreed that they must move away to another post. It was probably this move from Moultrie to Pensacola, as her letter would indicate.

She wrote more in detail about their arrival to her other sister in May, 1860.

'My dear Mary,

It does seem to me that I have done nothing but scribble ever since we came here. . . . I intend to ask for the return of all my letters describing "My Travels through the State of Florida", and then they can be published in royal octavo form, and assuredly will make quite a volume. The journey was a varied and adventurous one, by car and steamboat and stage, and took precisely six days to accomplish, and if I were not so tired of the subject I would fill some pages with an account of it, but I am sick as can be of it, and rather than write another word about it, I would close my letter abruptly, even at this early stage of the undertaking.

'Coming from Cedar Keys to Pensacola, we met in the steamboat a cousin of Captain Newton, a Dr. Newton, sister, and niece, whom we found to be very pleasant and agreeable people. One of the officers stationed at the Navy-yard, Lieut. Stark of the Marines, came on the vessel to meet them at Pensacola, and was consequently introduced to us. When we got to Warrington, Mr. Stark's acquaintance proved to be of some service, as we hardly knew, with baby, bird cage and servant, where to go at first.

'As we knew our boxes would not come for a month, we thought we would try to get board for a month or so, until we could look about us a little and decide what quarters to take. Mr. Stark told us that he knew of no place not full, but suggested that I and my accompaniments should repair to his quarters and wait there until Mr. Slemmer could ride up to the Barrancas Barracks and see Colonel Winder.

South. An idea of his character has been given in *Andersonville*, by MacKinlay Kantor.

'This we did, and although it was very ungrateful, I never have been so much amused as I was at Mr. Stark's efforts to entertain such unwonted guests. First, he saw us comfortably seated in his bachelor parlor, and then, after ducking his head in a manner impossible to describe (he is only twenty-five, and is intensely awkward and bashful,) [Carrie was twenty] he disappeared and returned, almost immediately with Lieut. Hebb, who shared his quarters. This satisfied him for a little while, but not long. A second disappearance was followed by his return with Captain Simms, the head of the Marine Corps here, and then the expression of relief which flitted across his animated countenance was beautiful to witness. It said as plain as face could say, "There, I have done my best for you, if you are not satisfied with *him*, you are indeed unreasonable.". . . .

'For four mortal hours I had to talk to those three strange officers, and it was with unutterable relief that I saw Addy return with Col. Winder, and Lieuts. Eddy and Gilman, to take me up to the Colonel's where we stayed for two days, and then went to boarding until the Winders went away, and left Addy Commanding Officer, when we moved into the Colonel's quarters, and we are now situated as comfortably as we could desire.

'With dearest love to all. . . .'

Caroline Buck, wife of an officer at Moultrie, wrote to her friend Carrie Slemmer in May, soon after they left there.

'I suppose by this time you are beginning to feel quite at home at Pensacola and begin to forget that Fort Moultrie was a very nice place. You are much missed. Indeed I can pay you the compliment of saying that you are more missed than any of the rest of us would be, should we leave. Your rocking chair, though I use it a great deal, does not seem to have the same effect on me that it used to have upon *you*. I am no more eloquent than formerly. I rock and rock, but the words don't come, and I almost begin to imagine that the chair had nothing to do with it. Have you a rocking chair now? . . .'

Another letter from Carrie to her sister Ellen, June 19th, 1860,

'My dear Sister,

The sun was so warm this morning that I concluded not to go to church and the consequence is this prompt response to your last letter. I do not like to stay home from church when I can help it, as Sunday seems so long up on this quiet hill, when one has nothing to do, and nothing pleasant to think about, and when we go down to the Navy-yard it seems to brighten one up to shake hands and chat with everybody. As we always have to ride both ways, we seldom get home before two o'clock, so that Sunday generally seems shorter than other days.

'I have just commenced to have weekly receptions in an unostentatious way, and I think the plan will answer very well. It is a very long walk up to Barrancas from the Navy-yard and the people do not like, when they take it, to find me absent and then be compelled to turn round and retrace their steps, so now I tell all the officers that I am certain to be home every Wednesday evening and I always invite two or three ladies to tea and then in the evening we either dance or play games. I have had three now, and they were all well attended, and everybody seemed to enjoy themselves very much, and then it is a very inexpensive way of having company. I never need to have anything but cake and wine, and that is no trouble.

'Mrs. Love gave a very pleasant dance at her house on Friday, and a couple of weeks since, a large party was given by Mrs. Gilman. The next morning Mr. Abert quite surprised me by sending up the *Pensacola Gazette* where I found in print that I had been "the center of attraction" the evening before.[1] So you see if the weather is warm, we are not likely to suffer from loneliness here. . . .

'I wish you could see how delightfully we are situated here, and what a charming house for a warm climate we live in, with its large rooms and high ceilings, its wide open hall and its long cool verandah extending round three sides; and the grounds are fit for a king. . . .'

Barrancas Barracks, Aug. 28th, 1860

'My dear Sister,

. . . As for letters, you would not have the heart to expect much

---

[1] Unfortunately none of the *Pensacola Gazettes* of these years are in existence.

27

from Barrancas, if you could realize the energy-destroying atmosphere we live in here. It is so delicious and makes one so good-for-nothing. I neither sew much, nor read much, nor do anything much, but talk. I have not paid a visit for three weeks, and when anything I care so much about is neglected, where do you suppose writing letters will stand? I think it is all a mistake about leaving Florida in the summer, and going North. As far as climate goes, I never want to leave the South again. The cool constant sea-breeze tempers the heat for us. The delicious long twilight evenings are just made for long walks and talks; and then when the moon comes up, we take such nice sails on the Gulf. In the Navy-yard on moonlight evenings, the people all go down to the wharf and amuse themselves with games and music, and sometimes we pay them a visit. Last evening all Barrancas, consisting of Mr. and Mrs. Gilman, Mr. Beese, an engineer officer, and Mr. and Mrs. Slemmer went down in a row boat, (not to the bottom of the sea) and had a glorious time.

'I have had a new amusement opened to me lately which I think perfectly delightful. On the anniversary of our wedding day, Addy made me a present of a very nice saddle horse, and as soon as the weather becomes a little cooler, I intend to scour the country, far and near. I have taken four or five delightful rides already, and have made myself a very nice linen riding dress. I anticipate a great deal of pleasure from this source this winter.

'Oh, dear, these mosquitoes! Banish them, and this country would be Paradise, but then one can't and sometimes they are almost unendurable. Just now they are presenting their bills with ferocious eagerness, as if I owed the vampires anything. I shall be so glad when winter comes so that we may escape these torments.

'We have been quite excited lately by the coming of a rumor, which said that the whole 1st Artillery regiment was to be sent to California in the spring, and of all things, that we would have to cross the plains to get there. We have heard nothing since the first report, to corroborate this, and so hope it may not be true. I for one do not want to go at all. I have no dread of the new country, and the distance, but the thought of the length of time we will probably have to remain and of the changes I shall undergo myself, and the changes I find on my return in those I leave behind, almost frightens me.

'Shall I know you when I see a dignified lady of thirty-six or seven, looking by no means old for her age, but still very different from the sister who was only twenty-six when I last saw her? I wonder how many children will surround her then, that will be utter strangers to me? And above all, I wonder if she will recognize me, quiet and subdued, with not a trace of the bloom and animation and flow of spirits, for which people used to flatter me?

'Frankly, I confess I am afraid to grow old. Age will come gently, almost imperceptibly, on you with your children's youth to keep you young; and your husband to love you, and, above all, for you to love. Jean Paul says that *love* is the real fountain of youth. As for me, I shall probably have but one child, I am content that it should be so, and though my husband's love for me never fails to surprise me, when I think of it, yet our tastes are too much at variance to bring happiness. . . .

'I sometimes think it would be pleasant to have a home with everything settled and comfortable around, where I might make some real friends, and keep them. This constant changing gets to be terribly monotonous with time. New places do not seem new to me, and the people that I meet are the same with only different faces. I should like exceedingly to be stationed near you, even if it were to take me to that cold disagreeable Mackinac [Michigan].

'Mary wrote to me about Pa, and my surprise at his having at last got a parish even if only for a year, overcame even my indignation at his wanting her to go with him. That is the only comfort I have in being so far away: he cannot come to see his daughter Caroline! I am very much obliged to you for asking me to come to Chicago but this climate seems to agree with me wonderfully, and Bertie, also.

'He is growing very finely and is a splendid little fellow, both mentally and physically, strong, sturdy and handsome. He is really sweeter and prettier every day, and sometimes he is *so* sweet, I could almost eat him up. He talks very well now and is a perfect boy, and very smart in every way. I do hope he will be worth something when he grows up. I do want somebody to be proud of so much.

'I wish you knew some of the people here so that I might write to you about them a little. I should like to introduce to you Mrs. Carrington very much. She is the best friend I have here and is an exceedingly cultivated and refined lady. The Virginia ladies against the rest of the world for me. I think she has perfect manners, and so does everybody else.

'My belleship, as you are pleased to call it, has died down woefully of late, since all the ships went out. Everything is very quiet comparatively now. Mr. Hebb comes up about once a week to play backgammon and Mr. Abert to take me out riding, and these are at present the only single gentlemen at the Navy-yard. We are going down to have a little dance at Mrs. Warrington's tonight. There are two other beaux whom I forgot to mention, neither of whom I can bear: Frank Shippy and Dallas MacIntosh. . . .'

CHAPTER II

For months the murmur of dissension had been rising throughout the South. Political leaders were conferring with each other on possible eventualities, and arms were being stored in secret places by the state governments. In 1860 volunteer companies began to drill on the parade grounds of many southern towns. At Warrington the local company swelled its ranks, drilling faithfully, and the workmen in the Navy-yard went about their work in a sullen mood. The secret organizations began to come out into the open and talk plainly of their intentions. Guards of the Navy-yard were doubled, then trebled, as a precaution against night prowlers and incendiaries.

The first spark that set off the conflagration appeared at Charleston Harbour, the Slemmers' previous post. On Christmas night, Major Anderson crossed over to Fort Sumter with his whole company in the twilight. The next morning Charleston was hopping mad, messengers were sent out to ring door-bells, and tell every family the news and the governor immediately demanded that the men return to Moultrie. Anderson replied that since he had been assigned to defend Charleston Harbour, he intended to do just that, although he was a Southerner himself. Apparently he did not want reinforcements, and shrank from civil war, enduring hostilities from the secessionists, but hoping that Congress would make some compromise that would save slavery and the Union together.[1]

When Slemmer learned, early in January, that State troops planned to seize all U.S. forts and other property in the South, and that Florida and Alabama troops were already planning to take

[1] Brevet-Major Abner Doubleday, 'From Moultrie to Sumter', in *Battles and Leaders of the Civil War*, Century, 1887, p. 46.

the Navy-yard and all forts in Pensacola Harbour, he must have realized the similarity of his position to that of Major Anderson's at Moultrie. If force were to be used against Pensacola, they too could withdraw to old Fort Pickens on a nearby island, Santa Rosa, and take their stand against the Confederates.

Addy also kept hoping that a civil war might be averted. These Southerners had been their close friends and they could not think of fighting them. He kept expecting that some instructions would come from President Buchanan. Lincoln had been elected, but did not take office until March, so directions from Washington were confused or none at all. Buchanan was an old man who loved the Union and could not bear to see it destroyed. He did not believe that a state had the right to secede, but at the same time he did not feel that the Union had any right to prevent it by force.

This was the atmosphere in which Carrie wrote her next letter dated January 5th, 1861. Since the first few pages were still mostly concerned with social gaieties in spite of the nearness of war, perhaps Addy had not yet told her of the imminent danger, or possibly she did not want to worry her sister.

'My dear Sister,

Having nothing particular to occupy my time and attention this afternoon, I do not believe I can employ the hour more advantageously than by answering your letter. The *Crusader* went out yesterday and at present I am insane enough to be very glad of it, although I dare say in a week's time I shall feel as sorry as everybody else appears to now.

'There never has been so gay a month in my life as the month of December A.D. 1860, and I don't believe in any other place there could be. "What Christmas can be as we grow older" was practically illustrated in a most delightful manner to me. We danced Christmas *in* at Mrs. Warrington's, and we danced Christmas *out* at a hop given by the officers of the ships in port, and every other night we met at some house and danced until morning. You will probably laugh at my silliness when I assure you that at every party your bashful and retiring sister Caroline was undoubtedly the woman whose hand was most sought after in the dance, and whose tongue was most eagerly listened to. The ambition to be a belle seems low and mean when one thinks about it afterwards, but its realization at the time is delicious. To carry away the palm from women much more handsome, much better dressed, much older and more experienced, gives one a pleasant taste of power at the time and leaves no sting afterwards.

'There is one lady here who is infinitely prettier than I am, besides possessing a wonderfully sweet disposition, and yet she is often sitting quietly by, while half a dozen of the best men in the room stand laughing and talking around my corner. Navy society is the most fascinating in the world, they are so glad to be on shore among their own people after being at sea that to talk to the officers is refreshing beyond measure. If I knew to a dead certainty that I should suffer years afterwards for my heedlessness now, I should still go on doing as I do. Life has little enough enjoyment in store for the happiest, and the few crumbs of pleasure that fall to my share I mean to accept thankfully and make go as far as possible. That I cannot have the whole cake I realize acutely enough, but I can stay my hunger for happiness now and then, and I should be a fool not to do so.

'I don't feel any call to be a saint just now. When I do, I will listen to it. At present I am content to be what Captain Moffitt called me the other night, "a charming little sinner." Imprudent I know I am, but no one ever suspected me for a moment of anything worse. I treat people in a friendly way, but I treat *all* alike.

'You say I resemble Becky Sharp, and, in one or two things, I confess the "soft impeachment", but her worst fault I am free of. She would do anything for money; I, nothing. I am surprised at your recent introduction to the enterprising young lady. She and I are old acquaintances. Don't you like her better than Amelia? I like Thackeray very much. Better than any living writer. . . .'

But here Carrie had to break off abruptly, since events were too exciting for her to sit still and write. Her husband had called a conference of military and naval officers at their home to consider what to do next. She heard them discussing their problems over and over: the attitude of the surrounding country had changed from hostile to belligerent, their nearest base of support was a month's journey distant by ship, their men were too few to man the forts and Navy-yard, let alone hold them against an assault. Should they run off and take ship to the north? Or should they quietly surrender to the larger force of men? Who would dare start such a thing as a war against friends?

Carrie listened as long as she could as they kept returning to the question of surrender or war, and after a particularly long silence, she jumped to her feet, saying, 'If you men won't fire the first shot to protect our flag, then I will!' Her enthusiasm was infectious and thus they decided to go ahead and withdraw to Fort Pickens and fight if necessary.

On Monday, January 7th, Addy called on Commodore Armstrong, at the Navy-yard, and asked his co-operation, but having no special orders to do so, Armstrong declined. The next day the first step was taken by the Federal men indicating their intention to resist, by the removal of the powder from the Spanish fort (the small original fort adjacent to the Barrancas Barracks) to Fort Barrancas, where on the same night a guard was placed with loaded muskets.

It was just in time, for about midnight a party of twenty men came to the fort, evidently with the intention of taking possession, expecting to find it unoccupied as usual. Being challenged and not answering nor halting when ordered, the party was fired upon by the guard and ran in the direction of Warrington, their footsteps resounding on the plank walk as Slemmer's company started for the fort at double-quick.

At last on January 9th an order came from General Scott, Supreme Commander of the U.S. Army, to Slemmer to do all he could to prevent seizure of public property and to co-operate with Commodore Armstrong at the Yard. The latter received orders on the same day to co-operate with the Army, but Armstrong was already so greatly under the influence of Captain Ebenezer Farrand and other secessionist officers of his command that he dared not take any very active part in aiding the Army, not even so far as to send over the Marines, as he had promised.

The excitement at the Yard and in the village of Warrington was intense and was increasing daily, and the Commodore was nearly distracted. He wanted to do his duty, and apparently saw it clearly while Slemmer was with him, but as soon as the Army officers left him, he became demoralized, and was thwarted in his plans by his own officers and others about him, who advised and warned him not to inaugurate civil war and bloodshed by aiding Slemmer in what they called 'the mad scheme of resisting the State authorities'.

Fearing that as soon as the determination to occupy Pickens became known, attempts would be made to prevent it, Slemmer decided to move at once, and the Commodore promised to have the *Wyandotte* at Barrancas to take them across at 1 p.m. that day. He did not, however, and Slemmer had to visit the Commodore twice more that day to counteract the influence of those about him. The steamer was again promised at 5 p.m. but did not arrive.[1]

On this day Carrie took a few hurried minutes to finish her letter to Ellen.

'The first sheet of my letter was written several days ago, and though I have only a few moments now, I will complete it for the next mail. You will know by this time that we are out of the Union. Addy is in Command here which gives him great responsibility. We intend going to Fort Pickens tomorrow, and will, of course, stand on the defensive. The feeling here seems very warlike. Fort Barrancas is so large that with only 45 men, nothing can be done. So Addy intends to move to a position which there is some prospect of holding. If he can find a good escort for me, he intends to send me north. . . . . We heard yesterday that some Mobilians were on their way down here to seize these forts and so command the harbor. Everybody in the Navy-yard is Southern so they will not meet with much resistance there.

'I think the Government is acting shamefully towards the Army, sending neither orders nor reinforcements, where goodness knows they are needed badly enough. Ft. Pickens, the position we intend to take, is the most important stronghold in this part of the Gulf and is about a mile or half a mile from Barrancas. I don't want to go there at all, as it will be so dreadfully lonely. We will not be able to go anywhere without a boat, as the fort is on Santa Rosa Island.

[1] Brevet-Lieut.-Col. J. H. Gilman, 'With Slemmer in Pensacola Harbor', in *Battles and Leaders*, p. 27.

'I cannot write any more, as Addy and some Navy officers whom I have been expecting are coming up the steps now——

'Love to all,

Your affectionate sister,

CAROLINE.'

Harper's Weekly, February 23rd, 1861, described Fort Pickens and included these sentences, 'Its ditch is usually so full of moccasin and rattlesnakes as to be a peculiarly bad place of transit. In fact the whole island is infested with them.' Loneliness might have been the least of Carrie's worries!

Lieutenant Gilman later described their movements. 'In a large flat-boat or scow, and several small boats loaded with our men, provisions, brass field-pieces, ammunition, tools, and whatever public property was most needed and could be carried, including, I remember, an old mule and cart (which afterwards proved of great service to us), we were towed over to Pickens and landed there about 10 a.m., January 10th. Lt. Slemmer's family and mine were sent on board the store-ship *Supply*, on which, a few days later, they sailed for New York.

'All our men were compelled to leave behind more or less personal property, those who were married leaving their houses and families as they were. Under such circumstances, when so many inducements were held out for men to desert, and when so many men in higher places failed, it speaks well for their character, loyalty, and discipline that none of our men deserted. No company of men could work better or with more enthusiasm, and they were not at all disposed to give information to those outside.'[1]

Carrie later described their retreat in *Harper's Weekly*. 'The exodus from Barrancas was made necessarily in much haste, there being little time except hurriedly to pack up the most valuable of our articles of furniture and wardrobe. No personal violence was offered to these retreating women and children; but the sudden breaking-up of so many peaceful households, and the violent separation of family ties, were cause of great distress. To many, the parting of husband and wife was as if for the last time, and

[1] Gilman, ibid., p. 28.

tears bedewed many a hardy cheek when the last goodbye was spoken.

'During the day and night of the evacuation of Barrancas, and the transfer of the garrison to Fort Pickens, every person, men, officers and their wives, performed prodigies of labor, and never obtained a wink of sleep for nearly twenty-four hours. The hard work fell about equally upon all, without regard to rank or sex. The ladies cheerfully performed their part throughout the trying ordeal.

'On the day following the embarkation of the families on board the *Supply*, Mrs. Gilman and Mrs. Slemmer, accompanied by officers from the storeship, went on shore under a flag of truce, to obtain a last interview with their husbands. Every step of their progress was met by armed officials. They were obliged, first, to obtain permission from the new Commandant of the Navy-yard, Randolph, who ten days before had resigned his commission in the Navy. This was very reluctantly granted, after appeals had been made to him as a husband and father. They then had to pass the Barrancas forts, whose Commander, after some hesitation, allowed them to pass. In this place, so lately deserted by these peaceful and happy families, all was now confusion. The un-disciplined soldiers or their understrappers had broken open some of the trunks and boxes containing the wardrobes and household relics of Colonel Winder, late Commander, probably in pursuit of clothing for their own use; and they saw ladies' dresses and family daguerreotypes scattered about with little regard to their vaunted respect for the rights of personal property. . . .'

Gilman had said that the withdrawal was not completed until January 11th, so that may have been the reason the wives had to return to the mainland from the *Supply* rather than to the Island, to say good-bye to their husbands.

Reports of contemporary newspapers were often inaccurate at this time, but there is the ring of truth in a characteristic remark made by Carrie reported in an article on Pensacola and its forts in *Frank Leslie's Illustrated Newspaper*, February 9th, 1861. 'It is said that after [Slemmer] had abandoned Fort McRea [*sic*] Mrs. Slemmer went thither to procure some of his wearing apparel, and, it being denied her, she indignantly left, saying, she herself on her return to Fort Pickens, would man one of the guns.'

Harper's Cyclopaedia of U.S. History says, 'Among Slemmer's workers were the heroic wives of Lt. Slemmer and Gilman, refined and cultivated women, whose labors at this crisis form a part of the history of Fort Pickens.' While an item in the Personal Column of *Harper's Weekly*, February 9th, stated, 'The gallantry exhibited by the wife of Lt. Slemmer, at Pensacola, is creating quite a lively sensation among the patriotic ladies at Washington. A suitable testimonial in her behalf is in contemplation.'

Another article in *Harper's Weekly*, February 2nd, said,

'MRS. SLEMMER ARRESTED AS A SPY

'The Mobile, Alabama, *Mercury* of the 23rd learns from a letter from one of Capt. O'Hara's Company, now at Pensacola, to his wife in Mobile, that the wife of Lieut. Slemmer, Commander at Ft. Pickens, had been arrested at Ft. Barrancas without any ostensible business, and the reasonable supposition was that she had gone there to take notes of the position of things and report them to her husband.'

This was probably just a rumour, since she was not in the vicinity long enough to help in that way. Neither did she ever mention it later, although she did say that when she went marketing in Pensacola, before leaving Barrancas, she was snubbed as being the wife of a Federal officer, and once was surrounded by an unfriendly crowd.

The men at Fort Pickens now felt sure that they would be attacked at any minute. The enemy was in possession of everything on the mainland and Fort Pickens was in a very dilapidated condition, not having been occupied since the Mexican War. Including the thirty ordinary seamen, they numbered only eighty-one men.

Just before sundown of the 11th, four men came over and demanded of the corporal on guard admittance to the fort as 'citizens of Florida and Alabama'. Slemmer and Gilman went to the gate and found Mr. Abert standing there, a civil engineer of the Yard, and one of Carrie's former admirers. With him were three officers whom he introduced as Captain Randolph, Major Marks and Lieutenant Rutlidge. Captain Randolph said, 'We have been sent by the governors of Florida and Alabama to demand a peaceable surrender of this fort.' Lieutenant Slemmer replied, 'I am here by authority of the President of the United States, and I do not recognize the authority of any governor to demand the surrender of U.S. property—a governor is nobody here.'

One of them exclaimed sharply, 'Do you say the Governor of Florida is nobody, the Governor of Alabama, nobody?' To which Slemmer replied, 'I know neither of them, and I mean to say that they are nothing to me.' Since they felt they were getting nowhere with the stubborn Slemmer, they soon left.

The next night a small party of armed men was discovered near the fort by the patrol, and a few shots were fired. The men at Pickens had little fear of an attack by day, but had every reason to expect a night attack, an attempt to surprise them and carry the place by storm. All the men had to work by day mounting guns, preparing fire-balls, and hand-grenades, and by night do picket or patrol duty or stand by the guns. They were completely worn out with hard work and want of sleep, not having had a night's rest since January 7th.

On the 15th, Colonel Chase, commanding the enemy's forces at the Yard and Barrancas, came over in a small boat with Captain Farrand, formerly of the U.S. Navy, and next in rank at the Yard to Commodore Armstrong, and landed at the Pickens wharf, where Slemmer and Gilman met them, and the following conversation took place, as reported by Gilman.

'Col. Chase: I have come on business which may occupy some time, and, if you have no objection, we had better go inside to your quarters.

'Slemmer: I have objections, and it could hardly be expected that I would take you into the fort.

'Chase: As I built the fort and know all its weak and strong points, I would learn nothing new by going in, and had no such object in proposing it.

'Slemmer: I understand that perfectly, but it would be improper for me to take you in; and, however well you may have known the fort before, you do not know what it now contains, nor what I have done inside.

'Chase: That is true, and I will state my business here. It is a most distressing duty to me. I have come to ask of you young officers, officers of the same army in which I have spent the best and happiest years of my life, the surrender of this fort. I would not ask it if I did not believe it right and necessary to save bloodshed; and fearing that I might not be able to say it as I ought, and in order also that you may have it in proper form, I have put it in writing and will read it.

'He then took the manuscript from his pocket and began to read, but, after reading a few lines, his voice shook, and his eyes filled with tears. He stamped his foot, as if ashamed of exhibiting such weakness, and said, "I can't read it. Here, Farrand, you read it." Capt. Farrand took it, and remarking that he hadn't his glasses, and his eyes were poor (they looked watery), passed the paper to me, saying, "Here, Gilman, you have good eyes, please read it." I took the paper and read aloud the demand for the surrender. As soon as I finished, I handed the paper to Lt. Slemmer, when he and I went a few paces away; and after talking the matter over, it was decided, in order to gain time and give our men a night's rest, to ask until next day to consider the matter.... The next day another refusal to surrender was sent the Confederates, Captain Berryman of the *Wyandotte* taking it to the Navy-yard. Immediately after this, I think, the *Supply* sailed for New York.'[1]

After a rough passage of almost a month, Carrie with her baby and Negro nurse, finally arrived in New York. Their ship had been crowded with passengers and about seventy prisoners of war whom the rebels had captured at Pensacola and dismissed on parole.

By this time the tension at Pickens seems to have relaxed for a while, and Slemmer was able to get newspapers and some food from the Navy-yard. A truce was made that as long as Pickens was not reinforced (the U.S. ship *Brooklyn* was now lying off shore) the secessionists would not attack. Carrie must have enjoyed reading some of the newspaper items during the next few weeks, such as:

[1] Gilman, ibid., pp. 29–31.

'Lieut. Slemmer, like his compatriot soldier, Anderson, has been placed in a very prominent position by the present crisis. But this was in the blood, which a brave sailor says is ever thicker than water, for his grandfather was a gallant soldier in the Revolution.... No immediate hostilities are expected, as by the last accounts he had concluded an armistice with the forces of the Seceding states.'[1]

'At latest date Slemmer was still in possession, and said he could hold Ft. Pickens. Lt. Slemmer enjoys the reputation of a cool, brave soldier, worthy of the important trust now committed to him.'[2]

'Lt. Slemmer is one of the kind of men that would wrap himself up in the American flag, and, if necessary, blow the whole thing to atoms. He does not look like a very extraordinary man, he is so small and insignificant looking; but when he says he will do a thing, you may bet your entire pile he will. I never saw a man in my life that could equal him in coolness. Amidst all the excitement he is as unconcerned-looking as if he had nothing to worry him in the world.'[3]

'MRS. SLEMMER

'This lady ... is now in her twentieth year. She was distinguished at school for great aptitude for learning, and excessive fondness for reading. Out of school though generally seen with some miscellaneous book in hand, yet in school she was probably never known to be deficient with her lesson. Her education has been very complete. Her intellectual faculties are of the highest order. Her mind is quick, strong and courageous. In face and feature she is extremely prepossessing, with very captivating manners. She is worthy to be the wife of an American soldier.'[4]

In March when General Braxton Bragg assumed command of

---

[1] *Frank Leslie's Illustrated Newspaper*, Feb. 16th, 1861.

[2] *Harper's Weekly*, Feb. 23rd, 1861.

[3] A letter from one of the officers of the *Wyandotte* appearing in the *New York Herald*, April 23rd.

[4] *Frank Leslie's Illustrated Newspaper*, Feb. 16th, 1861.

all the Confederate forces in this vicinity, Fort Pickens was almost lost by trickery. Bragg had arranged with a sergeant Broady to betray Pickens on the night of April 11th, for which service he was to be rewarded with a large sum of money and a commission in the Confederate Army. He had seduced a few of his companions into complicity in his scheme, and a company of 1,000 Confederates were to cross over in a steamboat and take the fort when the sergeant and his friends would be on guard. Fortunately a loyal man in the Confederate camp, Richard Wilcox, revealed the plot to Slemmer, and the catastrophe was averted by the timely reinforcement of the fort by marines and artillerymen under Captain Vogdes from the *Brooklyn*.[1]

Poor Captain Vogdes had tried to take charge of Pickens when he had first arrived on the *Brooklyn*, but Slemmer, who always seemed to have a good opinion of himself and in spite of the fact that he held a lower rank than Vogdes, refused to hand over his command, on the rather flimsy grounds that he had had no such orders from Washington. This finally came and the truce was then thrown to the winds. After a great deal of confusion Washington sent more aid, in spite of Secretary of State Seward's bungling and interfering.

At midnight on April 19th, the *Atlantic* and *Illinois* arrived with several hundred troops, five companies, and some horses, under the command of Colonel Henry Brown, with supplies of food and munitions of war. . . . It was not until the middle of May, however, that Slemmer and his exhausted little garrison were ordered to Fort Hamilton, New York Harbour, to recruit. The order came none too soon as scurvy had already appeared among the men. On the way north one of them died, and few of them ever entirely recovered from the effects of the severe physical and mental strain they had endured. Reinforcements continued to be sent to Pickens, and later efforts made by the Confederates to capture it never succeeded.[2]

There is an interesting letter from one of the Confederate soldiers, R. L. Sweetman, written to Slemmer from Mobile, Alabama, after the war, June 6th, 1867.

[1] *Harper's Cyclopaedia of U.S. History*, 1892, vol. 1, p. 517.
[2] Gilman, op. cit., p. 32.

'Lt. Col. A. J. Slemmer, U.S.A.

Dear Sir,

I would not have troubled you with your bill had my circumstances been better, but I have been unfortunate since the close of the War. I went into the Saw Mill business and the decline in price of cotton ruined me and now I am at work for the U.S. Quartermaster as a carpenter, so you can imagine how matters stand.

'I will with pleasure give you all the information that I possess relative to the Sergt. at Ft. Pickens, Brodie, [*sic*] the only one that I know anything about and personally I know very little, not having been over at Pickens but once, and that was a day or two before you went yourself, on which occasion I went over to ascertain the amount of ordinance stores, etc., on hand. The information I obtained from Brodie in a round-about manner, he not suspecting my object. I went over by request of some gentlemen of Pensacola to whom I made a report. Williams was with me at the time and it was the only time that we were together, he however went over on other occasions.

'I saw him today and asked him the particulars relative to the bribing; he says that no money was offered Brodie, but that Genl. Bragg offered him a Lieutenancy in the Army and at first wanted him to come over, but finally decided that it would be better for him to remain and he could be of more service there than at the Navy-yard. Williams was the medium through which Bragg communicated with Brodie and he is the only one that they tampered with. The correspondence between him and Williams you saw, and know more about it than I do. There were two of your sentinels bribed on the Island by Williams and two Confederate officers, which, I presume, you know something about and I think that was the only case which answered.

'There is a little circumstance connected with your command at Barrancas. If you remember, you put a small force in Ft. Barrancas on the night before you left for Pickens, and that force gave an alarm during the night, the long roll beat and several shots were fired. The next day it was reported that a force had been seen near the fort. Well, that force consisted of Williams and myself, making a reconnaisance. I was standing on the draw-bridge at the time the shots were fired, and you can say that *you fired the first* guns of the war. It is generally said that the first shot was fired at Charleston, but I contend that the first shot was at Barrancas.

'Times look gloomy in this part of the world. I hope and pray that they may improve. This country will take years to regain its former self, if ever.

'Very respectfully . . .

R. L. SWEETMAN.'

CHAPTER III

On May 29th, 1861, the *New York Courier and Enquirer* said, 'Lieutenant Slemmer arrived at this port on Saturday, and remained until Monday; but no more notice was taken of him, his brother officers and soldiers, than if they had done nothing at Pickens to uphold the American flag! If Major Anderson deserved credit and commendation, honors and promotion for moving his command into Fort Sumter . . . then was the conduct of Lieutenant Slemmer in transferring his command to Fort Pickens still more to be commended and still more creditable to the service and the country. . . . Lieutenant Slemmer was called upon to surrender his command to a force irresistible in numbers, and saw one of the senior officers of the Navy cower before the rebel forces, and, with his brother officers ingloriously pull down the Stars and Stripes and surrender the navy-yard at Pensacola without a blow. He was admonished by his senior and by his example that such also was his duty; but he scouted at yielding, resolved upon resistance, and in defiance of the advice and example of Commodore Armstrong, who should have been driven from the Navy with disgrace, threw himself into Fort Pickens and bid defiance to the rebel force. It was a noble act, and, like Anderson's at Sumter, worthy of high praise; and even more creditable, because he is a much younger officer than Anderson, was threatened by a much superior force, and was obliged to resist the contaminating influence of the surrender of the navy-yard, its garrison, and all its munitions of war by a senior officer of the navy, without a struggle and with abundant means of defense. By his gallantry he and his handful of brave men saved Fort Pickens to the country, and gave notice that they were prepared to be starved or be buried beneath the ruins of the fort, but that never would they surrender it to the rebels or permit their infamous colors to wave over its walls! They re-deemed their pledge, have been relieved, and came among us on Saturday last. On Monday evening Slemmer and his officers left here in pursuit of their families. . . . But let this pass; such is popular favor, and such the thoughtlessness of those whose duty it is to foster a sound public sentiment. Slemmer has gone, un-noticed and unhonored. . . .'[1]

It may have been because of this article that the New York City Chamber of Commerce some time later gave a banquet for several war heroes, including Slemmer. In addition to the keys to the city, he was presented with the Medal of Honor for his valour, for-bearance and fidelity at Fort Pickens.[2]

After a short rest, Slemmer was promoted to a Major in the 16th Infantry, assigned to duty as Inspector General, and ordered to West Virginia, under General Rosencrans. Again, Carrie had a finger in her husband's affairs. At the outbreak of the war, thou-sands of men from civil life were brought into the Army and made officers, some of high rank. This made Carrie mad, and she was determined that Addy should not be overlooked. So she set off for Washington with Ellen's husband, Charles DuPuy, requested an interview with President Lincoln, and succeeded in seeing him.

They were ushered into his presence as he sat at a desk on a platform at one end of the room. At first it seemed difficult to speak easily to Lincoln, but as Carrie stood close by his chair, she quickly put her hand on his shoulder, to help catch his attention. The President, always appreciative of any attention to himself, smiled and put his hand gently on hers for a moment. The ice was broken and they all talked easily. She told him her story, saying flatly that it was unfair to her husband that he should continue to be a Lieutenant when so many men from civil life were given commissions of higher rank.

Later Lincoln jotted down a note: 'List of officers I wish to remember when I make appointments for Officers of the Regular Army: Major Doubleday, Major Anderson . . . Lieut. Slemmer—

---

[1] War of the Rebellion. *Records of the Union and Confederate Armies*, Series II, vol. I, p. 54.
[2] *The Norristown Daily Times*, July 28th, 1897.

his pretty wife says a Major or First Captain.'[1] When Carrie wanted anything badly enough she went out and got it.

The new Major continued in poor health, caught typhoid fever, and was sent home by the Army Surgeon who despaired of his life. After they had returned to Addy's home in Norristown, where it took many months for him to regain a semblance of health, another blow came in early October, when their son Bertie, aged five, contracted diphtheria, and died.

From May until November, 1862, Addy was in the Tennessee campaign, Army of the Cumberland, until, near Murfreesboro, while leading his regiment at the Battle of Stone River, he fell and was wounded in the left knee. The surgeon wanted to amputate, but Addy with his usual determination refused to submit to an operation.

Within a few days of hearing this news, Carrie set out for Nashville, and at the same time began her journal, which helps in following her travels for the next three years.

'Jan. 11th, 1863. Being off to the wars again, it has occurred to me that I may find much amusement in the future if a few of my spare moments in the present are filled up by noting down passing events concisely as they occur, and then if they are worthy of it, and occasion offer, I can round out the skeleton at some future period.

'Left New York on Sunday evening with my mind full of anxiety about my husband who was reported wounded, and arrived at Louisville on Wednesday morning, where I received the information that Addy was doing very well, and would recover without any inconvenience, and be a *whole* man, in every sense, quite a consideration in these times of sharp Surgical practice.

'Leaving Louisville we began one of the pleasantest little journeys I ever experienced. Dr. Lyman of Boston took us under his protection, and as he is one of the few who redeem the race from contempt, that in itself was a pleasant circumstance. Handsome, well-bred, cultivated, with the tact of a woman and the

[1] Abraham Lincoln, *Papers*, ed. by David C. Mearns, Doubleday, 1948, vol. 2, p. 594.

strength of a man, it is a great gratification to know such a person. He was accompanied by two English officers, who proved to be both thoroughbred gentlemen, one a Lt. Colonel, and the other a Surgeon of the Scott's Fusileer Guards [*sic*]. This provided us with good company. . . .

'On the 16th it snowed very heavily, and ever since the weather has been impossible to move Addy to other quarters. Wonder what has become of Dr. Lyman and our English friends. They were to have been home on Thursday. Perhaps they have been taken prisoners by the enemy's cavalry, they infest the country between here and Murfreesboro. . . . Major Caldwell and some officers called while I was out. Dreamt about my darling Bertie last night.

'Jan. 20th. Received a call from Mrs. Heyward's sister, Mrs. Goff, and another in the evening from Col. Moncrieff and Mr. Baker. We went into tea together, and had a very pleasant evening in the parlour afterwards. . . . Col. Moncrieff gave me a bullet from the battle field. Hope we may meet again, some time. After parting with people we like and have been with constantly, there is a feeling of desolateness left behind. A few days will dissipate it, but such frequent partings tend to sadden and olden the character. I *feel* much quieter, however I may seem, than I did a year ago.

'There is one bereavement with me, night and morning, morning and night, which will never go until life and the capacity of enduring are gone together. The only thing in the world I had learned to love infinitely was my darling and he is taken away. Only to this book now and then, and to my pillow, can I tell this unutterable grief. It seems to me my nature in its emotions is made more lonely than most person's, or else I have suffered so severely alone, before, where I dared not show it, that I have taught myself to be secretive. . . .

'Feb. 19th. No news of any consequence this morning, except another gunboat ran the blockade at Vicksburg. The three doctors here yesterday, but did not stay long.

'Feb. 26th. Raining again. No news from the Army. Dr. Lyman called last evening, and Capt. Benton and Capt. Thompson, the evening before. I believe the rebel congress has refused to sanction

Jeff Davis' proclamation with reference to the non-paroling of officers. Read *The Channings*, very interesting.'

Even in the darkest days of the war, Carrie found her happiness in social contacts. While her journal is touched continually with notes of sadness, and filled with pages of copied poetry, some in German, she delighted above all in listing the names of the officers who called on her every morning or evening, evidently the accepted thing for ladies in those days. In all its pages she rarely mentioned her husband, never with any enthusiasm, and one wonders how he reacted to the constant circle of admiring men.

'March 5th. Have been seeing company all day, and feel tired. Lieut. Allen, brother of my classmate Leonora, was here. He told me she died a year ago. This is the third one gone out of my class, that I have heard about. Claude Brownrigg and Carrie Franklin are both dead. Perhaps they are the happiest ones of all. The old Hall was a good school for Heaven. Many date their first inception of true religious principles from the altar of St. Mary's Chapel.'

In March Addy was appointed a Brigadier General of Volunteers for gallantry in his action at Murfreesboro and in view of his former meritorious services. It seems strange that this promotion, coming as it did with no plea this time to the President, caused so little excitement in Carrie's journal.

'March 11th. Left Nashville this Wednesday morning at eight o'clock. Probably will not return as the paper of last evening said Addy was made Brigadier, and there are more chances of his being sent elsewhere. Dr. Bache rode down from the house to the depot, said he would be happy to send me his photograph. I shall be glad to have it, as with Dr. Lyman's, it will give me the faces of my four most frequent visitors and will serve to remind me of a pleasant two months in my life.'

'March 12th. Came to Louisville last evening and leave at twelve in the boat for Cincinnati. Mr. Phillips and Lieut. Jones, whom we met yesterday, have decided to go with us in the boat.

'March 13th. Left in the boat yesterday. Spent most of the time after dinner in the pilot house, with the gentlemen. In the evening had euchre and seven up, and afterwards a very pleasant oyster and champagne in the barber's room fitted up for the occasion. Slept very badly, and rose wearied and unrefreshed. Went to the Hotel this morning, and after breakfast, first took a walk with Dr. Lyman to a book store. Was presented with a set of Mrs. Browning's works, which I prize very highly both for the gift and the giver. Then took a ride with Lt. Jones and Mr. Phillips and afterwards a walk to see Cincinnati. Coming home found Dr. Lyman and Major Flint of the 16th in my room. Latter very refined and gentlemanly.' She then listed nine officers who came to call during the evening.

'March 14th. In the cars all day, talking mostly to Dr. Lyman. Must try to improve myself in walking and to cultivate repose of motion and manner. Read Jennie Grey's book about West Point, mere trash. . . .'

Arriving finally in Norristown, she settled down with a bad cold to arrange her belongings in the home of Addy's parents, and waiting for him again to recover his health. In less than two weeks she was writing.

'March 29th. Oh, how tired I am of this wearisome place, and I see no hope of any improvement. I should enjoy perfect solitude much better than this constant presence of uncongenial people.'

One wonders of which of the many officers she was thinking when she inscribed the following poem in her journal,

> *I say not regret me; you will not regret;*
> *You will try to forget me, you cannot forget;*
> *We shall hear of each other, ah, misery to hear*
> *Those names from another which once were so dear!*

Her journal reminds one more of a young schoolgirl's thoughts than those of a General's wife. Was it of Addy she was thinking when she copied out this final stanza of another poem?

50

> '*Now Truth has taken the place of Hope,*
> *And our hearts are like Winter hours;*
> *Little has after-life been worth*
> *That early dream of ours.*'

In the fall, Addy was well enough to return to duty, and on October 17th, Carrie resumed her journal from Columbus, Ohio.

'Tired, tired, always tired, now. I hope with the cold weather strength will come, or I shall be completely disheartened. Went out this morning and did not come home till dinner time. This afternoon Addy and I took a long drive through the woods, and had for our music the rustling of the thickly strewn leaves, a melancholy accompaniment. The air was as mild and delicious as a spring day, but in the effect there was all the difference between decay and promise. . . . Mrs. Cook came to see me yesterday and told me Major Coolidge was engaged to her sister. Perhaps before this he knows the secret we so often talked about—of eternity. The last battle was terrible.'

Carrie never forgot the immoral society she found in Columbus. Years later she wrote a tirade about the city in a letter to Ellen, February 18th, 1879. She began by discussing a girl much too young for one of her own former beaux, and continued,

'In my mind it is certainly against her that she comes from Columbus. I never was in a more dissolute society, more like the court of Louis XIV than is usually approached in modern times. It was there Kate C—— lost her reputation with Dick N——, and *his* wife with Major Somebody. And Will N—— and Mrs. N—— condoned the other's offenses. He had actresses staying in the house, and she had to chaperone them because he had some of her letters, which forced her to be complacent. An officer told me that you couldn't call on a young lady without being expected to kiss her, and it made general visiting a bore.

'There were some good people. Mrs. D—— and the K——'s and Mrs. P——, but I can't speak even for their young people. I know Miss N——, Mr. D——'s niece, was one of the young ladies who admitted affectionate behavior. Mrs. D—— did try to make a stand and not visit people who were quite shameless and open, but she was not strong enough. She came to the party given by Mrs. P—— for Kate C—— at her marriage, having previously refused to meet her.

'Will N—— and his wife had a reconciliation, and I cannot help thinking now the deplorable state of things is her fault. She was thirty-four when they agreed to take a new start, and if she was ever to behave sensibly, had reached the age when wisdom should have come. After the two children were born, and the youngest was ill with scarlet fever, she behaved so badly with the doctor in attendance as to give her husband all the evidence he needed to get a divorce.

'Of course in a place of this kind there would always be a great deal of groundless scandal; still, the whole tone was very low. The girls were frivolous and empty-headed, and the young men apt to relieve *their* intellectual dullness by drinking.'

Fortunately for Carrie they moved in December, back to Cincinnati.

'Dec. 8th. . . . Capt. Goddard and Capt. Todd came down to the depot to say goodbye. The former has quite won a place in my affections by his kind heart and his unvarying cheerfulness, and I was very sorry to say goodbye to him. Cheerfulness is a great gift, and makes friends everywhere.

'Feb. 18th, 1864. The days pass much more pleasantly here, with German, conversation, reading (read Mrs. Butler's *Life on a Georgian Plantation*, a very sad account of slavery. Am now reading Robertson's *Sermons* today) and taking exercise, they are none too long. Since we have been here, have seen Genl. Rosencrans, Genl. Schofield, Genl. Stoneman, besides others whom I did not know. Genl. Negley is very friendly, sent me candy while he was here, and now that he is gone, shows his remembrance by expressing a box of candied fruit from Philadelphia. He is to be back on Saturday, and I am very glad.

'When my German lesson is learned today, I intend to commence a set of cambric night-dresses. Wrote a long letter to Walter Wright on Sunday. I take a great deal of pleasure in this correspondence, because he knows more than I do. Ellen wrote me yesterday about Pa, which made me feel anxious and worried.

'March 4th. Got up feeling sick, but took a pleasant walk after breakfast with Genl. Negley and felt much improved in condition. Have been sewing when I find time. . . . It was a perfect luxury to take up *Recreations of a Country Parson* this morning. For a week I had hardly read a page, and habit makes some reading almost a necessity. I starve without it. Am occupied now in getting ready to go east. This climate does not agree with me, and I am going to try if more bracing winds will strengthen.'

In May, Carrie's father died, and she did not continue her journal until the next year.

'Jan. 16th, 1865. Came back to Cincinnati the first week in November after an absence of almost eight months, a greater part of which time was spent in a sick room. Went by my Doctor's orders to the sea shore in July, to Cape May, where I remained two months. My health is not yet restored, and I have been so often disappointed that I have given up counting the days before recovery, and have accepted ill health as a part of my present life. I like Cincinnati society much better this winter, perhaps because I know more of it. Have been to several parties. Genl. Negley has gone to California, sailed on the 3rd of Dec. Had an animated discussion with Judge Key yesterday. Queer as he is, his conversation is at least suggestive, and therefore not, as I find most persons', exhausting.

'Jan. 27th. Went to a ladies' dinner at Mrs. Pendleton's yesterday, and passed a delightful evening. The dinner was just as formal in its arrangements as if gentlemen had been present. No food was placed on the table, which was ornamented with a silver centerpiece, holding in each bracket a bouquet which we were to take possession of at the end of the dinner.

'First the waiters handed soup, then fish and potatoes, then roast beef with tomatoes, then quails with sweetbreads and some stewed vegetables. Then oyster patties, and afterwards dessert was placed on the table. Everything was elegant. In the evening we had a delightful time, sang little songs, recited German poetry, and scraps of English, and were much more sensible than if we had been compelled to confine our topics to the weak minds of men.

'I am enjoying my winter here exceedingly. Judge Phister, of Kentucky, sent me a bottle of apple brandy with his book *Charge to the Grand Jury on the Subject of Treason*. At a party at Mr. Anderson's on Tuesday, Governor Morton of Indiana was introduced to me. He came to see me yesterday morning and stayed two hours. He is a remarkable man. I am to have his photograph and any speeches or pamphlets that he thinks may interest me.'

As for entries concerning the events of war, they were surprisingly few. On April 18th, with no apparent feeling, she wrote, 'Mr. Lincoln was assassinated the night of Good Friday and Mr. Seward wounded. Judge Key brought Mr. Pendleton in to see me in the afternoon. The latter called again on Monday.'

The War ended at last, and in August, 1865, Addy was mustered out of the volunteer service. On January 4th, 1866, Carrie made her last entry in the journal, stating that Addy was stationed at Fort Schuyler, at Sackett's Harbor, New York, 'this miserable, forlorn place.' The last page shows a pencil sketch of two sad jonquils.

In the early winter of 1868, Addy was made Commander of Fort Laramie, Dakota Territory. Carrie felt far away indeed amidst the troublesome Indians, two days beyond the 'new city' of Omaha, which was at the end of the railroad. Her only pleasure was riding her horse, sometimes into the Indian territory. One night a barrel of sugar was stolen from the General's porch and the whole camp was sugarless for several weeks. One or two messengers, white men, had been murdered by the Indians, and accordingly a pow-wow was held. A treaty was finally made by which the white men agreed to stay on one side of the river and the Indians on the other. At the end of this meeting the peace pipe was lit and smoked, first handed to the General's wife as the only white woman present. Carrie later said, 'I fooled them, I only blew through it!'

On October 6th, Addy had a conference with another group of hostile Indians some distance from Fort Laramie, and returned exhausted to the fort. That night as he slept beside his wife he died suddenly of a heart attack. He was thirty-nine years old, leaving Carrie a widow at twenty-eight.

How little we know of Addy's personality or his character from any of Carrie's writings. Was there shock rather than sadness for her in his sudden death? Her feelings may have been lightened somewhat by the words of praise in his obituary which, after giving a complete biography, closed with these words:

'As an Officer and a gentleman, General Slemmer has always ranked high. No duty assigned him was ever shunned or slighted. The army has lost a valuable officer, and the community a valued citizen. . . . In the various positions to which he was called during the eighteen years of honorable service he stood far above the temptations of the hour, and exhibited in the discharge of his duties, economy and intelligence; also great zeal and uncompromising faithfulness, which was no less honorable to the army than to himself.

'The Regiment will wear the usual badge of mourning for thirty days. . . .'[1]

[1] *The Herald*, Norristown, Pa., Dec. 18th, 1905.

CHAPTER IV

—————◦⟩⟩⟩◦✦◦⟨⟨⟨◦—————

arrie now turned to her family for comfort, and visited Ellen and Charlie DuPuy, recently moved to West Phila-delphia. Here she found many children to take her mind off herself, for there were two sons, Charles and Herbert, and four daughters, Mary, Maud, Nellie and a namesake, Caroline Lane, with a fifth little girl, Emma, to come a few years later. She also visited her mother and sister Mary, or Polly, who never married, and lived also in West Philadelphia.

She continued her correspondence with many former friends, who could now openly declare their love for the appealing widow. One of these letters was from General Negley, March 14th, 1870, from San José, California, a most desolate cry of agony because of her refusal to marry him.

'My dear ——

What a pain of nights and what dreadful depression, day and night have I endured since Saturday, in place of a happy, happy future, in which all, yes, all was anticipated. I find myself midst a sea of uncertainty, no purpose, no one to sympathize with me, no one to receive the confidence I would have entrusted, no one upon whom I would confer my heart and hand, and all that the efforts of a life's heavy labour, has accumulated to be now enjoyed.

'Dear! Dear Carrie! I had but one thought and that was exclusively, wholly in thee. I thought I knew you well, and felt sure that in you I would concentrate all that I have, and all that I hope for in the future. I had but thought that all that was in the least objectionable and that had caused some little difference between us, I refer to your extraordinary business care for yourself, would be a recommendation when our interests might have become one. . . .

'There would have been no one point in which anything but happiness, yes, Carrie, extreme happiness could have looked upon us in the future. Oh! for Heaven's sake, be frank with me, tell me wherein I have so rapidly fallen from that high position I once occupied in your estimation, give me something tangible to answer, and I will respond to any and all, that all the world may say against me, dear, dear Carrie.'

Carrie later gave her reason for refusing him in a letter to Ellen, December 14th, 1876. After replying to some gossip about Negley, she mentioned his opinion of women in general and of his difficulty with them since they kept throwing themselves in his way because of his money.

'His own opinion of the characters of most people in society was such that he told me often, after I was a widow, that I was the only married lady he had ever known well to whom he would feel safe in proposing marriage. I am glad he did propose to me so often because it showed his respect and belief in me. If it hadn't been for the widespread scandal about him, I should have felt tempted, once or twice, to accept him simply because I should have had the children. But he had been too bad; and I doubted if he were not too old to amend, married or single. I am afraid he would have fallen a victim, as he used to call it, to any fast woman who chose to make advances to him.'

Another faithful admirer was Dr. Arthur Schell, whom Carrie had met in the Army and who later became the DuPuy family doctor in West Philadelphia. Many were the drives he took her in his buggy, with Carrie's face carefully concealed behind a veil lest people should recognize her and gossip. Widows were supposed to stay at home, or be seen only with other ladies. She trusted him implicitly and he had almost won her, when she discovered that he had invested some of her money unwisely without her knowledge and had lost quite a sum. That was the end of the doctor's becoming a member of the family, although they remained friends and corresponded for years.

Carrie soon tired of West Philadelphia and decided to travel to

England to visit her many cousins there. On May 20th, 1870, General William T. Sherman wrote her a letter of introduction to London circles.

'Dear Madam,

I promptly comply with your request and send you letters to Hons. Mr. Motley and Washburn, the latter replaced General Dix last year. I feel pretty well acquainted with Mr. Motley, less so with Washburn, but both can and will befriend you if you stand in need of a friend at Court.

'Should you simply desire the acquaintance of some gentleman familiar with matters and things in general, send this letter and your card to B. Moran, Esq., U.S. Secretary of Legation, London, who is, I know, especially courteous to all Americans, and especially to those presented by me.

'I feel pleased to see that you turn to me as your friend, and I hope you will never fail to call on the Army for acts of friendship. Surely I will always endeavor to do whatever I can for your benefit. Wishing you a pleasant passage across the ocean at this favorable season, and an agreeable sojourn in Europe.

I am with respect,
Yours truly,
W. T. SHERMAN, GENERAL'

So, armed with the proper credentials, Carrie set off for England, and soon the steady trickle of letters across the ocean to West Philadelphia began.

Aboard ship, almost to Queenstown, Sunday, June 5th, 1870
'Dear People at Home,

I never felt less like writing in my life, such as I have I will send you. Well, there is no use perilling soul as well as body when one goes out on the great deep, so I may as well confess to having been awfully sea-sick. . . . I never felt so sorry for having left home in my life, and I can't help wondering why anybody with the whole broad continent of America before him to choose, should ever bring such awful tribulation upon himself. . . .

'Our fellow passengers are not interesting, and I have not made the acquaintance of a single one. We have one Scotch Baronet on board, but he might as well be a Scotch scarecrow for all the interest we take in him. He sets great store by himself, too, and never talks to anybody but the Captain. If that is a mark of aristocracy, we are aristocrats, too, for *we* never talk to anybody but the Captain, either. I sit on one side of him and Mrs. Sharpe on the other, when we come to table, and consequently we have the seats of honor. I like Mrs. Sharpe very much, and could not have a better travelling companion. . . . On reaching London I am to go direct to a quiet Quaker house, where the expense will be only about twelve dollars a week, and rest there until I have some time to recruit my strength and look around me a little. . . .

'Dearest love to all . . .

CARRIE'

London, June 10th, 1870

'Dear Mother and Sisters,

. . . I suppose my letter from Queenstown has come to hand and told you I was very near London on Monday last. On Tuesday we steamed up to the bar, just too late to cross with the tide, and had to lie still from half past seven in the morning, till four p.m., waiting for high water to float us in.

'Standing on deck watching the tide, it chanced that the Baronet, who is not Scotch but English, and a Captain Dale of the Royal Navy, took position near us, and gradually joined in our talk. . . . Well, the old Baronet seemed to take a great fancy to me, and when we left the ship for the lighter which came up to land the passengers, he said the Captain had resigned his charge into his hands, and might he have the pleasure of seeing about a cab, etc., for me when we came to Liverpool? Mrs. Sharpe and I had quietly made up our minds that as not a soul knew us, it would be a sinful extravagance to travel first class to London when second class is just half price and almost as comfortable, but under these circumstances we thought we wouldn't mention it.

'Sir Clinton bought our tickets at the depot and being old and fussy of course made a mistake about the baggage, every bag and box of which was left behind on the platform, because he had not left himself time to pay the express charges. But finally we four,

Capt. Dale, Sir Clinton Murdock, Mrs. Sharpe and myself, were all shut up in one carriage and on our way to London. We had a pleasant five hours ride to London, through a beautiful, green hedge-rowed country, with daylight enough to see it almost up to ten o'clock and finally came into London tired out, and ready to eat chopped corn if nothing better was to be had. . . .'

After finding temporary lodgings, Carrie proceeded to see the sights of London, and to entertain new friends, including the recently acquired Sir Clinton and Lady Murdock. She knew her mother would be interested about her meeting her father's brother and wrote:

'My dear Sister,
Uncle Samuel has this moment left, and I may as well tell you of his visit while the maid is bringing up my dinner. With all due respect, I think Ma chose the black sheep of the family when she took Pa, for all the relations I have yet met, delight me. This uncle has a thin pale rather long face with white trimmed mustache and whiskers, and thinnish white hair, *not* bald on top, and dresses with the most exquisite neatness, which you know could not exactly be said to be Pa's distinguishing characteristic. He looks, talks and acts like a perfect gentleman. . . .'

After a few weeks Carrie visited another cousin, Jeannette Potts and her husband (always referred to as Mr. Potts) in Cambridge, and Carrie had an opportunity to write home about more interesting relatives. She loved the way Jeannette's sister, Anna Fison, made fun of family traditions and mimicked relatives, and said Jeannette was the beauty of the family. Both the sisters knew seven or eight languages well. Mary Fison was another sister living with the Potts in Cambridge. Carrie continued by giving details about Pa's father:

'Grandfather Reynolds was a remarkable man with the manners of a Courtier and no one, not even his wife knew anything about his belongings. He became a friend and convert of Wesley, and gave up his former life completely, and would never answer a question about father or mother, so that they know absolutely nothing of his family, except that Reynolds was an assumed name. From his education, manner and perfect knowledge of the world, they all are sure he must have held a high social position before he gave all up for religion. Afterwards, he lived the life of a saint, going about doing good, and a monk could not have been more of an anchorite. It used to worry his wife dreadfully, as she felt certain he could, if he would, claim a higher position, but he always told her such things were a snare and she had better be content as she was. They had plenty to live on and brought up all their children well. The daughters were very fine women, but owing to their Methodist associations had no opportunity to marry well....[1]

'On Monday I go to London, and leave in the evening for Paris, without some fresh news comes. Germany is an impossibility as even if I cared to risk annoyance and inconvenience, I should not be let in. They are turning all strangers out of the country, and I see the French Envoy has left Stuttgart, so I can't go there.... I am so provoked about the war [Franco-Prussian] as it cuts off all my pleasant plans for Germany. You will surely see me home in November, as I grow tired of constant travelling....'

London, July 25th, 1870

'My Dear Sister,

Charlie Murdock has laboriously copied out for me a tour of Switzerland arranged by a friend of his for the friend's mother, who was going alone. It was a very virtuous act, and one it would take an immense amount of friendship to induce me to imitate; he is a very nice youth, not painfully pleasant to look upon, if he only wouldn't drink so much wine at dinner, and make his breath smell so horribly afterwards, as he bends over me with photograph book or portfolio of engravings and surrounds me with odours *not* of Araby the Blest. He seems to have taken a fancy to me, but I can't return the favour so it's no use trying. I am afraid I shall always be

[1] The Rev. John Reynolds, Sr., 1760–1821. Was first a rector in the Church of England before becoming a Methodist minister. He and his wife, formerly Charlotte Oxenborow, lived in Norwich, England, where they entertained Wesley and brought up their family of twenty children.

addicted to low tastes, for I find of all the single men I have met on this side, I like Frank Beck the best, and he is only an underwriter at Lloyd's, and has even the distinction of my preference by playing a superb game of croquet, and always being quiet and gentlemanly. He has taken a degree at Oxford, and serves to make my stay here more pleasant.'

In answer to questions about Jeannette's husband, Carrie could not say a pleasant word. Mr. Potts[1] was a tyrant, a miser, and so mean to his wife. Now that she had seen how their marriage turned out, she vowed she would never marry General Negley, or Commodore Vanderbilt, either. They were all three complete egotists.

She had met Commodore Cornelius Vanderbilt, ruthless American railroad magnate and millionaire, while visiting friends at Saratoga Springs. She later said of this encounter, 'Mr. Vanderbilt was an old man when we met at Saratoga in 1869. His wife, Sophia, had died and evidently he was looking for a young thing to marry. He took me riding in his carriage on three or four occasions, and on one of these he asked me to marry him. I had no thought of marrying a man old enough to be my grandfather, so I turned him down. He asked me to think it over and said that if by next Saturday I had not changed my mind, he was going to marry Frank Crawford, a Southern girl. I again said No, and so he married Frank.'

In a letter from Cambridge she said, 'They are all of the same kind. But Jeannette is so sweet and kind, only having married Mr. Potts so that her brothers could go to college. But good seldom does come from evil and she has not even the happiness of an aim attained. One brother died at college, and the other after a wild dissolute life, became converted by some creature he married, without their knowledge, and is now a missionary to the FeeGee Islands, which requires no great amount of learning.'

After a rather lonely and uneventful trip to Switzerland and France, Carrie decided to settle in Cambridge for a long visit with the Potts, at their home, 15 Fitzwilliam Street.

[1] Robert Potts, 1805–85. A private coach in Cambridge, was famous for his edition of *Euclid's Elements* and was active in University affairs.

'My dear Sister,

I pay Jeannette two pounds a week for board against their will. I have a regular game of croquet every afternoon it doesn't rain, some of the college fellows usually dropping in to help make up the necessary four. One of the Trinity fellows, Mr. Clifford, is a perfectly delightful companion, writes poetry, was senior wrangler, and is considered a perfect genius in Natural Science, but like so many geniuses, has no nose to speak of and is weak in character, I feel sure.

'All these people here seem to me to lack something, backbone perhaps, which a business life gives (they despise business, and money, apparently). Jeannette is just like the rest: dreamy, poetical, imaginative, cultivated, but not robust, very intellectual, but lacking power, somehow. They all know a great deal more than I do, but I always feel as if I can tell them what to do.

'I never for one thing should have let Mr. Potts grow so utterly conceited, selfish and unreasonable, and the practical notions of most of these university people seem to need setting straight. "Knowledge comes, but wisdom lingers," I suppose, is what is the matter.

'Meanwhile the society is very pleasant, and Jeannette and I are planning to attend Prof. Sedgwick's lectures on Zoology, and Prof. Fawcett's on Moral Philosophy, and if I can, I want to gain admittance to Vernon Harcourt's course on International Law. Then, every Friday we are to go to Mr. Hudson's German readings; that is, we all meet together in his rooms to read Schiller, each taking our turn. . . .'

One of Cara's old Cambridge acquaintances, Mrs. Keynes, when ninety, recalled a story about Jeannette Potts, who took herself very seriously as a poetess. One day when she was taking a walk into the town (they had moved into a house on Parker's Piece) she was inspired to write a poem. Rushing into Peck's, the chemist's shop, she exclaimed, 'The divine afflatus! Give me some paper, quick!' Mr. Peck, much puzzled about her predicament, showed her into the lavatory.

'My dear Sister,

. . . I have, confidentially, lots of admirers, who of course mean nothing, but help to make the time pass pleasantly. The only two eligible ones are Vernon Harcourt, M.P., who is up here for a month to deliver his annual course of lectures, and who comes in almost every afternoon for a little talk. He is a widower and engaged to be married, so report says, and is between fifty and sixty years old; in addition to being considered the most disagreeable man in England. Six intimate friends once gave a dinner, and each agreed to bring the most disagreeable man he knew. Twelve covers were laid but only seven guests appeared, the original six *and* Vernon Harcourt. Each man thinking over his acquaintances pitched on V.H. as most perfectly meeting the conditions. I like him because people's ways never trouble me much and he is so immensely clever.

'Then, the other of the two is Arnold Morley, a youth only twenty-two years old, but the handsomest man I ever saw in my life, and good and clever. His father is Member of Parliament, and a very rich man, and if he, the son, were ten years older, and a barrister in practice instead of in embryo, why, then—perhaps I might grow tired of him if I knew him better! He comes to play croquet about twice a week, with an older brother, who is also nice in his way. I met them all up in Scotland at Mr. Porter's house. Don't you or Mary tell Philadelphia people about my going out, because it will sound very fast, in their ears, though without any occasion. I wear the same crepe trimmed black I should at home. . . .'

Carrie enclosed a note to Ellen from their cousin Anna, full of enthusiasm about Carrie.

'I am glad to have this opportunity of telling you how delighted we are to have Carrie with us, and how fond we are of her. I had always a desire to know my American cousins, but she surpasses all my fancies about them. She is so sweet and bright and good and pretty; however, it's no use attempting to describe her.

'Of course everyone is fascinated by her, but it doesn't seem to make the least difference to her. . . . It is quite amusing to see Mr. Potts with her. I know she has told you that he is the least bit of a Bear. Well, she leads him in chains, and he runs to fulfil her slightest wish. He went down into the cellar at ten the other night, and fetched up a bottle of his Trinity ale, sacred liquid that he only has out on grand occasions *for other people*, and what was more, finding us in the midst of an impromptu lobster supper, he actually abstained from having prayers!

'He saw the woe upon our faces as we gazed on our plates, and on the hot coffee, which the twenty minutes' devotions would have ruined, and went away. Quite an unprecedented occurrence. Carrie wanted to thank him in the fullness of her heart, but I suggested that gratitude on that score would shock him. She remarked he would be rewarded for it above. . . . Carrie's name in the University is *die Allerliebste* [the best-beloved], we find.'

Cambridge, Dec., 1870

'My dear Sister,
I am engaged now for all the dances at the Trinity Ball next June, and if you go and read this letter out loud to the Philadelphians, you will banish me altogether from their good graces, so don't do it. Truly a man is never a prophet in his own country. I never was so liked and courted in my life as I am here, and I don't flirt at all, but treat every one exactly the same.

'In my secret mind, I think Arnold Morley is my favorite, perhaps because he is very quiet and sedate, and seems hardest to win, but I am not as fixed as the poles, in my preferences, although you may not believe me, and sometimes I like Lance Stirling the best. The latter is not at all handsome, but Arnold has the face and figure of a god.

'My one *devoted* attendant, a much older man, Mr. Clifford, a fellow of Trinity, has gone off to Sicily on the eclipse expedition, begging so hard for my photograph to refresh his vision, that I had to give it to him, and I shall likely be in London before his return. He is a genius in Astronomy and Mathematics, and has an ugly face, but lovely disposition. Unfortunately like all men of genius, his moral nature is weak, and everybody influences his actions, though he influences their intellects. If I want, I can be

Mrs. Clifford, but I should have no guarantee that my husband might not take to any vice or excitement that pleased his fancy, because one feels in studying him that there is no resistance of any kind in his character.'

Although Carrie had thought she was completely fancy free, she evidently fell more in love than she had intended.

'My dear Sister,

You need none of you be afraid of my marrying an Englishman, though thereby hangs a tale, which I may tell you when I come home, if the soreness has all gone out of it. I look so young in this climate that I pass for only twenty, really, but I did not think it right to conceal my age from this man who was eight years younger. I don't think he minded that, because he is very fond of me, but when I told him about my health, and how any one who married me would have to be content with only me, and no children, he finally came to see the thing as I did, and agreed that it was best to part.

'It is rather hard lines for me, to have to give up the only man I ever loved in my life, and such a man! Almost perfect, mentally, morally and physically, but to have had my will now might have brought us both unhappiness after a while. But then I can't really think so. I feel sure I could have made his life happier than any other woman ever will, because I have so many companionable qualities, and he brought out all the best in me; but I will tell you the whole story when I come home. We said goodbye on Tuesday, after a long talk about impossibilities, and soon he will go off for three months travel on the continent, and out of my life forever.

'Just now fate seems a little grim, and I sympathize with Mantalini's opinion that life is a "demd horrid grind", but I can't have everything, and I seem just to learn to love a thing perfectly and then to lose it. First Bertie, and now Arnold. Just the thing one wants, one can't have. I don't care a straw to be great or rich, but I should like to have a husband and children to love.

'Don't write back anything about this, because I am doing my best to get over it, and the spot is too sore to touch. Meanwhile, I am very tired of Cambridge, where everything is permeated by his memory, and shall go back to London to my old lodgings, alone, in a few weeks. . . .'

On December 26th, 1870, she wrote that at three o'clock that day she would be thirty years old. This fact seemed to make her depressed, so that she found fault with everything, bemoaning the fact that so many friends had gone away for vacation, and even small irritations seemed more than she could bear.

'Anna is a generous whole-souled sort of a woman, but is so little my style in manner or ways, that she often drives me distracted and out of the room. She has a way of expanding her full chest, lifting her great bosom, and heaving immense sighs, when she reads, which nearly drives me wild sometimes. And when she sits in front of the fire and lifts her petticoats prudently away from the blaze, she has a habit of slowly rubbing her huge legs up and down the woollen stockings, until every nerve in me rebels against the sight and sound. It is the fault of my temperament, not her nature, which makes me often wish myself at the limits of the earth rather than in her neighbourhood.

'The side of her which makes her sing delightfully, read poetry like a poet, and talk so amusingly that we sit for hours listening, is always very pleasant to me. But it is as much as I can do to refrain from telling her about the other things.

'Just now, we are all joining in a plot against the male sex, laying "man traps" for a clergyman. Anna has given her fancy to a fellow of Trinity named Taylor, an exceedingly clever man and writer of books, with plenty of money and much reputation whom she has about as much hope of getting as I would the Prince of Wales. . . . He is a very shy fish to catch, first because he *is* shy, and then never goes anywhere in general society, never accepts invitations of any kind, except to the Martyns who are intimate friends.

'Jeannette has invited him to tea tonight, but no answer having come, whether he will come or not, only the night will show. I am to be used as a decoy duck, to try to get him to feel at ease, and to care to come often, and then I am gradually to draw off when he feels sufficiently at home and talk to other people, and leave Anna to entertain him; but *will* he walk into the trap and come to tea? Anna would make him a splendid wife, or anybody else, who hadn't nerves like fiddle strings. . . .'

Cambridge, Jan. 13th, 1871

'My dear Sister,

. . . Tonight Anna's "chosen" is invited for a game of whist, but the misguided man *will* prefer me, and as my share of the trap is to make him come familiarly to the house, it doesn't answer for me to stay out of the room. At my suggestion, another Fellow is to come; I am to start Mr. Taylor out of his bashfulness into a talkative mood, and then gradually edge out of the conversation, and occupy myself with Mr. Main. We plan everything beforehand, but, laws, it's no use. Anna might as well cry for the moon as for Mr. Taylor, and he has no more idea of marrying than of going to Egypt.

'I don't wonder she likes him, though like most of the geniuses here he is ugly and ill dressed. His head is furnished with any amount of knowledge, and he is the author of a theological work of great merit, I believe, *The Gospel in the Law*, besides editing a Mathematics Journal. Far be it from me to read either, but they impress me with the fact that he must be clever. We are a very united pleasant household of women, and it seems a pity that everything must break up so soon, and each one go her separate way. Poor Jeannette is desolate, and can't bear the thought of Anna's going to Oxford and me to London, but we are both to be back in a couple of months.'

The girls wanted to have a party, but since Mr. Potts forbade cards or dancing they decided to put on some plays, calling them Educational Charades for his benefit.

Cambridge, Jan., 1871

'My dear Sister,

The house is settling down into quiet after our grand effort on Friday evening, which we think a great success. Mr. Potts, instead of being disagreeable, enjoyed everything exceedingly, and what a load that was off our minds, only those can tell who have lived with him. We had a dreadful scare early in the evening, while getting the dining-room ready for the plays. Anna was at one end near the closet with cap and apron on, dressed for her part, and Mr. Walpole and I were pinning curtains up over a clothes horse to make one of the sides of the stage, when Mr. Potts walked in. We darted behind the horse, and Anna into her closet, and he surveyed an empty room solemnly for a moment and then walked out again.

'If he once forbids a thing, no power on earth, no amount of reason will ever make him reconsider, and his only reiterated answer always is, "NO, I have said NO." Until one feels like boxing his ears, as the only way of making any impression on his head. I never saw such a man before in my life; but he took the plays splendidly, though he wouldn't let us dance to the piano after supper. I had two splendid bouquets given me, one from Mr. Clifford, and the other sent by an American undergraduate named Gallatin, a boy of twenty-one, who belongs to a good family in New York.'

Cambridge, Jan. 30th, 1871

'My dear Sister,

Anna has taken her departure for Oxford, this morning, to stay perhaps till Easter, against our earnest advice. The "String" was really beginning to feel himself at home in the house, and manifesting a reluctance, once here, to tear himself away, heedless of "those to madness stung" (Mr. Potts) which I always consider a sign of progress, as I told her; but she had made the engagement to teach for a little while in the "sisterhood" to help them along, and had to go, with many a backward glance. . . .

'Monday evening Mr. Main was here, and we played a surreptitious game of whist, with an eye and ear on Mr. Potts' doings. The latter's first wife, among other unpleasantnesses, didn't like cards, so he never had them played in the house during her life time; and now, although he always takes a hand in the college rooms, and other houses, he won't allow us this simple, innocuous assistance to dull people and a dull evening. We play all the same, under *my* auspices, and when he comes in sometimes he sees four innocent faces looking up at him from a small round *empty* table. If he has eyes in his face he must know what the position means, but we don't openly brave him with the sight of the cards, and he has the singular trait to prefer this sort of thing, to our openly following our fancies.

'Here is an acrostic Mary Fison wrote about him one evening as some relief to an exasperated spirit.

ROBERT POTTS

'Roving, rough and rugged one
Oh, how hideous thou art,
Blaring like a mastodon
Ever scolding, rude and tart;
Raging like a wintry sea,
Thou art all thou shouldst not be.
Prating of thy mighty deeds
Of the wonders thou hast done
Till all thy audience secedes,
Tired and angry, one by one.
Sure 'tis time thy race were run.'

In February Carrie went to London and wrote about visiting the House of Commons with her friend Edith Sandys, who was soon to marry Carrie's cousin, Harvey Reynolds. 'We were very much in luck, for the University Tests' Bill was the principal subject of discussion. I couldn't have spent so long a time at Cambridge without knowing all the ins and outs, of what some people consider bulwarks, and others great grievances, so I was quite prepared to take sides, and to listen eagerly, and some exceedingly good speaking I heard. Bulwer Lytton[1] made an explanation first, which gave me a good chance to inspect him, and to discover what an old man he was, and then one after the other, Gladstone, Sir John Coleridge (a shining light in the Government, Lord Chancellor, or something) Prof. Fawcett,[2] Beresford-Hope and a lot more took part in the discussion; the whole was a great treat. . . .'

[1] Edward Bulwer-Lytton, first Baron, 1803–73. Novelist and dramatist, M.P.
[2] Henry Fawcett, 1833–84. The blinded Professor of Political Economy at Cambridge; later M.P. and Postmaster General.

'My dear Sister,

Polly's letter has just been forwarded from Cambridge . . . what she reports of Mr. Biddle's conversation makes me indignant, as such things always do. If I did think of marrying, everyone would say it was heartless and atrocious, but yet so prone do they consider the human heart to wish to do what is unnatural, that they are only surprised when one does not give occasion for the outcry, and think it is because one can't.

'I think it is extremely likely I shall never marry at all, nor do I consider my health such as to justify me in marrying. I am old enough besides to have come to some understanding of the true value of things, and should never marry any man however much he had to offer, whom I did not love, and at thirty a woman does not fall in and out of love with every other man she meets.

'I think people usually don't understand my character at all, and I'm sure I don't know why, as I never make any attempt to disguise. I continually get the credit of being worldly and I don't know any fault I am more free from. My faults are many, but that of over-valuing the world's prizes does not rank among them. . . . Of course one likes admiration, as one does fruit and other pleasant things. I never knew man, woman or child who didn't, in some shape or other. Jeannette said in Cambridge that I treated everyone with exactly the same manner, and that she could not tell which one I liked best, and I know no one there had the least idea I thought of marrying again, which I don't. . . .'

London, March 7th, 1871

'My dear Sister,

Last evening Mr. Nadal, Secretary of Legation, came in for an hour and asked permission to bring a Mr. Hale to introduce to me, a nephew of Edward Everett,[1] and it just occurred to me, didn't an Edward Everett Hale write a book called *If, Yes and Perhaps*, or some such thing?[2] Well, they are to come at six on Thursday, and

[1] Edward Everett, 1794–1865. American orator and statesman.
[2] Edward Everett Hale, 1822–1909. American author and Unitarian clergyman, wrote *A Man without a Country* as well as the book she mentions.

I shall get Edith to run over, so that she may entertain Mr. Nadal while I talk to Mr. Hale.

'On Sunday we made up an excursion to the Zoological Gardens, the thing to do for members and their friends in the afternoon, and just as Edith and Julia Sandys and Mr. Walpole were collected in my rooms to start, in marched Sir Clinton with the like mind to take *me*, so we added him to our number and had a very pleasant inspection of the beasts. *I* liked the monkeys best, but the others seemed to care for the elephants and giraffes.

'Wednesday. Well, here I am home from my dinner at the Stansfelds', and have had a most delightful party. Oh, don't say with Miggs the Immortal, "Why wasn't I born old and ugly?" but *why* do the old men always take a fancy to me, and the young men hold aloof? Dr. Rae at the Conways, and now tonight Mr. Armitage, both with amiable but uninteresting wives, and both with grey beards, talked to me so faithfully that no junior had a chance or chose to make a chance to create a diversion. Dr. Rae is getting me tickets for the Royal British Association [*sic*]. He is the great Arctic man who found traces of Franklin or somebody, and is a scientific light.[1]

'A celebrated artist, Mr. Welles, by name, took me in to dinner, and some nice looking soul sat opposite, but Mr. Armitage[2] was the chief attraction, at the end of the table in Mrs. Stansfeld's seat, with her on his other side. He is to get me in to the House tomorrow to hear the debate on the Army bill, and if his wife only calls on me, it will be what Anna calls having laid another nest egg, because they are very rich people, and everybody here who can afford it, entertains, and I do so enjoy these entertainments.

'Being an American, I suppose, makes me a sort of lion, and I am always the center of the gentlemen. I don't say these things often, and you must excuse me this once, I don't care about it afterwards, but at the moment it makes that particular moment pleasanter. Mrs. Stansfeld grew quite affectionate towards the end, and kissed me goodbye all because I made her evening go so well.

[1] John Rae, 1813–93. Scottish Arctic explorer; found relics of the lost Sir John Franklin's expedition.
[2] Edward Armitage, 1817–96. Historical painter; did numerous murals in fresco.

'Yesterday at Mrs. Conway's who should walk in but Robert Browning, the poet, while I was calling. That was lucky, but it was very unlucky to be hemmed in by two old tabbies, and have to talk to them, and worse, to feel that seeing me in a bonnet, no man would care to see me again. . . . Mr. Conway had written him a note to ask him to dine on purpose to meet me on account of my admiration for his wife.'

London, March 16th, 1871

'My dear Sister,

Mr. Nadal came in for a little while in the evening and is to take me to see the University boat races on the 1st of April. I gave him instructions about Barnes Bridge, and ten shillings to buy my ticket of admission to that favoured spot. I take him with me because there will be a lot of people there I know, and anyone belonging to the American Legation will be an exceptional escort. He is a great goose to be sure, but good looking and gentlemanly enough, and does not talk through his nose to the same extent as some.

'He has an affected hesitation in speech, and a fascinating, as *he* considers it, sort of half laugh, which always makes me feel like stopping short in speech and telling him then and there not to be an idiot, but the restraints of society are a great stumbling block in the way of improvement, and consequently he loses the benefit of a criticism which certainly would be of great use to him. . . .

'On Thursday he brought Mr. Charles Hale, brother of Edward Everett Hale, to call. Mr. Hale was six years Consul General in Egypt, and whether it was the climate, or the fault of the mother who bore him, he certainly is the ugliest man I ever saw, *awfully* ugly, with tusks of teeth, a stoop in his figure, and one who would nowhere without assistance be taken for a gentleman. But he made up for all by being fond of poetry, and telling most amusing anecdotes, and by sitting in the shade as a help to oblivion about some of his personal peculiarities.'

London, April 23rd, 1871

'My dear Sister,

Mr. Hale has just departed after spending the afternoon, and all

73

the intellect I had seems to have been expended on him, for I certainly feel very little inclined to write. I never saw a man so restless, or one whose trousers seem to trouble him so much. Every few minutes he gives his legs desperate pinches, in the hope of catching his flannel drawers, I suppose, and settling them more to his comfort. Then, he gets up and bends one knee and jerks, and then bends the other and jerks, and so on through the whole visit. Today he varied matters by seizing the poker and using it for a graceful toy, between times, until his legs needed arranging.

'He had a bad attack of illness while in Alexandria and may wear some specially prickery flannel as a preventive against cold, but his movements keep one in a constant state of watchfulness. He is good hearted and intellectual, of first rate family and with sufficient money, and a Bostonian, but it shows how all important appearance and manner are. I *couldn't* marry him if marriage were the sole object and aim of my life. He is very much in earnest in paying me attention, but he must see I won't have him, and two-thirds of the time I tell Harriet to say I am "not at home".'

In March Carrie was presented to the Queen, and after writing at great length about her dress and all the details of the event, she concluded,

London, March 28th, 1871

'I'm not sorry I've been, but I never could live long enough to want to go to another, and if they do send me an invitation to the Court Ball, I'm not at all sure I shall go. "The path of glory leads but to the grave," and very much more of this sort of thing would kill me.

'The Princess Louise wasn't there after all, but the rumour of her intention to be presented was the cause of an immense crowd. Oh, what histories I heard! First, Mrs. Hughes introduced me to a slim man with shocking teeth as Lord Stanley, and then pointed out his wife, a little stout vulgar Spanish woman, much older than he, who, it seems, married him when he was eighteen. Nobody had a suspicion but he was a bachelor, until his father died, when this creature came forward and claimed her place, and was today for the first time presented to the Queen. And so on, something or other it seemed to me about every one. . . .

'The Countess of Granville, wife of the Minister of Foreign Affairs, nominally presented me, but I was only too glad to be with Mrs. Hughes and her "Tom",[1] as Lady Granville had charge of too many to look after *me*. Now I must go to bed, I am tired out, so goodnight. The more I see of this sort of life, the less I care for it. It is, as Mrs. Judd said, perpetually getting oneself up in one's best to reflect glory on some Highness or other. I find I feel quite contented to live out my allotted portion of time in the position in which it has pleased Providence to place me.'

Carrie went back to Cambridge for May week and was soon writing of more admirers and proposals. Years later as she was having tea in the house formerly owned by the Potts, someone said to her, 'Oh, Lady Jebb, I understand it was in this very house that you received three proposals of marriage in one evening!' To which she replied, 'Nonsense, two of them were in the garden.'

Cambridge, July, 1871

'My dear Sister,

Last evening we had croquet in the College gardens, and afterwards supper in Pembroke Lodge with the Vice Chancellor, and oh, how some of the young ladies are trying to catch him.[2] He and Mr. Jebb are the two most eligible matches in Cambridge. . . .[3] The latter has just been a source of great commotion to Jeannette and me, because he began by writing her a note, to ask her if he had *any* chance with me. He said, "to tell you the truth, I have no hope, but I want to *know*." This led to a letter to me, but as I have kept the correspondence you shall see how a senior Classic does things in England.

'Everything he had to offer would have suited me well enough, but I couldn't have married him if he had been a King. He intends to persevere, but they all say that at first, because I always tell them

[1] Thomas Hughes, 1822–96. Author of *Tom Brown's Schooldays*.
[2] The Vice Chancellor at this time was John Power, 1818–80. Master of Pembroke, 1870–80. He died unmarried.
[3] Richard Claverhouse Jebb, 1841–1905. Classical scholar.

I can't marry again, and that they *won't* believe. I think a widow has a right to avoid giving offence by retiring on her bereavement if she chooses.

'I don't blame myself about Mr. Jebb, because I have always disliked him from the first. He told Jeannette he fell in love with me the first moment he saw me, and that it was all over with him then. She believes implicitly everything he says, being such a sympathetic woman, with a touch of sentimentality, but I feel sure he will marry some one else in a year, as he is evidently on the "war path".

'The Vice Chancellor is much more to my taste, only he is over fifty in years, and as old as the everlasting hills in all his opinions and ideas. I am not sure that half the time he knows when I am talking nonsense and when I am in earnest, and he is half in love with me and half afraid of me. As I don't want him, I don't care. I think I will send you Jebb's letter, only *please* don't let Polly tell anybody. It only makes those old maids hate me and try to detract from me, and offers are the last things to boast about. Do show Polly the error of her ways, in such things. To make people envy you is far on the road to making them hate you.'

Before Carrie returned to America she answered Jebb's letter in a pleasant and almost encouraging manner.

Cambridge, July 23rd, 1871

'Dear Mr. Jebb,

I cannot let your letter pass without sending you some answer and yet I hardly know what to say. I have read it several times and I will do what you ask, I will take it home with me and sometimes read it there, and I will confess to you now that sometimes it almost makes me doubt. You are right when you say that the men who usually awake in me a passing interest belong to a different type from yours, and perhaps, just perhaps, this may be the reason why that interest *is* merely passing. It has grown to be a common saying at home that I like people for a little while, and then weary of them, and certainly it would be comforting to find a cause for such change outside of one's defective nature.

'Perhaps like many who have gone before me, and many who

will come after, I ignorantly, for want of a better standard, or because the bias was early given, choose what is not good for me and so feel ever a need unsatisfied. I think force of character has had more attraction for me than acuteness of intellect, but to take daily pleasure in such companionship, one's imagination must continually play about the individual and keep his capability of decided action ever in view, daily life offering so few occasions for the exercise of such qualities, whereas I suppose the intellect that once charms never fails to charm.

'But I am writing in what they call at home my most didactic vein, a tendency they always implore me to repress, and because you have less freedom to complain is no reason why you should have the infliction. I do not say anything about your love, because I *cannot* write about love. It is a feeling from which I have considered myself so set apart, that almost repulsion arises at the thought of all that its reawakening would imply.

'Why you should care so much for me whom you did not know three months ago, I cannot understand, but I must believe in the depth of your love, and feel very sorry that I can in no way repay it. If I could, I would let you go on loving me, and if you so chose, wait and see what another year might effect, but I dare not, I am too uncertain of myself, too hopeless of a change, rather.

'Jeannette has showed me the poem you sent her, and I am delighted with it. I think I shall follow the example of the Hebrews in Egypt, borrow it from her, and carry it off with me to America. Having such an example, one's morality could not be questioned, and I should be saved the labour of copying, a thing my soul abhors, or I should not ask you to please excuse these blotted sheets.

'With thanks for the careful analysis of your letter,
Believe me, your sincere friend,
C. L. S.'

After Carrie returned to the States, Jeannette sent one of her own poems describing Carrie's admirers, and how tired she was becoming of being their 'nuss' (nurse). It is too long to quote in full, but the lines about R. C. Jebb, Mr. Clifford and the Vice-Chancellor, Power, mentioned in her letters, are given below.

'Jeannette to her dear cousin, Greeting—

Dear Carrie, the town is deserted,
The house is as still as a well,
And their privilege none have asserted
Of ringing up George to the bell—
That boy is as fat as a pigeon
(He always looked hearty of yore)
But he's now never out of the kitchen
For he's never called up to the door.
One man only now takes the trouble
To ring the front door-bell; and he
Is the postman—whose labours are double
To what they used lately to be.
For daily I'm deluged with letters
Showered in at each post by the truss,
From all who are wearing your fetters—
O Carrie! Who would be a "nuss"? . . .

First of all there's our hero from Erin
Who was bad with the "fidgets" you know,
He says he's as thin as a herring,
And expects daily thinner to grow.
His notes are half plaintive, half frantic,
And very didactic at times,
And he says that across the Atlantic
He meditates sending some rhymes.
Then begs for a line in a letter
Just the least consolation to shed,
And though the hay-fever is better
He says that his eyes are still red.
I must try, I suppose, on my paper
Probabilities vague to discuss
Something solid to forge out of vapour;
But, Carrie, who would be a "nuss"? . . .

Then came a short note from a Fellow
Of Trinity—oh such a hand!

78

A five hundred horse-power propeller
    Could only such writing command.
I know that you think he is clumsy,
    That his features are hewn out of wood,
But if fall'n from your table the crumbs he
    Might gather, I'm sure that he would.
Then I've had such a power of inquiries
    From that dear old, good-natured V.C.
And to cap it, all now we require, is
    One line from the "Heathen Chinee".
I doubt not they'd all be delighted
    To take you "for better or wuss",
But their hopes I suppose will be blighted—
    Oh Carrie, who would be a "nuss"? . . .'

CHAPTER V

In spite of the fact that Carrie refused Jebb, she must have been impressed by the fact that he had won the highest honours in Classics at Cambridge in 1862, was a Fellow of Trinity College and had friends among the leading literary figures of the day. Still she did not feel enough drawn to him to consider marriage. But he was determined not to give her up so easily, and after her return to America in August, 1871, wrote to her regularly for the next three years. She had made him promise never to mention love to her, yet his letters, a mixture of Cambridge gossip and philosophy, always mentioned those things most likely to impress her, living as she did with Polly and their mother in the unintellectual atmosphere of West Philadelphia.

Cambridge, Nov. 21st, 1871

'My dear Mrs. Slemmer,

The Master[1] and Mrs. Thompson had a large evening party in Miss Thackeray's[2] honour, and I was pleased to meet her again, for we are old friends. She is devoted to the memory of her father, and is always glad to see anyone whom she can in any way associate with him.

'The first time I met Thackeray was at Charterhouse on Founder's Day, Dec. 12th, 1862, the year in which I took my degree. Do you remember Greyfriars in *The Newcomes*? Thackeray was intensely fond of the real Greyfriars, and was always ready to like Carthusians.[3] He asked me and another man to dine with him the

[1] W. H. Thompson, 1810–86. Master of Trinity.
[2] Anne (Anny) Thackeray, 1837–1919. Later Lady Ritchie, Thackeray's elder daughter, author of *Old Kensington* and other books.
[3] Boys who, like Jebb, had been at school at Charterhouse.

next Sunday: and I so well remember the evening. The party consisted only of Thackeray and his mother (who died just before him), Miss Thackeray, the authoress, who sat at the head of the table, and hung on her father's words, Miss M. Thackeray[1] and Dr. Russell, the *Times* correspondent, who was very intimate with them.

'I was very much afraid of my host at first, as he talked constantly in a strain of ironical banter, but he was so heartily kind under it all that he soon made one feel at home. I remember his being asked how he spelt "ecstasy", and treating the question with great disdain. He had a dread of everything that bore the most distant resemblance to pedantry.

'Miss Thackeray is very like him in her kindliness, and in her anxiety to prevent conventionalisms from checking the manifestation of kindliness; but, in place of his constant irony, she has a sort of unaffected dreaminess which never leaves her. In fact the distinctive thing about her is that she is sentimental without either affectation or loss of humour; and in talking, just as in writing, passes rapidly from serious pathos to drollery.

'The party at the Adams' last night was very pleasant. . . . I sat next to Mrs. Adams which was enough in itself to make the dinner a success for me. Professor Adams[2] said a thing which seemed to me so true, and which was deeply impressive as coming from an eminent man of science. "The problems of the physical world," he said, "seem too hard for man's mind at first; yet they can be made out by trying; they seem out of reach, but they can be reached by standing on tiptoe. Had the system of the universe been constructed a little differently, the ascertainment of its laws *would* have been beyond us; as it is, we seem to have been given simple cases, examples just within our comprehension, of laws which might have been too complex for the grasp of the human intellect."

'How strange that to some narrow theologians there seems to be a conflict between science and religion! Can there be any attitude of mind more truly and more nobly reverent, more essentially religious, than that of the real man of science, the man who, like

[1] Helen Marion (Minny) Thackeray, Thackeray's younger daughter. She married Leslie Stephen in 1867.

[2] John Couch Adams, 1819–92. Eminent astronomer, predicted the position of the then unknown planet Neptune, for which credit went to Leverrier.

Newton or Adams, has moved in thought among *all* the worlds, and has come back declaring, "*All* thy works praise Thee"?

'For me it is one of the great happinesses of the happy life here that one can live with such men, not with men who are starving their minds or making their moral natures hopelessly ugly in order to be millionaires or, as the crown of their career, expectant baronets. Here, at all events, there is a true and a refined republicanism; for there is no rank except what culture gives; and the society is composed of people who have foregone the pursuit of wealth or rank because they preferred prizes of another kind. I have never been in a place where the men seemed to me, on the whole, so honest or so manly or so true to each other; for they are bound to each other by the ties of interests which can never become slack, and which no self-interest can ever dissolve.

'I forgot to tell you that a friend of mine who went to America with Mr. Hughes last year has written to me about a movement in London for restoring, by contributions of books from their writers, the Free Library burnt at Chicago. A great many men here have sent their books. D'Israeli, Carlyle, and a great many other celebrities are sending their works with autograph inscriptions. Probably there is far too much grave distress to admit of such a gift being felt as having any appreciable value; but I do hope it will be recognized as a token of cordial and widely-spread sympathy.

Ever yours most sincerely,

R. C. JEBB'

While Jebb sounds as though he might have been rather a solemn scholar, and while we are told he was extremely shy, he had, on the other hand, many lively interests. 'While at Cambridge he joined the A.D.C. [Amateur Dramatic Club], the Beefsteak Club, and the Whist Club ... steered a First Trinity boat, held a commission in the Volunteers, was an officer of the Union and the Musical Societies, spent much money, was amazed at his own tailor's bill, became an "Apostle", attended a continual round of breakfasts, luncheons, and dinners, but read during the Vacations, and incidentally got the Craven in 1860. . . . The usual life of a University Don followed, varied in Jebb's case by his appointment as Public Orator in 1869, by writing articles for the *Saturday Review*, and later on, leaders for the *Times*.'[1]

Jebb's family had for years been well known both in the Church and the Law. Originally they were English, but in the early eighteenth century his great-grandfather, Richard Jebb, had gone to Ireland to enter business. His third grandson, Robert, was R. C. Jebb's father. Reference books give Jebb's birthplace as Dundee, where his parents were visiting his maternal grandfather, Heneage Horsley, Dean of Brechin. However, his home was in Dublin, then Desmond, Killiney, nine miles away.

Jebb wrote to Carrie from Desmond.

April 23rd, 1872

'My dear Mrs. Slemmer,

I have been giving a lecture in Dublin, the first of a series of "Afternoon Lectures on Literature and Art" which go through the season. My audience, which the Dublin papers described as "large and very *fashionable*" (oh, epithet dear to the Irish soul!) listened with exemplary fortitude to my discourse which is going to be printed in some shape or other; and then, any day you run down to Chicago, you can read the copy in the Free Library, to which the British author hastens to present his immortal works.

'On your recommendation I mean to get the *Life of Benjamin Franklin*. A peculiar interest belongs, I think, to the scientific men of the *pre*scientific age; they were so alone, and seem the greater for being alone. The heroic isolation of Galileo is only in a less degree the attribute of such men as Franklin. Apathy, incredulity, ridicule present obstacles as great as, and far less stimulating than, actual persecution.

'How curious that you should have been reading, and liking, *Auf der Höhe*![2] Only the other day I was on the point of sending it to you when something, I don't know what, put it out of my head, and I did not remember it till I read the name almost with a start, in your letter.'

[1] *The Morning Post*, London, Oct. 31st, 1907. Review of C. Jebb's *Life of R. C. Jebb*.

[2] A novel of West German peasant life by Berthold Auerbach, published in 1865; it achieved great popularity.

His poetic style is especially evident in the opening of a letter written in August, 1872, to Carrie.

'I was so delighted to get your letter last night. I had just come back from one of those little dinner-parties which often make a pleasant ending to one of our breezy, bright August days, and there—the first thing the light flashed upon—was your letter! There it lay, it did not vanish when it was looked at; it stayed where it was, quiet, palpable, divinely self-possessed; like one of those good gifts of the gods which men used to find in the valleys and woods, or on wild mountain paths, where Pan or Hermes had passed; like a good young man's prosperity in the third volume; like anything happy which comes sudden and seldom into the hard world of fact. And then this bright windfall allowed itself to be touched, even to be read through, not once only; and how glad I was to find that you were well, after all that dreadful heat, and to hear all about your life in Erie, and the delightful Germans, and the ladies with limited conversational resources. . . .'

Cambridge, Dec. 3rd, 1872

'My dear Mrs. Slemmer,

When I came back to Trinity last night, I found a note from, whom do you suppose? Miss Thackeray, dated the Bull Hotel and asking me to dine there with her and some friends the next day. It was such a delightful party, the Freshfields, Miss Ritchie, Mr. Ritchie, Mr. Hallam Tennyson, the poet's eldest son who has just come up to Trinity, and Mr. Henry Sidgwick. Mr. Tennyson was to have come but had a cold and telegraphed at the last moment.

'We had fun; among other amusements, we marked some of our common friends for: 1) appearance, 2) heart, 3) intellect, 4) manners, 5) sense of humour. The worst of that game is that one can never forget what happened to the inventor of the guillotine. . . . You cannot think how charming Miss Thackeray is; it is the charm of a perfectly good heart and a great wit enshrined in a lady. . . .'

Jebb no doubt hoped to cause a jealous twinge in the faraway Carrie.

'. . . Mr. William Morris, the poet, dined in hall with his friend, Mr. Eric Magnusson, the Icelander, who has worked with him on the *Sagas*. Mr. Morris is a rough, self-centred, passionate, odd, almost wild man. Mr. Magnusson tells me that he and Morris agree in thinking that the supreme joy is to get away from all the restraints of conventional life, to Iceland, or to Central Africa. I can never quite believe in a man who *tells* you what a charming child of nature he is, what agony it is to him to have to dress like other people, to use knife and fork, and to wind up his watch.'

Cambridge, May 27th, 1873

'My dear Mrs. Slemmer,

It would be most natural to begin by telling you of the ordinary May Term doings, perhaps, but another subject is uppermost in my thoughts just now, an event in any life, and a large event in mine. I have met "George Eliot" (Mrs. Lewes), and found such great happiness in knowing her better.[1] Friendship is a word varying in largeness of sense with the largeness of the nature; and her friendship means a great deal. She and her husband came to Cambridge for a few days with one of my oldest friends, Mr. Frederick Myers.[2]

'I had known Mrs. Lewes before, but acquaintanceship sprang into friendship by one of those impulses which cannot be explained except by some hidden law asserting itself in a moment. . . . We had been talking about Sophocles, and she had said that she first came to know him through a small book of mine. I asked how he had influenced her, and her answer certainly startled me. Probably all people, or most people who have any inner life at all, sometimes write down things meant for no eye but their own. Long ago I was putting down in this way some things that had been passing through my mind about Sophocles, and this among the rest, that George Eliot was the modern dramatist, in the large

[1] George Eliot lived with G. H. Lewes for many years. After his death in 1878 she married John Cross, twenty years her junior.
[2] Frederic Wm. Henry Myers, 1843–1901. Poet and essayist, Secretary of the Society for Psychical Research.

sense, most like him and that he had told upon her work probably *in the outlining of the first emotions.* Her answer to my question was, "In the delineation of the great primitive emotions." Verbally this was an accident, but hardly in substance. Of course I did not tell her. But was it not curious? . . .

'Her husband is very delightful, he is accomplished, and he has a good heart. What I admire in him is his faithfulness in laying everything: knowledge, social power, reputation, all, at his illustrious wife's feet. . . . We went together to the Choral Festival at King's, and as I was walking with her, I heard some people whisper, "Mr. Lewes is here, but is *she* here?" He was close behind, but I doubted whether he had heard it. When we came out, he quoted it to her. . . .'

Cambridge, Nov. 25th, 1873

'. . . On the 15th the Humphrys had a dinner party, rather crowded. . . . I talked to Miss Grill. The possessor of this some-what disquieting name joins the sentiment of life's most glowing and gushing years to the experience of a period considerably more advanced. Well do I remember taking her in to dinner once, and her saying, in the most unprovoked way, while she was dining with apparently good appetite, "Mr. Jebb, do you think that women ever die of a broken heart?" I was so terrified that I could think of no answer but that "perhaps other organs may have some-thing to do with it". . . .

'Mr. Tennyson has been here. He came up on Saturday, the 15th, and stayed till Monday. On Saturday I met him at his son Hallam's rooms, and sat on his right hand at dinner. He talked very pleasantly of the old Trinity days; and in the evening he read aloud to us "Boadicea", "The Grandmother" and the two "Northern Farmers". . . . I like Hallam Tennyson thoroughly; he has a beautiful nature; and, now that I know him well, I wish more than ever to know his mother. Everyone says that she is perfection.

'My friend Frederic Myers has been here, too. He is interested in spiritualism at present; and for the first time in my life I assisted at a séance during his visit. . . . The case in regard to "spiritualism"

86

is a dilemma. Either it is deliberate imposition or it is some agency at present unknown. The "unconscious muscular or cerebral action" theory may explain moving or tilting of tables, but it will not explain *rapping*. At present I incline to think that it is deliberate imposture. But I have not evidence enough for an induction. . . .'

Jebb continued by describing his experiences with one of the spirits, whom he tried to believe was an imposture. Carrie, who later disliked Myers, was completely opposed to the idea of spiritualism, and would have nothing to do with it.

Cambridge, Dec. 26th, 1873

'My dear Mrs. Slemmer,

Well, on December 17th I went to town to spend two days with the Tennysons, and very delightful days they were. I had long looked forward to meeting Mrs. Tennyson. She is tall, slight, with the traces, they must be called so now, of a sweet serene beauty; she is as stately as consists with a grace which has nothing of rigour; gentle, of perfect courtesy; with a sympathetic insight which makes those whom she admits to the friend-circle feel at once at home by assuring them of being understood. Two people, independently of each other, described her to me by saying that she was a *châtelaine*; and the description is really happy, expressing as it does something of the sweet queenliness of a French mistress of the manor of the old régime, helped by some quaint felicity in her dress which would evaporate under male analysis. . . .

'One evening, some of our party of the day before met again at a little dinner at the Leslie Stephens'—Miss Thackeray, Mr. Robert Browning, Hallam Tennyson, etc. We were talking of English words that had no rhymes, and after instancing: silver, month, depth, and false, Mr. Browning asked for a rhyme to rhinoceros, which he presently supplied himself, as follows:

> "*Whenever you see a rhinoceros,*
>   *If a tree be in sight,*
>   *Climb quick, for his might*
> *Is a match for the gods, he would* toss Eros!"

'By the by, if you read the review of my translations in the *Fortnightly*, you may have noticed that Mr. Myers disputes my way of taking the lines in Browning's "Abt Vogler",

> *"For one is assured at first, one scarce can*
> *say, that he feared,"* etc.

Mr. Browning volunteered to tell me that I had interpreted the whole passage exactly as he had meant it, and that the possibility of Mr. Myers' version had never even occurred to him. Oh, that the shades of the departed could sometimes be evoked to decide points of this kind! The points which test an accurate instinct are generally *above* the logical sphere: they cannot be proved.'

Carrie received many letters from other admirers while in West Philadelphia. Several were from her young friend Walter Wright of Chicago, who had corresponded with her faithfully since the beginning of the Civil War, letters mostly concerned with books, both English and German, poetry and other forms of intellectual development. His last letter, February 11th, 1872, spoke mostly of love.

'My dear Friend,

You do not approve of something in my last, and call them "sentimental" and "without meaning", and I am at a loss to know why. As I remember what I said I spoke of the real regard we had for one another in days past, and expressed a wish that the old feeling might be brought back. How there is any false sentiment in such a wish, or how it is without meaning I quite fail to see. You may not share in the feeling, and I am sorry to know that you do not, but for my part I cannot but regret that the old affection has gone, and wish strongly it could be recalled.

'I must say also that I have always rejoiced in believing that the social intercourse between us was never of the "sentimental" kind but quite the contrary. You tell me that you have in you now "a morbid tendency" which you have to guard against, but I never perceived it in the old time, and always thought I never met a person with a nature more clear, bright and healthy than yours.

For myself, I may say no one ever called me sentimental so far as I know.

'Bear with me if you can while I say a word more about love. You tell me that to love is "to crave to secure one for yourself for a permanent possession and a dread lest the one loved might be lost to you and secured by some one else". Now such a feeling I must say seems to me not to be love at all, but only a compound of selfishness and jealousy. The spirit of love is a spirit of self-sacrifice, and it longs to do or to suffer all for the one it loves. To seek to keep one for yourself, and to minister solely to your gratification is not love at all, but only selfishness; the end of love is not to make yourself happy, but to make another happy. True love is utter forgetfulness of self, and entire devotion to another, and I hope you may find some one to love with all this devotion, and to be blessed with all the depth and fullness of joy it ever brings with it. With a nature so richly endowed I know no one who could be a greater blessing to herself, or to the one she loved, than you, if only once brought fully under the sway of this self forgetting and devoted love.[1]

'You speak of a certain "hardness" that I sometimes told you I feared was growing upon you. It is true I have felt that you had lost something of the quick feeling for all that is good or fair, the fine sense and appreciation of what is highest and best in nature and character, of which when I first knew you, you had so much and which I admire greatly and prize most highly. . . .

'Your friend,

W. W.'

While Carrie may have deserved the censure of this letter, it probably made her turn all the more willingly to Jebb, for he never criticized her in his letters, writing almost entirely of things of the mind, and about people, rather than analysing such things as love, which Carrie said she wanted to forget.

Another admirer was the the Irish poet, William Allingham, perhaps best known now for his poem,

[1] Many years later Carrie pencilled at the top of this sheet, 'Love as it was shown to me by R.C.J.'

> '*Up the airy mountain,*
> *Down the rushy glen,*
> *We daren't go a-hunting*
> *For fear of little men. . . .*'

In his last letter to her, December 17th, 1872, he said,

'Yesterday was a dark wet day here, but it's marked with white in my calendar because I found your letter on my breakfast table, as though dropt from the sky. I knew I should hear something someday, but could not guess when, or what. Now I can at least think of you *in loco*, the City of Quakers, namely, though I wish it were not so far away.

'I am very glad to hear of your liking England so well. I am not, for my own part, dissatisfied to have passed my youth mainly in the country, but now should be very unwilling to live anywhere but in London, unrivalled (at least for any person of English speech) in its multiplicity and variety of interest. One of my few ambitions, long ago, was to be friends with certain men whom I looked up to as the highest of their time, and in this, if in nothing else, I have succeeded beyond hope.

'You name Mr. Carlyle; the dear old man fulfilled his 77th year on the 4th of this month. We walked in Hyde Park, talking of many things. At one place he fell silent, stopped, and, while I went on a few paces, uncovered his venerable head and bowed it. I knew what this meant; it was the place where his wife died suddenly, in her carriage. Carlyle's piety, affection, and faithfulness are even deeper than his intellect and learning. I shudder at the thought of losing him. Yet it is one of his whims to declaim against *Poetry*! In conversation, however, he makes large admissions on the subject.

'Have you seen Tennyson's new volume? The poet himself called on me a few Sundays ago, and I had the pleasure of three evenings of his company, playing host to him one evening at the South Kensington Museum, which he had never seen before. He complained of the dullness of the country, and I believe if he had not two big houses tied to his legs, like cannon balls, he would come and live near London. I was several years in the neighbourhood of his Isle of Wight residence, and saw him often and intimately, with the greatest delight.

'It is presumptuous to speak in this connection of my own little productions. I am sorry that the new and enlarged edition of my poems is not ready to send you, since you so kindly consent to give my Muse hospitality, but rather than delay, I send you now by book post three little green volumes in the hope of their being lucky enough to greet you on or about New Year's Day. May the New Year be a happy one to you! And may it carry you again to England! "Wait till you are an old woman,"—no, no!! Do come in March or April, with the flowers of this very next Spring. I should be so happy to look forward to seeing you.

'Poor Mr. Froude, the shillelagh is whistling round his head with a vengeance! I only hope it will not descend in hard fact. I think I told you that I am managing *Fraser's Magazine* for him in his absence. He wishes to resign it to me on his return, and perhaps I may take it for prudential reasons; but editing is often disagreeable work, one offends so many people, by the rejection of articles; and besides, it cuts off much from one's time for original writing. . . .

'Yours sincerely,

W. ALLINGHAM'

At last the call of England grew too strong for her, and in July, 1874, she returned to Cambridge to find out what her feelings were towards her faithful Richard, or Dick, as she called him. When she was in her eighties she told a romantic story about how her final decision was made.

She said that at a dinner party, one evening, they had all been talking of guardian angels. 'Dick had made his proposal and I had made up my mind to refuse him because I felt I wanted to be with my mother. I was to arise early the next morning and leave before he could come to call or leave a note. As soon as I went to sleep, I had a vivid dream. It seemed that my guardian angel appeared before me and in earnest tones said, "You are making a mistake. This is your great opportunity and you will never regret it." The dream had such an effect upon me that I lay awake for long hours and finally fell asleep so soundly that I did not waken for my proposed early start. So that when Dick came the next day, my answer was decidely different. A strange thing, don't you think, how a dream changed my whole life?'

Whether this story is accurate or not, she did suddenly accept Richard, and the two were married on August 18th, 1874, from the home of his sister, Eglantyne, and her husband, Arthur Jebb, in Shropshire. Carrie sent the announcement from *The Times* to her family.

'On Tuesday, the 18th of August, at the parish church, Ellesmere, Shropshire, by the Rev. John Jebb, D.D., Canon of Hereford, assisted by the Rev. J. Peake, Vicar of Ellesmere, RICHARD CLAVERHOUSE JEBB, M.A., Fellow of Trinity College, Cambridge, and Public Orator of the University, to CAROLINE LANE, widow of the late General Slemmer, of the Army of the United States, and daughter of the late Rev. John Reynolds, D.D., of Philadelphia.'

Caroline Slemmer, London, about 1870

Eleanor Evans, 1818

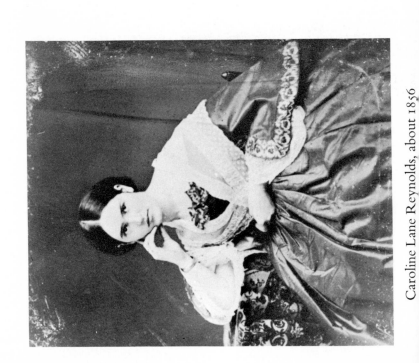

Caroline Lane Reynolds, about 1856

Adam J. Slemmer

Ellen Reynolds DuPuy, 'My dear Sister', about 1859

Fort Pickens, Santa Rosa Island, Florida.
Photographed by Herbert Spencer

Medal of Honor presented to Slemmer by the New York City
Chamber of Commerce, 1861

Caroline Slemmer, about 1862

Bertie Slemmer

Mr. and Mrs. Jebb, honeymoon, Llandudno. In wedding-dress and picture mentioned in her letter

CHAPTER VI

Two days after the wedding, Carrie wrote most matter-of-factly from Llandudno, Wales.

Aug. 20th, 1874

'My dear Sister,

Dick has insured his life for two thousand pounds and settled this upon me in the event of his death, and he has signed a legal contract to settle my own property present and prospective on me for my own separate use, he to have the use of the income for his life, in case I die first, but to have no rights at all in the principal which I am to will as I like. I told him that the state laws at home would have done better by him but he said what he wanted was me, not my money. . . .

'So much for the business. I have spent all my money and all yours, too, on my new things, and yet it seems to me I have to consider very thoughtfully what to wear in order to make my dressing look respectable. I had no time really to shop, so I went to the two most expensive places, ordered my things and left all the details to their own taste.

'My wedding dress is of two very delicate and closely approaching shades of grey silk and anything lovelier than the result you never saw. This dress with crêpe lisse sleeves and ruffles cost twenty-seven pounds, sixteen shillings, but then if you could only see the quantity of silk it took, with side pleatings double, so as to have the two shades in coquilles, down each side of a marvellous back breadth. It is lined in the body and faced in the skirt with white silk, but I won't go on describing. Dick and I are to be photographed today, *I* say on purpose that our friends may ever have my wedding dress in remembrance.'

After describing in detail two more new dresses, bonnets, under-clothing, etc., she continued,

'So much for the finery, which please to understand I have described for your benefit, and not because *my* soul therein delights. "Me mightier aspects move," just at present, and I grudged the time I had to give to shopping. Everything came home in time, though *just* in time, Dick having to bring up the wedding dress himself from London; and we left the Adams together to take the train for Shropshire. You know his sister Eglantyne married her cousin Arthur Jebb, the heir to three thousand pounds a year, and a country house, and it was to their place, the Lyth, we were going.

'When we got there, it seemed to me just like the novels we read of English life. The cart was at the station to take our boxes and my maid, (the latter not being in existence, left her place unoccupied) and for us a carriage with liveried coachman and footman. None of the places in novels are near the station, and no more was ours. We drove for a mile through the most beautiful country I have seen in England, full of lakes and with distant hills, and then up a grand avenue of trees, until we came out on the lawn drive, and so the front door.

'About six or seven of the two Jebb families came out to meet us, among them my present father and mother-in-law, Dick's sister Eglantyne, called Tiny, and her husband, Arthur, and his sister Louisa, our hostess since her father's death. They took me to my room and left me there to dress for dinner, which was to be at half-past seven, and, when it came, was very fine. In the evening we ladies talked together while the men remained in the dining-room over their wine, and for half an hour, after they joined us, and then went to bed. From Friday until Tuesday, the 18th, the time passed very pleasantly among a houseful of people.

'The weather had been lowering, indeed pouring, at intervals, so you can fancy how pleasant it was to see at least dry ground on Tuesday morning, even though the skies were overcast. From the carriage to the church door there would be quite a little walk, and I did not like Elsie's chef d'oeuvre to run a shadow of a risk of being wet. All the party preceded our carriage, in which Mr. and

94

Mrs. Jebb and I drove to the church. There Mr. Potts, who was to give me away, met me, gave me his arm, and carried me last up the aisle to the altar at each side of which everybody belonging to the party had been arranged, and where Dick and his best man, Basil Hammond, were waiting to receive me. Canon Jebb, Dick's uncle, assisted by the Parish Vicar married us.

'We went into the vestry afterwards to sign the register, still like the novels, you see, and then Dick and I drove back to the Lyth together. We had not time to do more than change our dresses and say goodbye. (I don't know what Dick had, he *says* tea, but for me a bottle of champagne was opened in my room by Lou, and chicken and charlotte russe were abstracted from the table ready set for luncheon.)

'We set off again in the carriage to catch the 12 o'clock train at the station, which we did, and which got us in to Llandudno about five. And after two days, from Llandudno I am writing. To-morrow we leave here for the Lakes of Killarney, where we are to visit an old uncle and two aunties and from there I shall write again. . . . Dick is writing a review of Buchanan's poems for the *Saturday Review*, and I am sitting half the time writing and the other half gazing out at the sea, and the two great bluffs which hold it in, the "Great Orme's Head" and the "Little Orme's Head". Both employments must stop now, for the carriage is here, and I not dressed. . . .'

A few days later the bridegroom wrote to his sister, Tiny, from Danesfort, Killarney, Ireland, the home of his Aunty Fan, Aunty Tye and Uncle Sam, all Horsleys, the maiden name of his mother. Jebb said,

'Well, we have been going through a series of festivities, Headley's, Killarney House, 5 o'clock tea at Beaufort, dinner party at Danesfort, luncheon ditto. Tonight there is a dance at Southill and on Monday we are going to the Upper Lake with Dick Herbert. . . . We go to Desmond as at present arranged on Wednesday. Cara is bearing the strain upon her social energies wonderfully. Just now she is playing piquet with Uncle Sam. . . .'

From now on Carrie will be referred to as Cara, her husband's

nickname for her; he also called her Carina and Carissima, deriva-
tives of the Latin word for 'dear'. She wrote again from Killarney, sounding definitely homesick and not a bit certain whether
she had done the right thing in marrying Dick.

Killarney, Sept. 4th, 1874

'My dear Sister,

All your letters, meaning yours and Charlie's and the children's,
reached me only yesterday morning. I really think if it were to be
done over again, I should never have the courage to take a step
which threatens to cut me off so much from home and country;
but everything was so hurried, that, the "yes" once extracted, I
had no time for reconsideration. One can only hope the hasty
marriage may turn out all for the best, though just now I cannot
help but feel unhappy when I think of all of you.

'One never sits down in sorrow when there is anything to be
done, and I console myself by making all sorts of resolutions. To
begin with, I shall post letters twice a week regularly, and if possible write at least a few lines every day. . . . Then, the children
must keep up their affection for their aunt by making her house
their second home. After this year I shall never be quite content
without one or two of them with me, but we can talk all that over
when I come back next August. . . .

'The parties and amusements still go on here, but I am in no
mood to enjoy them, and should prefer them at longer intervals,
even if I were. Tonight we go to a dance given by a Miss Wright
and tomorrow to a grand dinner at Murcross, one of the show
places at Killarney, owned by a Mr. Herbert. The Duke of St.
Albans and his bride leave there today, but the Marquis of
Bromont and his bride, the Duke of Marlborough's daughter, and a
great beauty, are staying in the house, and will be there tomorrow.
You know the Horsleys are an excellent old English family, equal
to the best, though now they haven't a tithe of the wealth of the
friends with whom they associate. . . .

Desmond, Killiney, Sept. 11th, 1874

'My dear Sister,

Nothing particular has happened since my last letter except

that we have again changed our plans and are now to stay at Desmond with Dick's father and mother for ten days or a fortnight instead of going for so long a time to Paris. Desmond is rather a small place, coming as we do from such grand houses, but a prettier situation I never saw. The house stands on a hill, and has apparantly nothing between it and the sea but sloping lawn and trees and shrubbery, and the view out across the bay from the dining-room window is simply perfect.

'Dick's father looks upon himself as an unsuccessful man, because I suppose he was not a Judge and because he has not made a large fortune as a barrister, but according to our notions we should consider him very comfortable. I suppose it must be rather hard to live within sight of a large castle where one was brought up, and to feel that one has not risen or been able to keep up one's inherited position.

'The Canon is the eldest son, and most of the property he came into he has squandered, or given away in restoring old churches. Mrs. Jebb says just as expensive a dissipation really as drinking and gambling. She is only afraid the chests of old family plate may go the way of all the rest, a fear I share with her, as some day Dick must come in for his share of that. The Canon is like your Uncle Charles, a widower without children, but with the unfortunate addition that he is a great scholar, with all a scholar's impracticabilities, and with a great fancy for restoring antiquities. When his wife died, he sold all her jewels of which she had great store, and gave the result to a church he wanted to help at the moment, to the great exasperation of all the younger relatives. No wonder we tremble for the plate!

'There is also a splendid library which old Bishop Jebb started with the idea of having a celebrated family library known as the Jebb Library to be inherited by the eldest son. It is worth now between five and six thousand pounds, and this the Canon has my full permission to sell whenever he sees occasion. It has hitherto only been a burden and expense to the unfortunate inheritor who has had to hire a house on purpose to hold the library, and to keep some one to attend to it. Nobody would be sorry to see the books go, if their departure could save the plate, except the Canon who thinks far more of them than he does of the silver.

'Mrs. Jebb and I get on capitally together. We spend our mornings in the drawing-room, me listening and she giving me all the family history, which I should never have heard from Dick himself till the end of time. I have the full and true account of all Aunty Fan's and Aunty Tye's lovers, and how the former was deserted by her's, for a great heiress whom he married and was afterwards miserable with, and how Aunty Tye had offer after offer, without ever for a moment changing her fixed determination. Aunty Tye is so lovely that one cannot understand how she contrived to escape matrimony at all.

'One of her old lovers, and latest I should suppose, as he is fifteen years younger than she, was staying at Danesfort while we were there and he said to me one day, "Old as Eglantyne Horsley is now, I have never seen a face or a character to compare with her, and until I do, I shall not marry." I thought to myself, "Well, Mr. Wellington, you will have to hurry up in the search or when you find her, she will not marry *you*, since I know for a fact that you are forty-eight years old." His testimony convinced me that the histories that Mrs. Jebb tells are not exaggerated.

'About the notice of the wedding from the *Times*, at first I thought I would get Charlie to put the notice in the *New York Times*, and in the *Army and Navy Journal*, but perhaps it may be too late now to be worth while. Jeannette gave old Mr. Jebb the D.D. to put in after Pa's name. She told me afterwards that there was a dissenting clergyman named John Reynolds in England and she was determined not to have people think he had been her uncle. Besides she said she distinctly remembered Pa's saying that some college had given him the title, or was to give him the title, and at any rate she thought there ought to be some way of showing he was an Episcopalian, and D.D. would be best. I didn't care, seeing that he was dead and gone, and that in America D.D. meant no extraordinary merit or ability, though if I had been consulted I should have left it out, not liking to assume more than is one's due. . . . Address your letters to my new name, "Petersfield House", after the 1st of October.'

After the honeymoon in Ireland and Paris, Cara wrote from this address in Cambridge; it was a furnished house they had rented,

98

and she was soon busily keeping house there and making more friends.

'My dear Sister,

. . . Fortunately Dick is very easy to please about his eating . . . in fact I wish he cared more about it, and less about sherry, as I am sure he needs nourishment and not stimulant, but one can't make an Englishman see this subject with *my* eyes. He has almost constant indigestion, and he has had two or three attacks of rheumatism, and is even now a little lame from rheumatic stiffness in the hip, and I am sure so much sherry must be bad for him. If he would only take claret, it would be better I am sure, but he won't and he laughs at my thinking he takes much sherry, only a small pint bottle a day and that at dinner, for he seldom touches wine before. I suppose I have an undue horror of wine, and that it may be necessary in this climate, but I can't make myself believe in any good results following its use.

'Today Mrs. Prettyman and Mrs. Walpole, her sister, have been spending the afternoon with me. The latter's two sons went out to Nebraska with fifteen hundred pounds apiece, were robbed and cheated in every conceivable way, lost every penny they had, and while waiting to hear from home, one took a place as waiter at a hotel table, and the other got work as a varnisher. They went through untold hardships. One of them had his foot frozen, and cut off his toes himself with his razor, and they were both at times without a morsel to eat, or a penny in their pockets. They were too proud to come home, and were only forced to do it by illness, both having dangerous attacks of congestion of the lungs. Still, they like America so much, they mean to go back as soon as they are strong enough. . . .'

'My dear Sister,

All this week I have been sitting up in state, which means my best clothes, to receive visitors and every afternoon from three to five the room has been crowded. I don't at all mind callers when I have got myself into the proper state of mind by preparation, and when I am dressed and ready, so that the week has been most agreeable.

'I could not possibly try to introduce everybody to you at once, so I shall wait to tell you about people until I have really become acquainted with them myself. Most of the visitors thus far have been ladies and their husbands, Professors and Professorinns, Masters and Mistresses of Colleges, etc., all the best society of Cambridge. One starts here with everything in one's favour, and Dick says he never saw the stiff old gentlemen and their stiffer wives unbend as they do to me. The Vice Chancellor took me into dinner as the bride, at a grand dinner given for us at his Lodge, and I thought him a very cordial pleasant old man, and was surprised afterwards to hear that he is considered to stand immensely on his dignity.

'Meanwhile, I like housekeeping under English auspices immensely. My cook comes to me every morning after breakfast and asks me about the dinner, and usually I go with her into the buttery and see what there is. We have three house servants and a gardener, and every scrap of the washing even to the towels, is put out to a laundress. Wages in the long run are quite as dear as at home. For instance, I pay my house maid eighteen pounds a year, $90, two pounds a year for her own washing, and eighteen pence a week for her money. The cook will have twenty pounds a year and the above allowance, and Martin the waiter, a boy of sixteen, seventeen pounds a year, and beer money and tea.'

Cambridge, Nov. 2nd, 1874

'My dear Sister,

I felt so tired and wakeful all night that I did not wake in the morning until ten o'clock, and as Dick would sleep on until the day of doom if nobody woke him, neither of us came down until half-past ten for breakfast. . . . In came Jeannette in somewhat of a fever of embarrassment. She had invited twenty-four people to a dinner party with the belief that half of them would refuse, fancy anyone taking the risk, and every single individual had been disengaged, and had accepted! Her drawing-room at the outside only holds eighteen, and her own family makes four to add to the twenty-four. The only thing was to split up into two, and make some excuse to half the people for deferring their day. . . .

'I never like to mix up my money and Dick's in any way, and I don't like to borrow from him just now while his balance at the bank is so low. His fellowship comes in some time this month, and then if all the bills are once paid, I shall see my way clear. I don't naturally like to suggest it to him, seeing that few people recognize their own deficiencies, but I should like nothing better than to take possession of his income, to manage all the affairs, to give him whatever money he wanted, and at the end of the year to show him how comfortably we had got on without anxiety or trouble. Now, money drops between his fingers, and his accounts are just as likely to show too much on one side of the book as on the other, an indication of how they are kept. When a bill comes in, he generally believes he paid it a year ago, which is always a painful condition of mind, when the receipt is not to be found. Well, all this preamble comes from the fact that I mean to order a Wheeler and Wilcox sewing-machine forthwith, to engage a woman to come to sew, and to have my brown serge suit made up at once. . . .'

At this time Cara's letters contained many passages of annoyance at the delay of one of her steamer trunks shipped from America after her wedding, containing many of her clothes and some jewellery. She never did receive it, and not for many years was the mystery of its disappearance solved. Among other things that Cara had asked her family to send was Adam Slemmer's Merit of Honor medal, awarded by the New York Chamber of Commerce. This was found by a fisherman at the bottom of the Susquehanna River near Rockville, Pennsylvania, in 1897. An article in the Norristown *Daily Times*, July 28th of that year, said,

'The widow of General Slemmer married an English gentleman named Jebb, and she resides in London. When Mrs. Jebb sailed for England about twenty-five years ago she wanted to take [her late husband's] medal with her to show it to her husband's folks there, intending to send it back to General Slemmer's father. . . . That trunk was placed on the deck of the vessel just before it sailed from New York and that was the last seen of it. . . .

'The trunk containing the medal was stolen and fearing it might be the means of detection, the thief, or the receiver of the stolen property, threw it into the Susquehanna River as he was crossing the Pennsylvania railroad bridge at Rockville, where all these long years it has remained until found by Mr. Vantz.'

Cara was finally forced to borrow £20 from her friend Mrs. Adams and went to London to buy 'jacket and hat, bonnet and furs'.

Cambridge, Dec. 15th, 1874

'My dear Sister,

I get no time to sew on anything but cushions and screens and drawing-room fancy work. Dick can't bear to hear the machine and dislikes any sewing that doesn't look what he calls refined, and as he is home most of the time, I consult his prejudices. He was dreadfully shocked the other day to find me sitting on the rug before the fire, eating a sweet biscuit for my luncheon and reading the newspaper. He said I seemed to have a natural taste for squalid things, and it is true I did feel very content and comfortable, only I should have felt much more "squalid" sitting upright in a chair, pinched with cold by a table. It amuses me, but I try to shock what he calls his refinement as little as possible, and after a while I think he will grow out of the morbid state of his nature.

'His mother and his aunts told me I must not pay any attention to his criticism, and that in time when he saw how well I got on with other people, he would give up his anxiety. A shy, self-conscious man cannot comprehend the ease and absence of terror another feels who is not self-conscious, and Dick is in consequence as much in terror for me as he used to be for himself.

'Mrs. Adams says I have made a most favorable impression on everybody, and that, heaven save the mark, Dick is thought to be much improved in manner, because less shy, since his marriage. I told him this and was amused to see how wrathful it made him. We get on very well together, chiefly, I must say, because I have so little sensitive "amour propre", but then he has enough for both, and more would overwhelm the family. You would understand the situation so much better if you had only met him, and after next summer I hope you will have that pleasure.'

CHAPTER VII

I t is an interesting question why Cara ever married Richard. She had mentioned that once the 'yes' was said, everything went too fast for her to change her mind again. Yet, after all her decisions never to remarry, he must have been exceptional to have so persuaded her. He was a difficult man to know easily or quickly, and had an extreme reserve that often repelled strangers or acquaintances.

To an immature person he seemed unimportant and too diffident to be interesting. Gwen Raverat, Cara's grand-niece, who as a child lived across the road from the Jebbs, said in her book *Period Piece* that 'poor Uncle Dick was the least considered in the Jebb household. I knew that he was a scholar of international reputation; but to our childish minds, he was a figure of extreme unimportance, a sort of harmless waif, who was kindly allowed to live in a corner of the Library, so long as he kept quiet and gave no trouble. He used to slip furtively in and out, and never recognized us when he met us. Margaret was astonished when he said Goodmorning to her on the stairs one day, shortly before his death. I suppose he was terrified of children.'[1]

However, when Cara's niece, Maud DuPuy, was visiting them in 1883, she wrote home: 'Dick looks very well and is glad to be home. I have really grown to like him very much and am not at all afraid of him any longer. He is so bright and witty when we are alone, and so devoted to Aunt Cara.'

Alfred North Whitehead, Cambridge mathematician and later well-known philosopher at Harvard, knew Jebb from a different standpoint. In his *Dialogues of Whitehead*, Lucien Price tells how he exclaimed at Whitehead's mention of Jebb's name: ' "Jebb? He

[1] Gwen Raverat, *Period Piece*, London, Faber and Faber, 1952, p. 91.

edited my Sophocles. I often wondered what he was like." To which Whitehead replied, "He was a delightful fellow and had a charming wife. She was not learned, but you wouldn't have wanted her to be. Her husband had rather a fiery temper which was carried off by the charm of Mrs. Jebb.

' "The place I came into collision with him was at elections of Fellows for Trinity, about which he felt very strongly. Each time we came out from such an election, Jebb was generally not on speaking terms with some one of his colleagues. I would have to say to my wife, 'I say, pet, do ask the Jebbs to dinner, he isn't speaking to me at present.' One of his performances which I remember best and enjoyed most was the time he rode into the river on his bicycle." '[1,2]

Like all shy people Dick was a figure of whom it was easy to make fun. W. H. Thompson, Master of Trinity, who was famous for his caustic wit, said of him: 'What time he can spare from the adornment of his person, he devotes to the neglect of his duties.'

But in spite of the jokes about him, Jebb was far more than a vain and difficult man. One of his contemporaries, Oscar Browning, one time History Tutor of King's College, Cambridge, said, 'In October, 1858, R. C. Jebb came up to Cambridge, a purely Celtic genius, like a flame of fire. We became friends immediately, and our friendship lasted through his life. . . . He was a marvellous scholar, in some respects the best that our country ever produced. His faculty lay in a perfect manipulation of the Greek, Latin and English languages, so that he could turn any English into faultless Greek or Latin, and any Latin or Greek into elegant and forcible English. . . .

'With all these qualities Jebb recoiled from being bookish. He had a number of friends entirely outside our own set, whom he never introduced to us, with whom he used to spend a commonplace, jocular, and rather fashionable existence. He was very particular about his dress, in the worst-dressed collection of

[1] Since Jebb was always known to ride a tricycle, never a bicycle, this was probably a slip on Mr. Price's part.

[2] *Dialogues of Alfred North Whitehead*, as recorded by Lucien Price, Little, Brown, 1954, p. 225.

gentlemen in the world. He used to tell me that his great ambition was to be a cavalry officer. . . .'[1]

A Glasgow student, R. P. G. Williamson, wrote: 'Jebb's wit was pungent but never harsh or caustic; we all got what we deserved and expected. He did not, "as others used," repeat his jokes from year to year. . . . Perhaps his most famous inspiration was in connection with a little accident that threatened the fabric of his class-room. The class of Logic under the kindly John Veitch, had its home in a room directly over that of the Greek class. Veitch used often to wind up his lecture with a quotation from a poet, generally Wordsworth. On one occasion, when his selection for quotation was from a book of his own on the Border Ballads, his students were moved to a patriotic fervour of applause; they stamped vehemently across the room and all down the stairs. Professor Jebb, who hated noise, looked up uneasily, then quietly remarked to his own class below: "Gentlemen, I fear that my premises will not support Professor Veitch's conclusions. . . ." '[2]

While opinions seemed to differ about Jebb as a person and as a teacher, all were agreed that he ranked extremely high as a scholar. The late Gilbert Murray, Regius Professor of Greek at Oxford, was a young man when Jebb was at his height. Before his death he wrote of the 'charming Lady Jebb' and added: 'Sir Richard was recognized as the leading Greek scholar of his day in England; faultless in scholarship and very sound in judgment. He had a high reputation in Germany, also.'[3]

But to go back to the newly-married Jebbs, what did Cara herself feel about him? Did she really regret having to live with such a sensitive scholar? During the first years of marriage there were naturally many adjustments they both had to make. Neither of them was young, she was thirty-four, he only eight months younger, and she soon found out that he had several habits of which she strongly disapproved. For one thing, he could not control his spending of money, something which to her was almost sinful; and secondly, she discovered that he drank more than she thought he ought.

[1] Oscar Browning, *Memories of 60 years at Eton, Cambridge and elsewhere*, John Lane, n.d., p. 43.

[2] C. Jebb, op. cit., pp. 188–90.   [3] From a letter to the author, Feb. 6th, 1954.

With her usual determination she set out to cure him of both faults, and because he really loved her, she succeeded. By taking complete charge of his finances, she eventually not only freed him from debt, but by continual saving and investing, was able when she died to leave over £8,000 to Cambridge University alone.

As for his other weakness, it is said that before they were engaged he threatened to take to drink unless she agreed to marry him. Although this may have been said jokingly, the fact remains that once, when she thought he had been drinking too much, she decided to leave him. She was all packed, ready to go, when he persuaded her to stay and presumably was more abstemious thereafter. Every morning at eleven she used to take his tea to the study, there to enjoy it with him, and thus it is said she helped him to break the habit that so much offended her.

While Cara probably admired him at first for his intellect, she unknowingly found her happiness in the very demands that he made upon her. He never spoiled her as Addy had done; she had to work to please him, thus becoming, herself, a more interesting, mature woman. They complemented each other well: the shy husband proud of his much sought-after wife, and she, the successful hostess, making it possible for him to accomplish the endless hours of study and writing that brought him fame as a great classical scholar.

In Cara's letters that follow, he appears at first as rather forbidding, for he wasn't sure of himself or of his newly-married wife. But eventually he mellowed under her cheerful influence and she grew to return his love more and more deeply, until, when he died, she was genuinely heart-broken.

CHAPTER VIII

Cambridge, Dec., 1874

'My dear Sister,

We have just had a visit from Leslie Stephen, the editor of the *Cornhill*, and the husband of Miss Thackeray's sister. He follows what I have learned to consider the type of the literary physique, that is of the men whose regular business, not their genius, lies among books. He is tall, thin, long-nosed, narrow-jawed, melancholy-looking, after the manner of Mr. Kirke who edits *Lippincott's Magazine*. Such men are in harness because they have not combativeness and destructiveness enough to make their largeness of intellect tell in life. I like Mr. Stephen very much and am pleased to know that he likes me, as you see by the enclosed note. . . .[1]

'My Christmas is a bright enough one, and I have great hopes of a happy New-Year. . . . I gave Dick a gold pencil to carry in his waistcoat pocket and he gave me a butter dish for Christmas, and an immense painted black satin fan for my birthday. These big fans are all the fashion in London, nobody carries anything else. He wanted to give me a seal skin jacket, but we are both as poor as church mice at present and I would not permit the extravagance. Think of fifty pounds for piano hire, and the same for cigars, and double that for books! Dick is very much mortified at his past extravagances taking up so much of our money, and promises always to consult me hereafter in matters financial.'

London, 1874

'Dear Mrs. Jebb,

I have written to Longmans to send you a copy of my little

[1] Leslie Stephen, 1832–1904. Author of many books and editor of the *Dictionary of National Biography*.

Alpine book; which I hope you will accept as a sign of its author's gratitude for your very kind reception. You will find a faithful chronicle of Morgan's Alpine performances in the chapter about "Passes".

'I trust that you will let us know when you are likely to be in town, as Thackeray and my wife are very anxious to have the pleasure of making your acquaintance.

'Yours very truly,

L. STEPHEN'

Cambridge, March, 1875

'My dear Sister,

Dick is going away for a few days to Ireland on the 18th, and when he comes back he is to find us established in the new house, 3, St. Peter's Terrace, a much larger and unfurnished house we are to rent. I have a first rate right-hand man in my upholsterer, so there is no use in Dick's staying. Besides, discomfort of every kind always upsets him, and I shall be only glad to have him escape the small amount of turmoil the moving of his books and book-cases will occasion.

'How I wish you lived somewhere near me! It would be such a joy to have you to croon over the things with; and today you and I might have gone to a big sale in the country. I can't go because Dick disapproves of my going alone, and Jeannette is away and there is no one else to go with me. . . . Yesterday the knowledge that I had a charwoman cleaning in the other house, and that another roll of things had come from Taplings, induced me to rise earlier than usual, in order that I might be in the body where my thoughts and plans were.

'One result of the conceited conviction that you can do things better than other people is that you are very apt to turn to yourself; and I was very busy and happy cutting off the lengths of carpet for my own room, when my upholsterer and factotum, Mr. Bennett, came in, and caught me in the very act. He looked so shocked that I yielded my scissors and my position at once, and took on myself the harder work of putting my ideas into his head. . . . He will never think so well of me again, having seen me on my knees doing what he considers his business. Luckily, I don't care. I had not the faintest intention of sewing or doing anything else to them. I have a real liking for cutting out anything always, it is putting one's plans into operation. . . .'

Cambridge, April 5th, 1875

'My dear Sister,
    . . . I wish you could find a cook who would be such a comfort to you as my Mrs. Bird is to me. I gave a dinner party on Thursday and left the preparation of most of the dinner to her, simply giving my orders, and everything was perfect. I got a girl in to help, paying her fifty cents, and I will tell you what Mrs. Bird had to do.
    'First, she made the rolls herself. (One is laid at each plate, you know, instead of bread. She makes excellent rolls.) Then she made white soup, she fried twelve filets of sole, and made the lobster sauce to go with the fish. Next we had two entrées ordered from the college, which are handed around one at a time after the fish plates are changed. The first entrée was 'timballes de foie gras', and then, when this was eaten, and the plates changed, the second entrée, 'sweetbreads stewed with mushrooms and truffles', was passed. With these Mrs. Bird had nothing to do, which gave her breathing time to dish the main dinner. She roasted the leg of mutton, boiled the turkey, made its sauce of oysters, and cooked all the vegetables, potatoes, cauliflower and celery, which go with this course. When we were through with this, she sent up the roast duck with its sauce, and then her labours were ended. Wasn't that a great deal for her to do well, with only one assistant?
    'I hired two waiters to help Martin, and everything passed off delightfully. We had a plum pudding from College, and after that a Charlotte Russe, then cheese which always comes in after the puddings here, and then the table was cleared for dessert. All the wine glasses, decanters, etc., were taken off, the crumbs brushed away, and then new decanters put on, and dessert plates. The waiters then handed round one dish after another, of the dessert, after which we ladies arose and left the room to the gentlemen. . . .
    'The arrangement of the table, with Martin and Ann to help, in the afternoon was a pleasure rather than otherwise. I filled the centre of the épergne with green laurel leaves and spruce, brightening it up with artificial roses which nobody suspected (flowers

are very dear in winter, and I felt no call to incur the expense when these would do just as well). Then we put candles in the branches, and on each side of the épergne we put china pots which held inside of them earthern pots, with primulas in bloom, which I got out of the greenhouse. Then we arranged the dessert dishes up and down the sides, with their pyramids of bright oranges and apples, grapes and candies, and you have no idea how pretty the table looked. The wine glasses, especially the red ones for hock, are an ornament in themselves, and four small sherry decanters, one at each corner, added their touch of colour.

'Entertaining here is a great pleasure, and no trouble to the hostess. We had games in the evening, and to crown it all, a row among the cabmen outside who got tired waiting for the guests to go away, a sure sign that your party is successful. Dick never shows to such advantage as when acting the host in his own house, and he says I am a good hostess.'

Cambridge, June, 1875

'My dear Sister,
. . . I do like Cambridge very much, and my home here is quite pretty and satisfactory. Dick grows more and more fond of me as the months go on, and I am getting more used to the tremendous change in country, habits and association. An assured position is a great help to any social gifts one may have, and here all the women seem thus far to like me very much. Mrs. Adams, my intimate friend who really is almost as fond of me as if I were the sister she always wished she had, tells me thus far that I have given offense to none, and that she hears but one opinion. . . .

'Term is over now and we have settled down into quietness with a little variety furnished by a set of spiritual séances, the most arrant nonsense and imposture in my mind, but it amuses these great geniuses who think they can see some distances into a mill stone. Henry Sidgwick and Fred Myers, the latter the author of a poem called "St. Paul", are the head of the investigation as they call it, but they both seem as easy to delude and as anxious to believe as any infant.

'This is no affair of table turning and question answering. The medium, in this case a boy of sixteen, whose father and mother sit in the circle, is tied with tapes and laid on a mattress in a cabinet with a curtain over the opening instead of a door. He is supposed to be tied so that he cannot come out of the closet, and while he is entranced the spirit makes itself evident by a faint tall light. I have only given them my company twice, finding sitting in a dark room for two hours rather dull, since I had no faith to bear me up.

'Dick said today the spirit came out and kissed all their hands, but today the medium for some reason or other was not tied, so Dick is of the opinion that the spirit was neither more nor less than the boy on his knees. Human nature is certainly a very credulous thing, and eager after novelty. Fred Myers is a complete convert to the existence of spirits able to materialize themselves through the presence of a medium, and he now spends all his time in sitting in these séances, most of which are failures. Next week they have another series in London, and so on. . . . These men consider this to be the great discovery of the age, by whose development they will render themselves forever famous.'

During the spring of 1875, Dick had suddenly been faced with a new decision to make, which Cara later explained in her book, *The Life of R. C. Jebb.*

'Hardly had we swept and garnished the St. Peter's Terrace house, collected our furniture in it, and settled down comfortably, when a startling proposition came from Glasgow. Would Mr. Jebb stand for the Greek Chair in Glasgow University which Dr. Lushington was about to resign? If we decided to stand, his election was practically certain. The decision was difficult. Work in Glasgow would no doubt be heavy during the session; but then there was the glorious six months' vacation. And the work in Cambridge was by no means light, when we added to it that of examiner for London University, and of leader-writer in *The Times*, the latter work undertaken on his resigning the Trinity Tutorship.

'On the other hand, Cambridge had been his home for seventeen years. He loved every stone in Trinity . . . almost every face he saw was familiar, and friends met him at every turn. No wonder the decision was long in coming. It was not till the 8th of June that he announced his intention to stand for the Scotch Chair.

Even then he did not burn his bridges. His Alma Mater was very kind; she gave him a year's leave of absence, permitting him to retain his offices; so that if the work and climate in the North proved too severe, he could come back happily to her arms.'

'My dear Sister,

Dick has at last decided on his resignation of the Public Oratorship. This once gone, his Fellowship and Lectureship drop from him like a garment when the string breaks. . . . I can't help feeling sorry now the deed is done. He is simply wretched. I could do nothing with him. Every afternoon after a morning's brooding, he would send for some friend, now one, now another, to ask if some way of retraction might not be found. Some way would be suggested which only gave him the torture of going through the grounds of decision again. Day after day saw this process, until at last it did become too late. His intended resignation was published in all the papers, the candidates for the Public Orator office issued their circulars, and committees for canvassing, were organized. He vacates an office, important on many grounds, though very poorly paid. . . . Well, Dick felt so wretched that I persuaded him yesterday to leave all his engagements and to take the night train for Ireland. He must be back on the 15th to present some Bishop for his degree, but even six days absence will do him good. . . .

'I have decided, pretty nearly, to come home after all this summer. I shall stay here to see whether Dick is elected or not, and then sail. The election takes place on the 14th of July which will make me not arrive much before the 1st of August. . . . Don't say anything about Glasgow until the election is certain. Dick delayed so long before agreeing to stand, that two of the electors, we think, grew indignant, and promised their votes to the Oxford man. Dick wouldn't have thought of standing if Sir William Thomson[1] had not asserted that his election was perfectly certain, which I suppose it really is, only now he must take some trouble. He must

[1] Sir William Thomson, 1824–1907. Later Lord Kelvin, eminent physicist and Professor of Natural Philosophy at the University of Glasgow. His discoveries in transmission of electrical currents did much in making the Atlantic Cable possible.

see D'Israeli and Orr-Ewing,[1] who have votes and are in London, and may perhaps run down to Glasgow for a few days to see the two recalcitrant Scotchmen.

'I am very desirous now that we should succeed. The writing for the *Times* is ruinous to other writing, and hurried work always, and yet without that resource we should not be able to live here. Glasgow is near the prettiest scenery in Great Britain, and living three miles out of town, the distance of the New University buildings, we shall escape much of the smoke and dirt. And we shall have six months of the year to go just where we like.'

Leslie Stephen wrote a letter to Dick in which he urged him to leave Cambridge. One word is illegible.

South Kensington, May 12th, 1875

'My dear Jebb,

... I hope you have duly decided the Glasgow matter. I have half a feeling that you ought to go, but my feeling is due to my impressions of Cambridge. We enjoyed our week there exceedingly and a great part of our enjoyment was due to you and Mrs. Jebb. To that my interest is entirely against your going. Still, Cambridge generally always makes a rather melancholy impression upon me now. So many of my friends are dead, or mad, or have turned old fogies, or taken to drinking, that I feel as if there was something unhealthy in the place. A few people, like Latham, become acclimatized, but they are hardly models for mutation, and a few, like Fawcett, are strong enough to resist, but everybody has not such strength. Others seem to me to grow sick about my time of life in one way or another. That, however, is due in great part to the idiotic rule of celibacy; and yet perhaps in some part due to the worry —— with idleness which always seems to me characteristic of Cambridge. However, you have settled by this time and you are so much better up in the facts than I am that I should assume your judgment to be correct.

'I apologize once more for bothering you and am,
ever yours truly,
L. STEPHEN'

[1] Archibald Orr-Ewing, Member of Parliament; lived near Glasgow.

In July, after learning that her husband had been unanimously elected to the Greek Chair, Cara sailed for the U.S. alone, returning in October. Dick met her at Liverpool in a downpour and together they made the trip to their new home by train.

Glasgow, Oct., 1875

'My dear Sister,

On Wednesday we drove out to see our future home, which proved to be, as far as house and situation went, in every way desirable. It is the largest house I have yet called my own, with handsome windows, plate glass, large square hall, broad stairs, etc., indeed so imposing in size that my soul shuddered at the amount of furniture it would take to make it habitable. . . .

'We both at first feel homesick for Cambridge, and every letter we get from there shows me how completely Dick has become identified with English University interests. He says he looks on this as a sort of banishment, and that the true coming home will be when he is made Greek Professor in Dr. Kennedy's place, if that ever comes, and only he is rich enough to accept.

'Just now he feels profoundly happy in the knowledge that all his debts are paid, though disliking the novel sensation that results from having very little money either in his pocket or in the bank. He says he never was out of debt before since he took his degree. I promise him quite as pleasant a feeling when he first finds himself a Capitalist, but he suspects I mean to try to make him economical, and he rebels instantly against anything that points to more than being a little beforehand with the year's income. We want to do no more than pay all the furniture bills this winter.

'Iddie Butcher, daughter of the Bishop of Meath, was married on the 26th and is now Lady Monteagle. Lord Monteagle is an Irish peer, with an income of £7,000 a year, a seat in Parliament, a house in London, and another most beautiful one at his country place in Ireland. Nobody ever suspected her of making such a brilliant match. In her neighbourhood there is a very beautiful girl whom I met, clever and attractive, the daughter of Dean Somebody. Lady Somebody gave her a couple of seasons in town and everybody looked upon her as the one who ought to marry brilliantly, while any intelligent and well-placed clergyman would have been thought even by herself quite a suitable match for the Bishop's daughter. But you can't calc'late, as widow Bedott says. The brilliant young woman is still unmarried at thirty, and Miss Butcher, the simple unassuming woman, is Lady Monteagle, with fortune and position assured. Fanny, her sister, has just sent me a piece of the wedding cake, and a long letter about the wedding. It poured all day long, but marriages must mostly be unhappy if that is any omen in this country, though I had sunny weather for mine. . . .

'I was delighted to get your letter, I was wondering why you wouldn't write. Whatever you do, don't make your new black silk short. That fashion is as dead as last year's butterflies.'

Glasgow, Nov., 1875

'My dear Sister,

I went into the town hall on Thursday evening with Lady Thomson to hear Sir William give a lecture on navigation to the Glasgow public, with illustrations by maps and instruments. Dick had a seat on the platform. For the first hour I listened and looked with great interest, the next half hour I spent in watching the lecturer, occupied in a sort of hero-worship, and the *next* half hour I was too sleepy and tired to think of anything but hiding my yawns from Lady Thomson. The poor Lord Provost who sat in the most prominent place was in a dreadful case. Imagine a man like Charlie O'Neil listening to a lecture on Navigation, about which a politician cares as much as he does for Milton's *Ode on the Nativity*. This little fat man fidgeted and yawned, and threw his head up and sank it down, and I am sure secretly pinched himself often, in the effort to keep awake before the world. It was watching *him* that set me yawning.

'Sir William Thomson is called here the greatest mind since Newton. He has made a large fortune by his different inventions and without his active brain to obviate difficulties the cable would not have been a success when it was. He has a nature as large and broad and noble as his brain. During the whole lecture he never thought about himself for a second. He was possessed with the delight of giving, and he moved up and down the stage, pointing out his maps, and showing his instruments, as he went on talking, exactly as if his audience was a class instead of a thousand people. Lady Thomson adores him. She is his second wife and is a woman of Mrs. Bryan's type both in looks and manner, and is also very tall, very gracious, a perfect lady, and not very intellectual. His first wife was wonderfully clever they say, but not nearly so handsome and presentable. He was very happy with her, and is very happy now, though he has no children.'

Cara and Dick went to stay with his family in Ireland for Christmas.

Glasgow, Jan. 4th, 1876

'My dear Sister,

Our holidays are over and here we are once more at home, rather to my sorrow, as I miss the full household. I got a little tired of Mrs. Jebb's enumeration of Dick's manifold perfections, and youthful triumphs; people always forget that with opportunity everyone likes to use his own judgement in forming opinions. But I grew sufficiently expert in turning the conversation when I got bored.

'I preferred her stories of her own youth, though even here I guessed that she rather magnified her own attractions. Dick thinks she sacrificed everything for his father, but I take a different view. When she married him, his father was a prominent Judge in Dublin, living handsomely, entertaining largely, and in every way a man of mark; he is mentioned as such in *Greville's Memoirs*. His uncle was a Bishop, while her father was only a Dean with a Scotch living. I think she thought she was making a very good match, and so she was.

'She has had absolutely nothing to do all her life. She has had her own maid to dress her, a pony carriage, and every comfort, and has had a far less occupied life than either of her sisters. The father has been the unselfish one, working hard at his profession in order that she might bring up her sons to be as helpless as young princes. The consequence was that when Dick and Eglantyne were young, they were wretched. They wanted to be richer, they wanted servants in livery, a pair of horses, a title, and everything that would make them of as much consequence as the people they associated with. Dick says these things used to make him very unhappy and envious, until he got some sense.

'The one I like best, next to the old father, is a brother I never saw before, called Bobby. He looks upon himself as the black sheep in the family, because while all the others are intellectual and fond of study, he can't bear it. He likes hunting, shooting, fishing, horses and dogs, is full of fun when he gets over the idea that you don't look down on him, and has quite as much common sense as any of the rest, in spite of his dislike of books.

'I have written so much about him because I want you to help me in a plan. Would Charlie please find out what entrance examination is necessary for a medical student to enter at the Philadelphia University, and everything that a man intending to study medicine in Philadelphia would have to know? All the family want Bobby to study medicine, but here Latin and Greek are necessary to take a degree, and he won't study either. He says they are not the least use, he hates them, can't remember them, and the very idea makes him ill.

'Three years ago he went out West to Iowa, partly because his health was delicate, partly with the idea of farming, and went through all sorts of adventures; sold most of his clothes, lost the rest, was robbed and taken in in every way, being a trusting youth. He supported himself partly by shooting game, until he was almost frozen, and when he arrived in New York, had but fifteen cents in his pocket.

'It was snowing, and he wandered up and down trying to find the address of old servant of his father's, who he knew would lend him money. He remembered that it was somewhere near the upper part of Fifth Avenue, and I think he showed some acuteness in finding him. Bobby tells the whole story most graphically.

'He felt sure that Mooney, the servant, being an Irishman, would be of a sociable turn. He spent one third of his fifteen cents for a glass of beer in an ale shop, for an excuse to ask the keeper if he knew a man named Mooney. He didn't, and Bobby went into another shop, drank another glass of beer, and asked the same question, fruitlessly. Then he tried another way of getting a night's lodgings, being half dead with cold and fatigue, and nothing on his feet but a pair of patent leather shoes.

'He went to a boarding house, and asked if he could have a room. The landlady said he could. "But I haven't got any money, and can't pay you until I find Mr. Mooney." To use Bobby's words, "She must have been a horrid brute," for she began to make excuses, his pride took umbrage, and out he went again. Into a third shop he went, bought another glass of ale, by this time too tired to care what happened, and asked again for Mooney. This keeper did know a Mooney, but not, Bobby thought, his man, and as he was turning to leave, up stepped an Irishman who said he was Mooney's brother, and that his brother had been very anxious about a young gentleman and was just on the point of setting out for Iowa to look for him. Bobby was taken in and warmed, comforted and given a bed, which he said was the softest his bones had ever touched, and the next day his troubles were over. Mooney had money for him from old Mr. Jebb, and he took his passage by the next steamer.'

Glasgow, Jan. 31st, 1876

'My dear Sister,

Dick's *Attic Orators* are out at last. This morning an immense package came by parcel delivery, which proved to consist of ten copies for presentation. I would send you one, if the two volumes were not almost too big to be carried by post, so you must wait. Macmillan seems to be sure of its success, but Dick himself talks in the gloomiest way on the subject, not that he thinks his book *bad*, but he looks upon the world as unappreciative and cold. It will be reviewed in all the principal weeklies and if they are unfavourable, Dick will be simply miserable, though he ought to know by this time what reviews amount to. . . .

'I never went out so much in my life before. Tomorrow night after a dinner party we go on to the Yeomanry Ball, if I am well enough to dance. The Duke of Hamilton heads the invitation, and all the county people will come. I am sufficiently exclusive not to go to the Assembly Balls, though if I were a few years younger, I fancy the exclusiveness would not stand much in my way. It is only when you have too much, you begin to make a choice.

'Dick has a great idea of social success and likes me to go to everything. We receive a good deal more attention from the

118

country people than would come to our share simply from the position as Professor. The Napiers would never have called on us for that reason, for instance, but they know Dick's family in Ireland. Then, I seem to be considered rather a help in entertaining, and am often asked to slow parties at houses where they do not owe us a dinner, because of that. We and the Ramsays[1] and the Thomsons are the aristocratic part of this hard-working University.

'Dick pines for Cambridge often. I can only keep him here by holding out the Greek Professorship there as a means of probable return in the near future. I, too, like Cambridge much the better as a place of residence. The mere fact of a garden to work in adds considerably to my happiness, and now that I have had my fill of society, this taste grows on me fast. Then this is such a detestable climate, and Cambridge having no smoke, has so much sunshine.

'Still, I think if Dick were to turn back now, he would be thought to have failed here in some hidden way known only to himself, and we should both feel very sheepish. To go back as Greek Professor at the larger place would be simply taking another step up on the professional ladder. Dr. Kennedy being by far the oldest professor at Cambridge must resign before long and then comes our chance.

'Mrs. Adams writes us long letters, which never fail to rasp Dick, and even me sometimes, though I more often laugh. She *will* write to him about his successor before he has made up his mind to resign. Naturally, when he finds his place at Cambridge considered so desirable by others, he feels inclined to keep it himself. She seems to like to stir people up, and when she treads on none of my corns, and I haven't many, it amuses me to see how she contrives to aggravate Dick. Like most Irishmen, he has keen wit, but he has no humour, and often is a great help to me in the way of amusement when he does not know it. He has enough strong points to afford to be laughed at sometimes, though not if he knows it.'

Cara wrote as though Dick would get the Greek Chair in Cambridge within a year or two, when Dr. Kennedy died. How-

[1] William Ramsay, Professor of Latin at Glasgow University.

ever, that much loved Professor neither resigned nor died for fourteen more years. How sad the Jebbs would have been had they known they were to wait so long before returning there permanently.

Glasgow, Feb., 1876

'My dear Sister,

Dick has just come up jubilant over a letter he has received by the last post from Reeve, the editor of the *Edinburgh Review*, and no wonder! Reeve is Clerk of the Privy Council, the editor of the *Greville Memoirs*, and a very distinguished individual generally. He says Macmillan has sent him Dick's *Attic Orators*, he has read them with great interest, has put them into the hands of one of his best reviewers, and that a review will appear in the *Edinburgh Quarterly* some time in the summer. To be reviewed in this is a tremendous step up for a young writer. Dick is accustomed to the *Saturday* and the *Spectator* and to bear being noticed in them without undue elevation of spirit, but this about the *Edinburgh* is great good news, it means a matter of twenty-five or thirty pages, many extracts and real consideration. . . .

'This afternoon I am going to Mrs. Macnaughton's who has asked me to a spelling bee at four. I accepted partly because I thought it would be kinder, as we had to refuse her dinner invitation a fortnight ago, and partly because I thought it would be fun. I have been having Dick ask me hard words ever since breakfast, in preparation, but they will be sure to have hunted out a lot of their own, which I shall have to spell in an impromptu manner.

'Later. The spelling bee was very amusing. A long list of hard words had been prepared out of the dictionary, which one of the gentlemen read out. Every time a mistake was made, the erring individual dropped out of the circle, until we were all out. The same process went on for three or four rounds, and I must say we were all a set of remarkably good spellers, always excepting two or three Army officers, who invariably went down at the first round. One of them couldn't spell "siege" given him on purpose, I think, as a word he must know. Not the least abashed, he said he always wrote with a dictionary to save his memory, which had enough else to exercise it, without troubling about "e's" and "i's". We all made mistakes sooner or later, Mrs. Col. Bainbrigge the fewest, so she got the prize, a volume of *A Kempis*. I should give a spelling bee myself if only I had my big drawing-room, one couldn't find a cheaper or more amusing entertainment.'

Cara seems to have been annoyed at the interest shown by her family and the rest of the United States in the H. W. Beecher affair. This American minister and writer was accused of immorality.

Glasgow, March 14th, 1876

'My dear Sister,

I dare say Henry Ward Beecher *is* guilty. I suppose the temptation of a man so much made of all through life must have been great. He is evidently weak and vain, and the mere fact of his having special gifts as a preacher does not indicate special grace, too. I should think you would all be tired to death of the whole thing, and the newspapers would turn their attention elsewhere. I feel much more indignant about Grant's shortcomings, myself, thinking with the ancients that there are times when public virtue is far and away the most important consideration.

'We have only dined out once since my last letter. Tonight we go in to Lady Thomson's where my chief amusement will be a game of chess with Miss King. Chess has been a great amusement to me all winter. Hardly a day passes that I don't have a game either with Mrs. Blackburn or Mrs. Nichol, and we are all very eager to beat. I am now three games ahead of Mrs. B. and I don't mean she shall catch up again. Tell Polly I advise her to find out some one really fond of the game to play with. She will find it as great an amusement in winter as croquet is in summer. . . .'

Glasgow, March 20th, 1876

'My dear Sister,

Dick has been in bed with his rheumatism since Friday. He has been blistered and physicked and kept on low diet and water and tea, and is just now beginning to feel the benefit of what Emma [Charlie's sister] would call heroic treatment. The doctor says he

121

may get up tomorrow. It takes all my motive power to keep him supplied with books from the study, as he is writing and reading for his *Primer*, and usually thinks of one book of reference at a time. He has taken possession of the best bedroom in the third story, and the two flights of stairs are steep. The maids are wise since neither of them has yet succeeded in finding a book for him! The moment I dispatch this to you, I must go up again, in case anything should be wanted, and then get ready for Mr. Nichol's lecture.

'Mrs. Lee and I always walk in together, and today Mrs. Blackburn has offered to go with me, not knowing that I have Mrs. Lee for a companion. I expect wigs on the green. The only other time I saw them together (Dick sends for the black ink, I continue with the red rather than mount from my present seat, the study, to the dining-room) they seemed mutually to exasperate each other, and ever since I know from seeing a good deal of both, there has been no love lost. Mrs. Lee told me she would never meet that woman again if she could help it. They are both lively, agreeable, positive women, hence my intimacy with them, but neither is the least conciliatory.

'Mrs. Blackburn is good-tempered, self-complacent, and often most aggravating even to me; as for Dick, I don't know how often I have been told "that woman shall never enter my doors again" He says she snubs everything he speaks about. She doesn't, she is only chiefly occupied with stating her own views, which prevents her being the absorbed listener most agreeable to that natural despot, a state of the case I present to him which does not soothe. However, his wrath is quick to depart, always, and she is to dine here at our next and last big dinner party.

'There seems every prospect of peace after all the hubbub. Russia does not care to fight just now, apparently. I am almost sorry, believing that a European war would be a great lift to the United States.'

That such an attitude toward war could exist only eighty years ago seems incredible!

When the Jebbs returned to Cambridge at the end of term in April, they decided to keep their home there indefinitely to be used each year for part of the six months' vacation. In June they went abroad with a close friend, Gerald Balfour, brother of the statesman, Arthur Balfour, and Cara wrote on the 24th from Perugia,

'My dear Sister,

The first remark I am inclined to make before I pass to more thrilling details is that there are mosquitoes in Italy! Two or three have made my afternoon nap an impossibility. One has just been successfully killed and I find him in all respects like his trans-Atlantic brethren. Indeed many things about this climate made me almost forget I am not in America. The clear blue sky, sudden thunderstorms, very positive sun, large hotels for boarders, might all of them be exactly represented in Saratoga. To be sure there is the slight difference of frescoed ceilings, and larger rooms, but the former need not be looked at if you wish to indulge the illusion.

'When we got to Turin, letters were found from Mr. Oscar Browning, a great friend of both Dick and Mr. Balfour, asking them to take a little detour from the straightness of their path, and to come to meet him at Milan. So to Milan we went, arriving there at one o'clock. Mr. Browning was anxiously awaiting not us, but them. I retired to rest and they arranged that first he and Mr. Balfour were to walk and talk together, and then he and Dick. Why they couldn't all have joined I suppose arose from the fact that both Dick and Mr. Balfour would have wished to absorb Mr. Browning and neither would have had any patience with the other.[1]

'In the interval, Dick took me to see the Cathedral, a most magnificent spectacle. On our way we walked through a long beautiful arcade, a perfect joy. It was Sunday and the streets were

[1] Oscar Browning, no relation to Robert, was a Fellow of King's College, Cambridge, and, as mentioned before, a famous tutor there. He was very fat and once quoted in a letter to a newspaper a celebrated poem about himself, which he said was composed by a friend:

> O.B., oh be obedient
> To Nature's stern decrees,
> For though you're only one O.B.
> You'll soon be two O.B.'s. (obese)

filled with people going to and from church. No one had bonnets on their heads, nothing but small squares of lace, or else the mantilla with one end over their heads. . . .

'Now we are settled in Perugia, and the three gentlemen (we have made the acquaintance of another Englishman who is here improving himself) have started for a three mile walk to see an old Etruscan tomb. I am staying at home perforce, having a festered toe. Two or three American people are the only other guests of the house besides ourselves. One of them we have spoken to, but the other party is odious. Of them we have taken no notice; they survive and appear quite content with themselves, absorb the conversation at the dinner table, disgust Dick and Mr. Balfour and the other Englishman, whose name we do not know, but amuse me immensely.

'All of my companions would suffer a soul change into something quite new and strange if they only had the least shade of humour to soften the asperities of their characters. They would also gain in companionableness. I would give a small sum cheerfully every day of my life to have you or Polly to sympathize in the things which I find so amusing. The one American we condescend to notice is an old gentleman with a humourous twinkle in his eye. His name is Greenough, he comes from Boston, and is a brother of the sculptor.[1] A lady was with him the first day, but has since either gone away or is ill in her room. It seems not to be good breeding to ask questions of people you accidentally meet. If they choose to tell anything about themselves, it must be volunteered information, so whether she is wife or sister or simply some governess he has brought back, I do not know.'

[1] This was Richard Greenough, 1819–1904. Horatio Greenough's brother. While Horatio was better known, Richard was the more popular sculptor in New England.

CHAPTER IX

Cambridge, July 17th, 1876

'My dear Sister,

I have just had a visit from George Darwin, a son of the great Darwin, and himself a man distinguised for ability. He is a Fellow of Trinity, a mathematician and writer on scientific subjects. I was very much interested in his visit, having read eagerly everything his father has published. The father has had ill health for twenty years; all his work has been done while struggling with dyspepsia in its most aggravated form. The son, who inherits the disease, says there is some comfort in the knowledge that it seems not to shorten life, but actually to lengthen it, one had to take such care of oneself that other diseases were avoided. Polly's favorite saw occured to me, and was repeated, that "creaking doors hang long". Mr. Darwin promised to send me some papers of Mr. Galton,[1] the "Hereditary Genius" author, who is a cousin and great chum of his.

'Tomorrow we start for Surrey to spend a couple of days with the Tennysons. The distance is only an hour and a quarter by train from London, but even for this I wish we had cooler weather. It is 90° in the shade! Dr. Lushington has just written to ask us to his place. I don't want to go, for the women are my portion in this life, and Mrs. Lushington is too singular for anyone to enjoy her companionship. The Misses Lushington, the single sisters, are muteness itself, according to Mrs. Sellars' report. They stopped growing at twenty, and dress like the picture in the *Lady of the Manor*. They either knit or look at the carpet, but never talk.

'Have any of you yet read *The Life of Macauley* by his nephew?

[1] Sir Francis Galton, 1822–1911. Scientist, founder of the science of eugenics, a term which he coined.

I have just reached the second volume, and am only from a stern sense of duty not reading it at this moment. It is simply delightful. The reviewers call it "a life without a lady", and you certainly do gather the impression that for such a confirmed novel reader he had wonderfully little impressionableness. Henry Butcher[1] told me that Lord Macaulay was once very deeply in love; he proposed, the lady would have nothing to say to him, and that was the end. He devoted his affections to his favorite sisters, and never again gave a thought to matrimony, writing about women only for the study of character. The heroes and heroines became as real in their family circle as living individuals. When his sister first married, her husband hardly knew what to make of all the queer people she seemed to have met and known and about whom she and her brother were constantly talking. Do get the book out of the library.

'I have taken up French again and mean now really to study it until I make some progress. I felt so ashamed of my ignorance as conspicuously displayed in our Italian tour. I couldn't even ask for a bath without calling in an interpreter, and I always had to pay for a cake of soap, though I carried some in my tin box, because when the women asked me in their language, I never knew what they said, and they took silence for consent. Tell little Mary she ought to study it an hour every day. In this country if you know only one language you are thought not to belong to the educated classes. My German has just saved me, but you need French so much in travelling.'

Cambridge, Aug. 1st, 1876

'My dear Sister,

The *Times* gives me one very sad piece of news. The Bishop of Meath,[2] father of all the Butchers you have heard me speak about, whom we met in Ireland, cut his throat on Saturday in a fit of delirium. He had been suffering from a dangerous attack of Capillary bronchitis and congestion of the lungs for ten days, but was thought to be almost convalescent, when suddenly on Friday

---

[1] S. Henry Butcher, 1850–1910. Son of Bishop of Meath, Classical scholar, succeeded R. C. Jebb, 1906, as M.P. for Cambridge University.

[2] Samuel Butcher, D.D., 1811–76. Bishop of Meath, Classical scholar, Trinity College, Dublin.

night delirium set in. The family stayed with him all night, only leaving for a short time on Saturday morning for breakfast, I suppose. He sent the servant out of the room, wrote the word "mad" on a piece of paper, and then cut his throat. When the family came upstairs, he was still alive lying on the floor, he smiled at his wife, and then died.

'Henry Butcher had just taken his bride home for their first visit, and they must still have been at Ardbruccan House. Two marriages and two deaths that family has known in the last year. Mrs. Butcher's brother died suddenly of heart disease, and now her husband still more shockingly. Iddie, the daughter who married Lord Monteagle last autumn, has been nursing *him* almost ever since, without anybody knowing what was the matter. She has had terrible anxiety; but at last the doctors have found out that a small bone at the lower part of the back was dislocated, and he is on the way to perfect recovery. He got into such a state that he had to be carried about, and his suffering was almost constant while they were abroad.

'I don't know what you may think of *Daniel Deronda*.[1] In my opinion as a novel, it is altogether a mistake. It is like a valuable old painting whose subject is roasting and torturing the martyrs; it shows great genius but makes none but painful impressions. It rests such a burden on the brain that you can't even hope any good to anybody may turn up in the 8th volume. Perhaps *Harper* may not have carried you on simultaneously with the publication here, so that you don't know as much about it as I do. Mr. Tennyson has had the whole plot laid before him, but he said he had promised not to tell, and nothing could persuade him to gratify our curiosity.'

Cambridge, Aug. 17th, 1876

'My dear Sister,

Dick's Uncle Richard Jebb, the Vicar General of the Isle of Man, came on Saturday. A most amusing old soul he is. He began at breakfast with anecdote, description and narrative, and he kept on one constant flow of funny and interesting talk until bedtime. His stories about people whose careers he has followed were as

---

[1] By George Eliot.

127

romantic and far more thrilling than fiction. To be sure he had the advantage of having Irishmen for his subjects, who beat the world in recklessness.

'I cannot conceive why the Vicar General himself has not had more success in life. He began well with an eminent father, good connections, an excellent start in his profession as a barrister in London, and I think first-rate ability. He ends as Vicar General, a legal place, with £600 a year. As Mrs. Jebb says, so many little obscure ingredients seem required to make success that you never can tell which one is lacking. He is much more Irish than either the Canon or Dick's father, and looks not the least like them. Indeed, none of the three brothers give you any idea that they come from the same family. The Vicar General's and my father-in-law's unselfishness have stood in their way, I think. They are both as generous as the sun.

'The Canon, on the other hand, is a mass of good-humoured selfishness, and the stumbling-block in *his* path has been boundless self-indulgence. He sent a letter round to all the family last winter, a most pathetic epistle. He announced that his end was drawing near, that from signs not to be disputed he could not last through the winter, that mental trouble was torturing him in this solemn time when his thoughts ought to be turned to other things, etc. Well, the gist of it was that he had overdrawn his bank account. Dick's father sent him about two hundred pounds, his own money, and needless to say the Canon immediately took more cheerful views of his symptoms, his illness had been sciatica, and is now as well and lively as ever. It does seem that somebody is always found whose virtues fit into the vices of somebody else, so that both are able to keep in constant exercise.

'Dick's father and mother were here, too, and left on Tuesday for the Lyth, and I quite miss her company. She says now the doctor assures her her heart is sound, but she can't walk or do any-thing on account of queer feelings in her head. She complains of her eyes a great deal, but I saw her reading a whole afternoon without difficulty and without glasses, which inclined me to think she was better off in that respect than most people of her age.

'There is such a difference in people about complaining! Things that come to everybody in the course of nature, seem to some people quite peculiar and special in their own cases, and they make loud claims for sympathy and indulgence, at what everybody has to bear. The old gentleman I think much the feebler but nobody takes any notice of his ailments, himself included.

'Heneage, Bobby Jebb's twin brother, is engaged to be married, did I tell you? To a Miss Geraldine Russell, a young lady, well-connected, but the daughter of a clergyman and poor. The family were startled at first, but they like it now, as they think it will give him an incentive in his office work. He has been taken as an articled clerk by an old cousin in Boston, who is very rich and has an excellent business as Solicitor, and he will eventually become a partner. It was a splendid chance for Heneage who was drifting about aimlessly. He had been educated at Oxford for the Church, but chose to feel some scruples as to his own orthodoxy which prevented him from taking orders. A most provoking thing, his mother said, as he was really very good and religious, and just cut out for a clergyman.

'Poor Bobby, my favorite, has failed again in his chemistry, and is going to give up trying to be a doctor of any kind. His mother thinks it will just end in his living at home with them while they live, and on the income of the four thousand pounds he will inherit afterwards. She says if he were a daughter, this would be the natural thing, and she sees nothing else to be done. He can spend his time lying on the sofa, or taking long walks with his dogs, fishing and shooting, as comfortably as any Irishman in existence.'

Danesfort, Killarney, Ireland
Oct. 30th, 1876

'My dear Sister,

All the family here are a good deal disturbed about the health of Dick's brother Heneage. From what I make out he has had what we should call simply a cold for two or three weeks. He straightway imagines himself threatened with consumption, throws up all his law studies, and rushes off home. The last time I saw him he was threatened with heart disease, now it is lungs, and the next, I suppose, it will be the liver. His mother has brought them all up to pay the greatest attention to themselves, and such nervous people about their healths, I never saw. Heneage feels sure nothing short of going abroad will set him up completely, so now they are all casting about to find a travelling companion for him. Dick wrote to John Jebb, the cousin with whom he is studying, and it is from his reply that I draw my own opinion that Heneage is more frightened than hurt. They certainly are not a family of soldiers, nor does such spoiling at home make life any easier for them.

'Aunty Fan is at this present moment doing Dick's packing for him, perfectly delighted at the opportunity of doing *anything* for him, while he is walking about in the garden smoking. He will thank her very affectionately, and she will feel herself rewarded. I, with sterner views, remember old Commodore Vanderbilt's dictum, "Civility don't cost nothing." Whereas breaking your back over trunks does. It will take me some time to get him back into proper habits after all the coddling here. Aunty Tye and Uncle Sam take my view, but Aunty Fan waits on him like an affectionate dog.'

Glasgow, Dec., 1876

'My dear Sister,

I saw the Thomsons for the first time since our return. He and Lady Thomson, who goes everywhere with him, were at Inverary, the Duke of Argyle's place, when Queen Victoria was there. Lady T.'s account of the arrangements was very amusing. The Queen always dined alone, but came into the drawing-room for a little time every evening. The moment she was announced, the Duke and Duchess stood at the door to receive her and everybody in the room rose to his feet, and total silence fell. She never sits down among people, so they stood during the whole time she was there. Nobody liked to talk to anyone else. The Queen moved about, followed by her daughters and suite, and made remarks to different individuals, until she left and people could again breathe freely. Her daughters always came back, and stayed the rest of the evening. Lady Thomson thinks she must be a dull woman or she wouldn't set so much store by her dignity. Louis 14th was every inch a king, and yet he had a lively court, and so did George the 4th.

'Did I write to you about my visit to Milliken? The wedding had to be put off at almost the last moment. Miss Aymée caught the measles, was pronounced positively to have them by a Glasgow doctor on Sunday, and as the quickest way of telling everybody at once, a notice was put in the morning papers that on this account there would be no wedding on Thursday.

'Poor Lady Napier! She had the drawing-room all waxed, emptied and trimmed for the ball two weeks ago, all the musicians, waiters, supper, wedding breakfast, etc. were engaged for the 16th, and now all the expense and trouble will have to be done over again. When I told Sir William Thomson the news, his pity and sympathy were instantly given to the bridegroom. I don't care a bit for him, it is poor fat fussy Lady Napier on whom the brunt falls. He will have quite enough of matrimony before he dies. Miss Aymée is evidently attracted by the title and the fortune and will use both without much regard for the weak little man who gives them to her. I noticed several things about her that suggested she had no notion of settling down to a quiet country life for eight months in the year. Sir George Clark has a London house where he goes to stay for the season. All these rich people have London houses. The wedding is now fixed for the 4th of January, they think the risk of infection will be gone by then.'

Glasgow, Feb. 27th, 1877

'My dear Sister,

We have just had a letter from old Mrs. Jebb, announcing the serious illness of Uncle Richard. In that family the mole-hills are so very high, one hardly knows what to believe whenever anyone is said to be ill. I like this old Uncle very much and shall be sorry to hear of his death. He was exceedingly agreeable and amusing company and as generous as the day. If the Canon were to die, a feeling of relief would communicate itself to the whole family, but he flourishes as a green bay tree.

'On Saturday we went for a couple of days to Edinburgh to visit the Sellars. Among other pleasant people, I was made acquainted with Mrs. Ferrier, the daughter and widow of two celebrated men.[1] She looks like her father, Professor Wilson,[2] and

[1] Her second husband was James Frederick Ferrier, 1808–64. Scottish philosopher, professor at Edinburgh.

[2] Professor John Wilson, otherwise known as Christopher North, 1785–1854. Scottish writer, critic and poet.

has his joyous temperament. Chained to her chair with paralysis brought on by a walk of eight miles when she was not strong, but not connected in any apparent way with the brain, seeing always opposite her on a sofa her only son, a very handsome man of thirty, dying of consumption, she yet greets all her visitors with a bright face and cheery welcome; and time passes away like magic in her presence. One day the nurse, in moving her, fell on her foot. Mrs. Ferrier swore. "Why, ma'm," said the nurse, "if I did not see you I would think I was tending some *bad* old man." "Only a wicked old woman," said Mrs. Ferrier, good-humoured at once.

'Her eldest daughter is the wife of Sir Alexander Grant, Principal of Edinburgh University, who fell in love with her the moment he saw her, when she was a beautiful girl of fifteen, he was thirty. They made him wait three years before her mother would consent to the marriage. She is very pretty still.

'You will be pleased to hear that in this country age is properly respected. An old lady may even make a good match should she be so minded. The Hon. Mrs. Norton, poetess, novelist, etc., born in 1808,[1] is about to marry Sir William Stirling-Maxwell, Bart., aged fifty-eight or nine.[2] The marriage had to be put off as the bride was ill in bed with the gout, but they are only waiting till the spring. It seems that he has been in love with her almost since boyhood. Twenty years ago he married somebody else, since he could not get her (her wicked husband would "still live") and now at last, Lady Stirling-Maxwell having died two or three years ago, and Mr. Norton, one, the marriage is to come off.

'He is very rich and Mrs. Norton not, and people suppose she wishes to provide for her son. *I* think it the end of a long romance and he wishes to have her called by his name at last. She was a good deal talked about thirty years ago, but Mr. Norton was such a wretch that she had the sympathy of society, and the divorce laws were such that she could not get rid of him. People think the Queen will be very annoyed. She gave the Garter to Sir William not long ago, the first time it was ever bestowed on a commoner,

[1] Caroline Elizabeth Sarah Norton, 1808–77. Grand-daughter of Richard Brinsley Sheridan. Celebrated for her wit, beauty and misfortunes.
[2] William Stirling-Maxwell, 1818–78. Scottish writer, connoisseur and collector. Chancellor of Glasgow University, 1875.

and she will be displeased at his marrying a woman so much talked about.'[1]

Glasgow, April, 1877

'My dear Sister,

We went to the Bachelors' Ball last night and for a wonder enjoyed ourselves. My day has entirely gone by for expecting attention from any of the marriageable men; but there are a lot of old fogies, enough to fill up my card pretty promptly, who come with their wives and like dancing, yet feel doubts about the views young ladies take of them as partners, now they are matrimonially shelved. The oldest of them pick out the quadrilles and lancers on my card, and the waltzers take their steps carefully, stopping for breath when the space becomes slightly crowded.

'Do read the *Life of Mrs. Gilbert*, if you can get it out of the library. It does one good to see the possibility of such a woman. Mr. Gilbert was good in many ways, but his wife was an angel of wisdom and temper to stand his sentimentalities about his first wife. When he was away from home, he would write verses to *her* memory and send them to his second wife to admire. His *in*appropriate verses she calls them in one of the sweetest letters I ever read. She was a sister of the authoress of *The Scottish Chiefs*, and indeed the whole family wrote and worked and were wonderful for ability and energy. . . .[2]

'Charlotte Tennant, another Glasgow girl, or rather near Glasgow, married Lord Ribblesdale on Saturday. I almost gasped the first time I saw her after hearing the report of her great beauty. Prominent pale blue eyes, sallow complexion slightly reddening at the nose, hair much like the complexion, and a long face do not make a beauty in our American eyes, even if all these have the advantage of being lifted about five feet seven inches from the

[1] The marriage was evidently too much for them, since, having been married March 1st, she died on June 15th, and he the next year.

[2] The book Cara was referring to was *The Autobiography and other Memorials of Mrs. Gilbert*, edited by Josiah Gilbert, published in 1874. Mrs. Ann Gilbert, 1782–1866, one of the Taylors of Ongar, the second wife of Joseph Gilbert, wrote many books of verse for children, including *Original Poems for Infant Minds*, in collaboration with her sister Jane Taylor, not Jane Porter who wrote *The Scottish Chiefs*.

ground on a willowy graceful figure. These English people value tall slenderness more than any other nation. I suppose because the generality incline to fat. It was Charlotte's figure and youth and money that made her a peeress of Great Britain. She will look well at the head of his table, and he hasn't brains enough himself to look for any other gift, such as liveliness of intellect or superfluities of that kind.

'Her grand-father is charmed with the marriage his illegitimate son's daughter is making and will give her anything.[1] He is an old scamp who never married but who had the sense to bring forward his housekeeper's and his son, and to educate him exactly as if there were no bar sinister. The eldest grand-daughter I told you about long ago, just one of the prettiest and most taking of little women, as superior to this tall Charlotte as gold is to brass. She, too, made a very good marriage with Mr. Grant Duff, a young man and an old Scotch family.'

Cambridge, May 26th, 1877

'My dear Sister,

And now for a piece of news. Miss Thackeray is going to be married very shortly to an undergraduate by name Richmond Ritchie. He is a cousin of hers, and is either seventeen or twenty years younger than she; he is twenty-three or four. Everybody considers him fortunate in spite of the difference in age. Her charm depends not at all upon either youth or beauty and is very universally felt. He will be sure to be proud of her, and is himself so silent and so peculiar that he looks even ten years older than he is.[2]

'Callers came in and made me miss Tuesday's steamer, and took up all my time before dressing for the garden party at King's. I like garden parties the best of all entertainment. Nine out of ten dinners are nothing worth mentioning but eating. At garden parties you always have games of some kind, either croquet or lawn tennis.

[1] John Tennant, the grandfather; Sir Charles Tennant, Charlotte's father.
[2] Richmond Ritchie, 1854–1912, was seventeen years younger than Anne Thackeray. He became Private Secretary to a succession of Parliamentary Secretaries of State for India and was made a K.C.B. There were two children of the marriage.

'The latter is the most played now, and the nicest of all. I am just learning and it is certainly livelier movement than I have indulged in for many a day. The gentlemen play splendidly as well they may, practising in college grounds every afternoon. Do any of the children or their friends play, or hasn't it crossed to America? You need a level and rather larger ground than in croquet, and asphalt is better than grass unless you can have a very smooth lawn. I bought a little grass-cutter which I can use myself, since which our little grass plot is in much better condition.

'The girls *ought* to play lawn tennis if they can find a place. They couldn't have better exercise. A set costs a good deal, as the best bats are sixteen shillings a piece, besides the net and balls, but if they liked I could bring over a set as a present for two of them instead of anything else. I don't like to play with anything but a real tennis bat, the little things that come with the sets are no good.

'When I finish this scrawl, I must go over to see Jeannette and Mary Tovey who is staying with her these last few days. English people are very fond of jaunting about to see their friends and relations; they seem to me the most restless of nations.'

Glasgow, Nov. 23rd, 1877

'My dear Sister,
... Dick has been busy writing and delivering two lectures in addition to his regular work. In the second he was rather unfortunate. It was a carefully written historical sketch of Bulgaria from the beginning, leaving out, in my opinion, the only time when that province possesses much of interest, the present. He read through a long German book and got most of his facts in that laborious manner. Well, what did the Lord Provost do in introducing him but say that Professor Jebb had spent his summer travelling in Bulgaria, had used his own powers of observation and intellect, and was coming before them this evening to give them his own fresh ideas, instead of a dull and dry discourse gleaned from books. Dick said he didn't know what to do. Not having an impromptu mind, he did nothing, but read his lecture under a cloud and gave me the benefit of his hitherto smothered wrath when he came home.

'Another of our diversions has been the Gaelic Ball. I have finally given up an amusement in which I never shone, dancing, and should have stayed at home if Dick had not made a point of my going. You have heard, probably, of Capt. Cameron, a South African explorer.[1] Well, it seems there was a row after we left. I thought him a little jolly myself when he was talking to me. He must have gone on drinking more champagne, for report says he kissed a married lady he was dancing with, she screamed, her husband rushed up, knocked Capt. Cameron down, and there was great commotion generally. He apologized humbly the next day, said it was all a mistake, that he only stumbled against the lady. I shall hear the whole story from Mrs. Dennistown on Saturday, since it happened before she left.

Glasgow, Jan. 8th, 1878

'My dear Sister,

Gerald Balfour[2] wrote to Dick that he could come to us from the 9th, with a dash, meaning an indefinite stay, depending upon circumstances such as his enjoying himself, I suppose. Although he is one of my favorites, I wish he had chosen next month instead of this for his visit when I hope to have more energy. If only he played chess or cards, and was not so intellectually above all such drawing-room amusements.

'Outdoor games his set play with all the eagerness of duller mortals, but these are healthful exercises. Dancing they despise, nor do they confess to any interest in the youth of the other sex. If you win a place in their esteem, it is at the cost of much mental effort and adaptation. This describes the younger set of Dick's friends.

'Those of his own age only ask from you an admiring silence or occasional echo, like Fred Myers, their search being for sympathetic appreciation. These talk much themselves and though

[1] Verney Lovett Cameron, 1844–94. Naval officer, African explorer. Sent by the Royal Geographic Society to relieve Livingstone, but finding he had died, Cameron recovered his papers and proceeded to the Atlantic, the first European to cross equatorial Africa.

[2] Gerald Balfour, 1853–1945, younger brother of A. J. Balfour, whom he succeeded in 1930 as second Earl. Went into Parliament, became Chief Secretary for Ireland, then held other Government posts.

their entertainment would seem an easy task, it isn't. They have a keen eye as to the way in which you listen, are put out in their carefully worded sentences if you interrupt (woe is me!) and yet detect instantly any absence of mind you may slip into.

'Well, Mrs. Sellars' third daughter is staying down at Row with her cousin Mrs. Hamilton. She is like her mother, bright, witty, full of fun and conversation, and withal sparklingly pretty and eighteen years old. I suggested to Dick that I should ask her for a week from the 9th. "No, that would never do." "Why not?" I asked, loath to resign such a pleasant way of getting help. "I assure you," with a solemn shake of the head, "You may take my word for it, in England it would never do."

'Of course this is all nonsense, and he knows nothing about it! Gerald Balfour would never for an instant suspect me of a match-making plan, and no other objection could possibly arise. What course ought a submissive wife follow? Certainly not argue the point. *We* know you only wear out your energy and never get your own way by argument. And, of course, if you make a good plan you mean to carry it out.

'The next day I seized a fortunate moment to say that at any rate we might ask Mrs. Hamilton to bring Eppie to dine with us on the 9th, and make them the nucleus of a little party to welcome our guest. Here, you know, it is always the custom to have a dinner party to meet anyone who comes to stay with you. To this Dick agreed without hesitation; and as they can't return the same night, I shall try to keep them over luncheon on the 10th, and make up a party to go to lawn tennis at the rink in the afternoon. This will dispose of one day. In writing to the Sellars in Edinburgh about our own visit on the 25th, I said I hoped she would lend us Eppie for a couple of days before she left our neighbourhood. If she can't come, there is no use in bringing Dick over to an invitation; if she can, by that time he will have quite forgotten that he thought there would be any impropriety in the matter.'

Glasgow, Feb. 6th, 1878

'My dear Sister,

We had a really delightful stay at the Sellars'. At the dinner party on Tueday, Lord Rutherford Clark took me in, and Lord

Deas sat on my other side; these are both law lords, who, like Bishops, give no titles to their wives, and are much more interesting than mere lords by birth. Lord Deas is one of the oldest judges in Scotland, and to my surprise I found him delightful. He had known Sydney Smith,[1] and Christopher North, and most of the Edinburgh celebrities of their time, and once carefully guided into the path of reminiscence, he went on smoothly talking in a most interesting manner. The other is a much livelier companion where topics of the day are concerned, so I had everything.

'When we ladies returned to the drawing-room, I carefully eschewed retired corners and nooks by the fireside. The centre ottoman was occupied while I was being introduced to one of the ladies, but I held my ground, cordially but firmly keeping up the conversation *standing*, until a chance came to turn away. "No, ma'm," I thought to myself, "I'm not going to talk to old tabbies *this* evening, with such a lot of clever men to listen to." When she moved on to her corner, I took possession of an easy chair, after a thoughtful survey of the room, in what I considered the most accessible place, a view events proved to be correct.

'First came up Prof. Masson, famous for his large edition of Milton, and with him I had a nice little talk about women's rights. Mrs. Masson is a strong advocate, and carries her husband with her entirely. Then, Dick brought up Prof. Geikie, the geologist, a nice little red-haired man. He has written two *Primers* in Macmillan's series, and was naturally delighted with the large sales. He told me how many copies were sold a year, what money he received, etc., and though the conversation can't be said to have been on the highest levels, I found it very interesting. My two Lords came back to me, and indeed sooner or later every man in the room was presented, showing the great advantage it is to have a good position in the drawing-room.

'On Wednesday dear old, or rather middle-aged, Dr. Lightfoot[2] came. There is a man! He is very plain, with some disagreement of the eyes, but you forget it all when you hear him talk, he is so able, so strong, so good. I noticed that he took no wine. He said

[1] Sydney Smith, 1771–1845. An English divine, celebrated for his wit and delightful humour.

[2] Joseph B. Lightfoot, 1828–89. Eminent Biblical scholar.

he thought a couple of years ago he would try what effect total abstinence would have, and that he found himself if anything better since than before. He always feels a slight pang when champagne passes him, but has no other feeling to contend with. You see that if he decides that any course is wise, no wish of his own or anybody else would shake him.'

Glasgow, Feb. 21st, 1878

'My dear Sister,

We duly went to the Calico Ball last night, a most amusing and enjoyable affair. I was too lazy to take much trouble about my costume, and was half inclined to regret that I had not, when I saw how bright and attractive most of the others looked. My blue velveteen was set off with a broad Queen Elizabeth ruff under the chin, a few strings of pearl beads were draped across the chest, and there I was.

'Dick had a brand new Cambridge volunteer's uniform, cap and accoutrements all complete, to be worn on this one occasion only. He had knee breeches of grey, bright red stockings, shoes with silver buckles, and felt every inch a soldier. He said the Muscovite would fly in terror at his view. Though I am bound to say he didn't, at least there were two or three Russians there with tall shakoes and everything else, and they kept their ground very well.

'Poor Mrs. Blackburn was in despair. Mr. B.'s brother-in-law seized this most inopportune moment to die, and according to custom none of the family ought to go out for a few weeks. Mrs. B. had painted a calico dress for herself in exact imitation of a mummy case over in the museum. Miss B. had her peasant's dress all complete and now all their trouble threatened to be for nothing. But they rose superior to custom, and went and danced and enjoyed themselves all the same. Mrs. B. said it was not a relation she cared much about. She has said this so often in similar cases that people begin to wonder if she has *any* relations she cares for. A niece died just before the Napier's Ball last year, and she made the same remark. I suppose if any of her own children died she would have to stay in a little.'

After returning to Cambridge in May, Dick went off to Greece while Cara visited in London. Following a visit to the National

Gallery, she wrote to Ellen mentioning the Latin hexameters Dick had composed for a Burne-Jones painting which was meant to form the decoration of a room in Arthur Balfour's house. 'Burne-Jones comes nearest to Raphael of any in these times. Dick wrote some Latin lines for a panelled painting of Perseus. I was pleased to see how prominent they were made in large gilt letters across the top half way down. . . .'

CHAPTER X

Cambridge, June 20th, 1878

'My dear Sister,

I have had a most pleasant week with Fanny and Augusta Butcher, two really delightful girls.[1] They made their own amusement and mine, too, and I found no refusals to any invitations to meet them. We have had some party either for lawn tennis or dinner every day during their stay.

'Fanny is a wonderfully attractive little thing. To my knowledge she has refused two eligible offers. An exceedingly nice man here, a fellow of King's, son of Canon Prothero of Westminster Abbey, showed her a great deal of attention, and I only hope it means something.[2] I think she would have him and they are so bright and companionable with each other, that it would be sure to make a happy marriage.

'Fred Myers is a goose, and we can't help all looking upon his affair as a sort of comedy. He is very companionable and with an insidious nature. Fanny says her mother is so afraid of him that she believes if there were no other way of keeping Eleanor, another sister, from his influence, she would leave London altogether. English people believe in prevention. Thus far he has had small chance of seeing Eleanor alone, and can have hardly made much impression on her affections.

'Dick comes home tonight. He has written so cheerfully from Greece, that I had hoped the journey would have given him a

[1] Fanny and Augusta Butcher were the second and third daughters of the Bishop of Meath. The eldest daughter, Iddie or Elizabeth, had married Lord Monteagle, as already related. Eleanor, of whom much mention is made in later letters, was the youngest daughter and the beauty of the family.

[2] (Sir) George Prothero, 1848-1922. Later Professor of Modern History at Edinburgh, and then Editor of the *Quarterly Review*.

complete renovation; but he says the night journey from Paris to London tired him more than all the rest. He caught cold, could not sleep in the train, and the hay-fever, after entirely departing in Greece, has come back. I shall see for myself how he is, and shall be very glad to have him home again.'

Cambridge, July 2nd, 1878

'My dear Sister,

My poor Dick's illness proves to be Typhoid Fever, I have seen no one but Mrs. Adams and Jeannette as people here seem to think it contagious. We have two doctors who both say the case is progressing favorably. Still, it cannot help but be an anxious time. I have written today to ask Aunty Fan to come, thinking someone of the family ought to be with me. I wish I had Dr. Schell to consult. These doctors won't tell me anything. . . .'

Cambridge, July 15th, 1878

'My dear Sister,

My letter today can only record another week in the sickroom. Since the hemorrhage of eight days ago, there has been no bad symptom, and after Tuesday the recovery will be certain. Aunty Fan has been with me since Monday and is a great help in every way. . . .

'Charlotte Waring has come to live with Jeannette for the next three years, if she doesn't get married, says Jeannette. A tall, stout widow of fifty-three or four *usually* remains faithful to her husband's memory, I comforted Jeannette, who wants her to stay and keep house for her. . . .'

Cambridge, Aug. 13th, 1878

'My dear Sister,

Well, Dick's chest is pretty nearly well, now. The pneumonia is gone, there is no more talk of consumption and the cough has almost disappeared. But the convalescence is in many ways more trying than the disease, made up as it is of boils and abscesses and neuralgic pains. First there was a boil on the back which I had to poultice night and morning, and of which you would have thought *I* was the author, so many exclamations did I get when I had to

142

open it. Fortunately for me, Dr. Latham was twice as rough, and caused a great deal more pain when he squeezed it, or I don't know what would have become of me.

'The doctor told me, what I never knew before, that Dick's liver was larger than it should be. One thing I fear, that he will never be a robustly healthy man again. He has taken a resolution of total abstinence which will, I hope, keep every tendency at a stand-still.

'On Tuesday we get our invalid carriage and start for Ireland, where, for the first time in my life, I shall be glad to be. It will lighten my labours wonderfully to have somebody to keep Dick company, so that I can get out for air, and be free to lie down a little after luncheon, a habit now become almost a necessity. From there my letters will cease to be Jeremiads and I hope more amusing....'

Desmond, Killiney, Sept., 1878

'My dear Sister,

I have done nothing but rest and vegetate since we have been here, and wait on Dick who has been made rather helpless by an abscess under the other arm. Today I encouraged him, by not being there, the best way, to dress himself, which he did without the least difficulty. From this time, unless another boil comes, I shall resign my position as valet.

'We go to Killarney on Friday, a change I am quite ready for. They are all most kind and nice, but a month at a time is quite long for a visit in any house except one's own home. Even Dick pronounces it "rather slow", and felt very wrathful when he thought they weren't going to be able to take us in at Killarney.

'Just for a few days, fear of a domestic crisis arose in Aunty Fan's mind; and under its influence she wrote that much as she should like to see her "darling Dickums" (she always treats him like a child of four) she thought if he were to travel now, it might bring on a relapse. Then she took up four pages with cases of convalescents who had over-exerted themselves, and different medical opinions she had heard.

'Very indignant her "darling Dickums" was! "That's all bosh about my health. I can't think what Aunty Fan means," and so on.

So the poor lady wasted all the trouble she took in sugaring her pill. We women knew that the real difficulty was a change in housemaids, quite a good enough reason for old Mrs. Jebb and me. A letter today says the new house-maid has just been inducted, and that Aunty Fan is anxiously looking for us next Friday. So now all is serene.

'Danesfort, their home, is a much livelier house than Desmond. Two old maids and an old bachelor have contrived to keep themselves much younger than the father and mother of this family. Aunt Fanny besides has the social gift. It seems impossible for anything to be done without her; in sickness and in health, she seems to be the chief help of the whole neighbourhood. It isn't intellectual powers, she hasn't any, or great moral superiority, for she is as good as her neighbours, and no better, but just the social gift and a capability of filling a breach. She is a thin, wiry little woman without an atom of laziness in her composition and proud of her activity.

'I always think of the two Aunties as Martha and Mary. Everybody likes Aunty Tye the better. When Aunt Fanny goes away, Aunty Tye and Uncle Sam always have a sort of jubilee; and in old days the father always cared least for his most useful daughter. When he was ill, it was Aunty Tye he always wanted to be in his room. Aunty Fan does all the work, keeps the money affairs straight, manages everything, but then she insists on everybody being pleased in her way instead of theirs; she keeps up a strict domestic subjection which makes the house seem too straight for perfect freedom. Aunty Tye is intellectual and very gentle, with a willingness to allow for individual aberrations, which comes I suppose from the larger mental grasp. I know I like her a hundred times better, but still when Dick was so ill, it was Aunty Fan for whom I sent.'

Desmond, Oct. 22nd, 1878

'My dear Sister,

All the papers are full just now of this dreadful failure of the City of Glasgow Bank. Luckily we deposit our money in the Union Bank, so we are safe. When banks break here, it is the shareholders who lose, not the creditors. Every shareholder will not only lose every penny invested but have to pay a thousand pounds' share. It is pitiable to think how many people this will ruin. Affairs will be very gloomy in Glasgow, I fear, and indirectly this will affect us; the number of students will be much reduced by it. None of the directors, who have all been taken up for conspiracy to deceive and defraud, are people we know. They say every one of them will be imprisoned with hard labour, a somewhat different treatment from what holds good in America. I don't think Jay Cooke[1] ever went to prison!

'Aunty Fan has again elected to be very anxious about Uncle Sam's health. He, good man, seemed to be as well and hearty as a stout man of sixty-nine could be. He was merry and brisk, with an excellent appetite, and general appearance of hale vigour, with only the slight drawback of a commencing cold in the head the day we left. Ever since, she has written daily accounts of the state of his health, mixed with comments on his obstinacy in refusing to send for a doctor.

'I suspect him of being as timid as another whenever anything is really the matter with him; witness his fancying he had heart disease, and getting almost ill from the notion. He came down to Dublin to consult the best doctor. After sounding him and examining him all over in Aunty Tye's presence, the doctor leaned back and said, "My dear man, would you just tell me what made you think you had heart disease?" He was as sound as a bell! Too sound, for he had an attack of gout some time afterwards. He wouldn't tell the doctor it was all Aunty Fan, whose constant attentions would end in driving anyone into every mortal disease.

'I wouldn't live with her for all this world contains, good and energetic and helpful as she is. She would drive me out of my senses. She wants me to sit up all night now and watch Dick, apparently. She says she would never be happy to leave him out of her sight. I told her there was much more danger of my dying suddenly than there was of his, but that I would rather do it, and so would he, I dare say, than never to be left a moment in peace. His

---

[1] Jay Cooke, 1821–1905. American financier, his company marketed huge Civil War loans of the Federal government; when his New York branch closed its door in 1873, it precipitated the great panic of that year.

heart is very strong, and I don't think there is much of any kind the matter with him now. He is very tired of doing nothing, and is looking forward with eagerness to the commencement of the session.'

Glasgow, Nov. 4th, 1878

'My dear Sister,

I have been all the morning sitting in my chamber counting out my money, and I can't make it tally with Dick's numbers by £2.10 shillings. I am forced to believe that either that amount is wandering about the floor of his class room seeking an owner, or else he has given too much to some students in change. This year we wish to keep our accounts exactly. The Government is always sending papers to be filled out, and when you only know in a hazy way what you have left, and not what you received, you have to put a "say" before each sum: "say a thousand pounds," as Dick always did in his accounts. This year we can know what comes into the house at any rate, for it is instantly delivered to me, and I count it over, lock it up, and jot it down on my memorandum tablet in my desk.

'The number will probably not be very large this year because of the widespread ruin from the City of Glasgow Bank failure. Dick says he must subscribe fifty pounds to the fund for the ruined shareholders and I agree with him. Poor Mr. Stuart's eight daughters, all brought up with every luxury, are behaving beautifully. Four have taken places as governesses, people are glad to get accomplished ladies. The others are studying to be telegraph clerks. They will marry better and sooner than if they had all the money, as force of character and high tone are of value all over the world.

'I have been so busy helping Dick to keep him from overworking that I haven't had time to think of my own dressmaking. We were comparing roll-book and class maps until eleven o'clock last night. In the morning I was showing Eliza over the house, counting the linen with her prior to her taking charge of it, and I could not get a moment to read the paper even, before Dick came in. Not that I dislike it; I enjoy having plenty to do, as long as other hands carry out the plans under my superintendence; and have come to believe that occupation is necessary to happiness.

'Wednesday. Dick brought me in another lap full of dirty notes from his students, just at this point in my letter, and I had to stop. . . . The class looks very promising. . . .

'Dick and I are both very well this autumn. He has lost the sallowness which made me anxious about his liver, and since we came here, has been too busy to feel whether he is depressed or not; and is in fact particularly happy. Another instance of the good effect of work!'

Glasgow, March, 1879

'My dear Sister,

. . . Dr. Lightfoot has been made Bishop of Durham. The highest See next to London, with a seat in the House of Lords directly he is inducted; and yet so differently are people constituted, that he hesitated for some time before accepting this great dignity, and feels very sad now that he has been made to believe that to accept was his duty. In his case, all the other things have been added. He is the best and ablest man I have ever known, hence too wise to be ambitious, too good to be greedy of wealth. He feels that he must give up his favorite home, Cambridge, his most congenial work, he will not have time for study and literary work now, and must henceforth devote himself to the unity of the Church.

'It is a sign how much he is needed that the place eagerly sought him, while the Church is full of men who would have given their eyes to be Bishop of Durham with £7,000 a year; able men, too, only the very wish for advancement shows they lack the wisdom which is a part of his large intellect. Dick congratulated him, and his answer was pathetic in its brevity and sadness. We shall miss him very much in Cambridge.'

Glasgow, March, 1879

'My dear Sister,

The weather has cleared wonderfully in the last month, and now we have bright sunshine and a good hope of spring. The March winds blow away all the fog and smoke, and everybody is saying what lovely weather. I begin to see that December and

147

January are the only months really to be disliked in this climate. Now, not only is the ice gone, but the frost is all out of the ground as well, and rarely is the mercury down even at its lowest to freezing.

'Lawn tennis has started again with the usual happy results. I wonder people don't start it in America. It really is the best game I ever played, and with thorough amusement and exercise three afternoons a week, life takes on a different hue. If only I could persuade Dick to play I feel convinced his depression would vanish like magic, but he has the unfortunate Cambridge habit of wishing to do everything that he does extraordinarily well, and he can't bear to be beaten. He says when we have a ground of our own, where he can play in absolute solitude, and his first efforts be unseen, he will promise to learn. May only his joints not grow old and stiff, pending this acquisition. . . .

'Now for a piece of delightful news for us: Dick is to be made LL.D. of the Edinburgh University, so henceforth will be Dr. Jebb in Scotland, and everywhere but at Cambridge. That University recognizes no degrees but its own, and it never confers its own members. This is a point of etiquette apparently. Dick had been away at St. Andrews since Friday, he and Dr. Lee having gone there for change of air and a game of golf. His letters had accumulated and he was looking them over on his return, telling me any news in rather a dignified way. (He was offended because I hadn't written to him. If I had written, the letter would not have reached him in time, there being no delivery on Sunday. But it seems he had done what I had not given him credit for, he had walked to the Post Office. Dr. Lee had got a letter, and he had not, and he didn't like it.)

'Well, after all his letters were read, he left a big brown paper one unopened, guessing it to be a book he had ordered and forgotten, and not feeling this a fit moment to confess to a useless purpose. I said, "Dick, you have forgotten this big brown envelope." And behold, it was the announcement from the Edinburgh University! Never was anything more unexpected. A scholar values honours of this kind immensely, as they help him in his literary career, and recognitions; and Edinburgh degrees are the most prized of all the Scottish universities. . . .'

Cara thought possibly Charlie's nieces, Mary and Ellen, might come over to college at Newnham or Girton, Cambridge.

Glasgow, April 27th, 1879

'My dear Sister,

... They would enjoy the life here immensely, and would be capable of the study. A very nice young teacher from some place near Philadelphia comes over every summer to study mathematics. There are several Americans in lodgings in connection with Newnham Hall, and Mrs. Adams says they are all nice. I know one at Girton, a Miss —— I cannot remember her name, though it is as well known as Sturgis or Aspinwall. She is very rich since her father's death, keeps a pair of horses and a manservant for her own use, and will, I have no doubt, with her fortune and position, marry here as her sister has done. Oh, yes, her name is Miss Minturn.

'A girl would need at the very lowest £100 a year to go even to Newnham and a hundred and fifty would be better. Girton is dearer still, and costs almost as much for a girl undergraduate as Trinity College does for the other sex. There is a marked difference in education of women in the last ten years. Every kind of advantage is thrown open to them and arranged for them, and as a reaction from husband-hunting, they are throwing themselves into all sorts of things that promise an interest or a career. It is the shape now taken by the sensible part of the Woman's Rights' party. Some who have no taste for study join training homes for nurses, and go out afterwards as Lady nurses. It must greatly increase the happiness of many people.

'Edith Reynolds says that Julia, her sister, is so much better and happier now that she really has something to do after college, than when she was rather fretting because she did not somehow get married. She was pretty, too, but as long as the law is against two wives, there are scarcely men enough to marry half the women, and with the best of qualifications, one half must turn to something else. I am afraid Philadelphia is getting to be in somewhat a similar case. . . .'

'My dear Sister,

Again I am a steamer late, but the burden of that family party on Saturday ought to be sufficient excuse for anything. Mr. Potts is simply dreadful! He button-holes people remorselessly and recounts his own deeds and sayings until weariness and anger reach their height, and yet without rudeness he can't be shaken off.

'Nobody ever does ask him to dinner, and I felt so sorry for him that for once I thought I would try what I could do to make him tolerable. I chose Saturday, because Dick had to be at Oxford, and I knew that I could not bear his annoyance in addition to my own. Well, it ended in my letting everybody else take care of themselves, and devoting myself to Mr. Potts. You may imagine what a bore he is, when I tell you I was so exhausted that I counted the minutes till the time came for the people to go, watched the door in hopes the carriages would be announced, and could hardly speak the few pleasant words necessary in dismissing the guests, voice and eyes and brain were so worn out. . . .

'On the night before, we dressed ourselves to go out to dine at the Provost of King's. There we met Mr. and Mrs. Spencer Walpole, M.P. for the University, and very much they were interested in seeing me. They knew that their nephew, Charlie Walpole,[1] had been a very eager old beau of mine. The family had been troubled about the danger of an American wife. Mrs. Walpole said to me that her nephew had been a great admirer of mine, and asked if I had seen his wife. I hadn't, and was glad to hear of her. She is not pretty, is older than he, Mrs. Walpole believes, although she says she is younger, and since the birth of her baby this year, has become large and still older looking. It was a comfort to know that I wore my red satin and was looking my best!

'On Saturday afternoon I went with Mrs. Stanford to see an old Roman pottery place, unearthed by some gravel diggers. Professor Hughes and Mr. Jenkinson had been grubbing away all day,

[1] (Sir) Charles Walpole, 1848–1926. Chief Justice, Bahamas, then Gibraltar. He proposed to Cara in 1870, and as a widower, several times after Dick died, even when Cara was seventy-seven. He married a second time in 1922, and committed suicide four years later.

searching for broken vases, and whatever remains they could find of the Roman occupation. Professor Hughes knew exactly the kind of places where the most hope existed of finding things, the kind of soil, height of layer, etc. Mrs. Stanford preferred looking on, but very soon the fever seized me and I fell to grubbing like the others. To my lot it fell to get the greatest treasure of the day, an old Roman comb, which I gave to Prof. Hughes. Their effort in this digging is to find some coin which may fix the date of the Roman occupation, believed to be in the 3rd century. . . . '

Cambridge, July 8th, 1879

'Dear Polly,

We are very festive this week. Eleanor and Augusta Butcher are with us since Saturday and everybody is inviting them to something. Eleanor is not pretty, but has a most attractive face, which fastens your eyes, and fascinates you. I don't know at all whether Gerald Balfour has made any impression, yet am inclined to think he has; she is more silent and shy with him than with others, a good sign. He makes no effort to conceal the attraction she has for him, talks to her at dinner parties all the evening, never speaks to Augusta, nor does anything but openly show his intentions. Although I must say he does not do his courting in a very eager way, as far as I can see, steady as it is. I never catch any words of sentimental talk; it is always about music, or political economy, or philosophy, something to which the whole world might listen. . . . '

Cambridge, July 19th, 1879

'Dear Polly,

Now for gossip. Alas, alas, I am afraid Eleanor's chance of Gerald Balfour is less now than before her visit. He called yesterday; when I offered to read him part of her letter, he said it would not bore him neither would it interest him. Needless to say, I refrained. He is full of earnest thoughts, works hard for hours every day at Mental Philosophy and Metaphysics, and she is full of humour and fun. This last attracted him at first, afterwards grew wearisome when he tried to strike a deeper sympathy. Still, she is very pretty, and that is a power. Dick thinks she is really interested

151

in him, and her frequent notes and letters to me, I can't entirely set down to my attractions. Yesterday he talked about Hegel the whole time, I must say in a most interesting way, but he carefully avoided leaving the abstract.

'This afternoon I am to take Miss Foster to see a four game of real tennis played between Gerald Balfour, George Darwin, Mr. Mortlock and Mr. Austen-Leigh.[1] Poor Miss Foster is a cousin and shy admirer of the latter, why *will* people set their fancy on impossible objects? She has no more chance of winning him than you have of the Emperor of China.

'Afterwards I go on to Mrs. Clark for a game of my own tennis; yesterday I was at the Burns' and on Monday they will all come here. It is a cheap way of seeing one's friends and much pleasanter than set dinner parties. I have a cake, a plate of thin bread and butter, and tea all set out on a table in Peterhouse Garden, and Kate in her pretty cap and apron to wait on everybody. Most of us play, there are two nets; those that can't, sit and look on or talk, whichever suits them, and nobody is bored or exhausted.

'Dick won't play which is a great vexation to me. All the afternoon he sits and writes away at his article on Thucydides for the *Classical Book of Essays*, and he never gets any amusement at all. Still, it seems to make him happy which is the great thing.'

Cambridge, Aug., 1879

'Dear Polly,

. . . Gerald Balfour came yesterday as usual, Sunday afternoon visit, and of course the topics were tender. Eleanor Butcher has still a chance, but he confessed that he got a little tired that Sunday when he and she walked about the Roundabout together. He wishes to see more of her before he begins to pay her attentions from which he could not honourably draw back. Julia Sandys did not like him. She admits that he is good to look at, and an interesting being, but also a "nasty, cross, disagreeable, odious thing!" He was playing lawn tennis with her, and answered rather sarcastically what I must say was rather a silly question. . . .

[1] Augustus Austen-Leigh, 1840–1905. Great-nephew of Jane Austen, the novelist. Later Provost of King's.

'Fred Myers is somewhere in America now, probably at New-port. He took letters to all the Adams' of Boston, and expects to see the pleasantest side of American society. Henry James' story in the *Cornhill*, "The International Episode", struck his imagination as presenting a very attractive picture of American young ladies, and I am sure he has gone over with many ideas of amusing him-self. *He* does not see that his girth is wide, his hair thin, his thirty-five years fully printed on face and figure, and that the only kind of person fitted to *attract* him, would scorn him.

'We are having a most pleasant summer in Cambridge. I am very busy all the time, and very happy. I don't see why there is so much to do; I only know that the day has in it never an hour too much.'

In the fall they made their annual trip abroad.

Paris, Oct. 20th, 1879

'My dear Sister,

I wish I could tell you something that might be of use about the French fashions, but I am waiting myself to make my winter coat and dress until I can see the *Bazaar* again. At the Théatre Français they wear the most magnificent dresses I ever saw in my life. All the long ones have princesse backs, many of them with long basques and pockets in front, cut steel buttons, jet fringes on the tablier, etc. I see that café au lait coloured silk is worn again. Skirts are made so scant and short as to require very little material. Large plush hats are very much worn and also ones of black velvet.

'Sarah Bernhardt looked lovely in a large soft one of the latter, in her character of Mrs. Clarkson, the other night. She is a most superb actress, and whatever I see her in, I always make up my mind to try to remember how it was made and to have one like it for myself. A white silk of hers would not be bad for a wedding dress for your Mary.

'We are enjoying our visit to Paris extremely. I know you don't like descriptions, and leaving these out, there is little to write about. I spend my morning in the Louvre looking at pictures. We leave on Friday for London and the next day to the Harry Jebb's place, Firbeck Hall, in Yorkshire. You and Polly shall have a description of it next week. All I know now is that thirteen gardeners are constantly kept to take care of the grounds. . . .'

Firbeck Hall, Oct. 29th, 1879

'My dear Sister,

. . . This is an immense house, in size like a hotel, with gardens, hot houses, conservatories, stables, and all the appointments of large wealth. Harry Jebb, Dick's cousin, has it for his life and 13,000 pounds a year. At his death the landed property all goes to the son of Gladwyn Jebb.[1] The old lady who last owned it did not like Gladwyn, so took this way of showing her preference for Harry, and yet preserved justice in the next generation. According to English ideas, the eldest male branch is heir and ought to get almost everything. Harry's son will have a good deal of money, and no right to complain. . . .'

Glasgow, Dec. 25th, 1879

'My dear Sister,

I send you all much love and greetings of the day. To observe Christmas day would be to these Presbyterians an encouragement of popery and prelacy they are bound not to give. All the shops are open and work goes on just as usual. New Year's Day is their festive season, when they get drunk without reproach, and bow to nothing except the pavement. These maids are all a thoroughly satisfactory respectable set, but two years ago, I found Jessie in a very muddled and dazed condition the morning after, at the time of my usual visit. "First foot" still is a great institution in Scotland, and the first foot always carries a bottle of whiskey about with it, to treat the newly elected sweetheart. It tries to arrive as soon after midnight as possible, and a good deal of tramping about the town goes on. My servants are to have a supper; I have told them they may ask in a couple of friends apiece and have a little party. Dick will be away and I am to dine early to leave them free.

'I wouldn't tease Nellie about talking. She ought not to talk

[1] The son who inherited it was Sidney Gladwyn Jebb, father of Sir (Hubert Miles) Gladwyn Jebb, Permanent representative of Great Britain, 1950–4, at the United Nations. Now British Ambassador in Paris.

much at her age. What can a girl of fifteen have to say? I was inclined to be very silent at her age, though afterwards I acquired the
habit of talking a great deal.'

Cara was surprised to hear of Fred Myers' sudden engagement
and received this letter from him in answer to her query about his
fiancée.

London, Jan. 21st, 1880

'My dear Mrs. Jebb,

Very many thanks for your most kind letter. I shall, if all be
well, be most charmed to come to you at Cambridge in May or
June with my wife that is to be. I don't like describing her in any
way, feeling that in my position it is out of place; but in answer to
your question I will give a few facts which may save you further
trouble. . . .

'Eveleen is the third daughter of the late Charles Tennant, some-
time M.P. for St. Albans, and of 2, Richmond Terrace, White-
hall. . . . The second sister, Dorothy, aged 23, is known as a
promising artist; and in the Academy of 1875 there were pictures
of the two sisters, separately, by Millais, Eveleen being then 17.
A drawing of Frank Miles, entitled Vanessa, and sold in the shops
was taken from Eveleen, but I am glad to say is not sufficiently like
for anyone to recognize her from it. She is just 22. And here my
category of facts comes to an end: the rest I hope you will learn
from personal acquaintance.

'I will add, however, that my engagement was a surprise not to
you alone, but to everybody, my acquaintance with the young
lady having been of very short duration: and that subsequent
acquaintance has constantly increased the sense of thankfulness
with which I receive a blessing which seems to me as incomparable
as it was unexpected. . . .

'Yours most truly,

F. W. H. Myers'

Edinburgh, March 6th, 1880

'My dear Sister,

My week in London proved thoroughly pleasant from the first
to last, good weather, good health and everything. And now we

are here visiting the Sellars'. In London we went to see Henry Irving in the *Merchant of Venice* and one who, as far as the organs of sight are concerned, is much more interesting, Ellen Terry. She certainly is beautiful, the most beautiful woman I think I ever saw, and on a grand scale. "Divinely tall and most divinely fair." She looks like cousin Gertrude Sandford, but with a longer neck and more slender figure, this last beautifully rounded and absolutely perfect. Her smile is glorious, and her acting so natural that you almost forget it is acting and fancy Portia is there before you in the life. I could not sleep afterwards for thinking of her. Irving, too, as Shylock is a thousand times better than in *Hamlet*. It struck me he had taken Tennyson for his model of an old man and often the voice and words were exactly an imitation of that gruff deep-toned poet.

'We had a good-sized dull dinner party last night, and are looking forward to another tonight which Mrs. Sellars promised shall be more amusing. I wish you could see her drawing-room, so pretty and so comfortable. Morris papers on the walls, Burne-Jones' photographs, old china, old carvings, Indian silks everywhere. None of the daughters are married, much to their mother's surprise; but Edinburgh seems to me a worse place for settling even than Philadelphia. Year after year on our visits the same young ladies appear after dinner for the evening part of the entertainment, each year a year older and less blooming. . . .'

Glasgow, March 23rd, 1880

'My dear Sister,

On Friday, the night of the Gaelic Ball, Mr. Peile, a man who was at school with Dick, and Miss Peile, came to stay till Monday, an awful ordeal. We took them to the ball, and to my horror I found that Miss Peile, fat, forty-five and plain, still liked round dances and expected to have partners provided! I said on entering that I was not strong enough for much dancing and should limit myself to the squares and polkas. "Then," said she, "you can turn over anybody who asks for a waltz to me. I am *very* fond of waltzing." Fancy my feelings! I simply did not do it. I know so many officers and people through the lawn tennis club, that of course I had plenty of partners. The elder ones I introduced to her, but not

Mr. and Mrs. Jebb, honeymoon, Paris

R. C. Jebb's parents, Emily Horsley Jebb and Robert Jebb, at their home, Desmond, Killiney, Ireland

The three Butcher sisters, Augusta, Fanny and Eleanor.
Taken by their friend Mrs. Frederic Myers

Eleanor Butcher

Harper's Bazaar fashion plate enclosed in
one of Cara's letters

Springfield, the Jebb home in Cambridge

A drawing-room in Cambridge of this time

Cara Jebb, about 1880

Nellie DuPuy, portrait by Cecilia Beaux.
Owned by Mrs. E. D. Reed, New York City

one of them *dreamt* that such a set looking body had any aspirations, and with that valuable principle "the greater good for the greater number", in my mind, of course they were made no wiser by me. Dick was bound to do his duty, so she got two or three dances with him.

'We came home at half past two, waiting the last half hour on account of our frisky guest, who *had* secured a partner for that dance, and was not inclined to let him off. She came up to me as I was talking at the moment to a nice young Navy Officer named Cavendish, and asked if I would mind waiting, as she had *disappointed* him for the last dance from having been at supper. The amazed look on Mr. C.'s face was very amusing, and I saw him view with interest the man who came up to carry her off.

'Both she and her brother are most uninteresting people, and I feel sure that I must use some exertion to prevent Dick's good nature from making them too intimate with us. He is always inclined to accept an invitation which must then be paid back in kind.

'Her father was the Curate at Hatfield twenty years ago, (they were all ten born there) so I made her tell me about the Salisbury family and the Balfours' father and mother, interesting to me because I like all these young ones so much, and because two sides to a story is an amusing variation. But I find it hard to keep Miss Peile to the subject, as she shows a constant inclination to wander off to the Peiles and her own brothers and sisters, all whose affairs she has put me in possession of, with amazing frankness.

'Her brother Horace, visiting here with her, was married to a woman twelve years older than himself, who died in five years, and to whose memory he is still faithful. He wants to marry again, she is sure, but not without money; his first wife had £40,000. Middle-aged and uninteresting as he is, she seems to think he has only to throw the handkerchief; and what stands in his way is that he is no lady's man, and though he would like to marry in general, never thinks of anybody in particular. I could tell you pages more about him, and then go on to the other nine brothers and sisters, but I won't.

'She is upstairs packing now, so any points I am not clear about, she will have time to settle after luncheon! She told me today she could feel herself visibly growing fat on so much good living.

They kill their own sheep, and she says it is nothing but mutton, mutton from one month to another. "We kill a sheep and eat straight through it." '

'My dear Sister,

Mrs. Caird came on Saturday just as my time had come for writing, and sat on and on till long after the hour for the American steamer. She wasted another hour for me yesterday, to my infinite weariness. A lady in whom she is interested is giving a course of lectures on singing to ladies in her drawing-room. Mrs. Caird told me her story, and mentioned this as one of the ways the unfortunate woman had chosen to help a small income. Of course I had to say I would take a ticket, though I know and hope to know no more about practical singing than a Choctaw; and yesterday I went to the first lecture. She is welcome to my guinea, but never again to my presence.

'The first part was very much like a funeral at the Slemmer's. When I entered, the room was half full of a lot of middle-aged fusty-looking women, dressed mostly in black, sitting uneasily on the arranged chairs, talking to each other in spasmodic whispers. (My own opinion is that these early ones were most of them admitted free, friends of the lecturess, to ensure an audience.) Then the silent entrance of this lady, the solemn placing of manuscript and footstool, and general preparation, almost brought the tears to my eyes, it was so very funereal.

'As she went on, I could have wept for another cause, from weariness and vexation. Even her voice ended by exasperating me beyond bearing and when at *last* she stopped, I rushed away without waiting to be introduced to her, with a hasty excuse to Mrs. Caird about having an engagement at three. It was dreadful! Really, some of these charitable people ought to be put into confinement. . . .

'We are all delighted with the result of the elections, and especially that Gladstone has got in for Midlothian. Nobody talks of anything else, and I find myself reading the speeches and taking as much interest as anybody. I hate Lord Beaconsfield, he is such an out and out sham. . . .'

CHAPTER XI

Cambridge, June 3rd, 1880

'My dear Sister,

Well, I have been confided in again, this time by a man I had learned to look on as a tardy lover. To my great surprise one of my favorites here, a fellow of King's, Mr. Prothero, towards the end of a call the other day, after talking about his faults and defects, told me he had been in love with Fanny Butcher for years, but had feared to propose at first, and afterwards had felt not justified in proposing. I know Fanny likes him, and believe she has for this reason refused all her other suitors, but of course I only gave him general encouragement.

'The result is that he . . . has now started by the first train to London. I was touched by the absolute candour and truth with which he told me his income, his prospects, and all his affairs. . . . So Fanny has got her lover, unless I am very far wrong; and now I wonder what will happen to Eleanor? She is lovelier than ever, in an exquisite highbred way, which throws such a bar-maid beauty as Mrs. Fred Myers completely in the shade. . . .'

Cambridge, June 15th, 1880

'My dear Sister,

We had a delightful visit from the Lionel Tennysons.[1] She is a niece of Lady Augusta Stanley of whose death you probably read, and is an altogether good and charming woman. The Tennysons are a lucky family and Lionel came in for his share in getting such a wife. They have asked us to dine with them in town on the 20th to meet Mr. Lowell,[2] very nice of them. Lord Selborne is to be

[1] The poet's son.
[2] James Russell Lowell, 1819–91. American poet and Minister to England, 1880–5.

there and lots of distinguished people whom I shall like to meet.

'Thursday night I went to sleep with the Butchers where Fanny's engagement to Mr. Prothero was the chief interest. She had only seen him three times in the last two years. I asked her how she could know her own mind so instantly. She said whenever anyone else came near her somehow he never seemed as nice as Mr. Prothero, and though not the least unhappy about it, she knew from that that he was her standard. Everybody including me thinks her very fortunate.

'Now I wonder again if Eleanor will renew her impression on Gerald Balfour? Mrs. Lionel agreed with me that no girl in the world would ever refuse him.

'Polly will rejoice with me at Grant's defeat. Did I tell you he was very drunk at a dinner party in Calcutta and insulted an English lady who sat next him? Sir Henry Maine, Master of Trinity Hall, told me, who got it direct from a member of Council who was present.'

Cambridge, July 25th, 1880

'My dear Sister,

At last I have met the great Arthur Balfour[1] and rather to my surprise I found I liked him very much, for he is a young prince in his way and almost as much spoiled. He is not so handsome as Gerald, but is sweeter and less positive in manner; I don't wonder everybody likes him. He seems to me by nature the best in a family all of whom are best. He has a simplicity of character which not all the circumstances of his life have quite succeeded in really spoiling, and a singular sweet fineness of expression. To set against this is the undoubted fact that he is very indifferent to everything, a man who does not pretend to be, but what is far worse, really is bored with his life. He, like all the rest, has a cold emotional nature, and probably that one essay he made in love has exhausted his power in that direction. He is a man that almost everyone loves, so George Darwin told me, who comes in contact with him.

'I think the sadness arises partly from the fact that the spirit of the age prevents him, a naturally religious man, from being religious, except on the humanitarian side. Even people who believe in

1 Arthur James Balfour, 1848–1930. Statesman and Prime Minister, 1902.

heaven, find it difficult to believe that the next life can be one of perfect happiness without effort. They see in the immortality of the soul only the possibility of struggle and aspiration of labour and often weariness, such as they have here, and they can't imagine an existence which is to be a complete break and change from this.

'All the Balfour family take hold of the end of religion they can be sure of, the helping of people here. Their mother, Lady Blanche, belonging to a different generation, was absorbed in dogmatic religion, and they inherit her unworldly nature, without the power of her unquestioning faith, so they miss her happiness. I should like very much to see more of Arthur, but I shall not have the chance, as he only comes to Cambridge to be quiet with his sisters and to avoid society.

'Dick comes back from Oxford for good tomorrow, thankfully, after having gone through steadily a thing he had got to hate: a course of lectures to strangers. One secret of his success is that he can make himself do disagreeable things. His imagination makes something appear desirable and when he finds in sober reality it proves to be disagreeable, he goes on with it, even though no great harm would come if he gave it up. He says college life now would be intolerable to him, and I must say he was more deeply impressed with the discomfort of college rooms, than with anything else that had befallen him.

'Yesterday the dressmaker was here and she had grown so used to my lead, that left to her own devices she seized the opportunity to cut my brocade train all wrong. Luckily it will not show when plaited up and hung, but I shall always feel that the bias seams are in the wrong place. The white damask, cut out thoughtfully and slowly by myself, is a perfect beauty; the whole front covered with white bead braid and bead fringes, which gleam and shine and move and give an altogether brilliant effect. The enclosed picture is the design I followed for the front, taking the other part from a white satin wedding-dress in another number of the *Bazaar*. . . .'

Cambridge, Aug., 1880

'My dear Sister,

I have just seen the beginnings of my neighbour's troubles in the arrival of the first doctor next door, whom I take to be Dr. Paget's brother. This meeting of the Medical Association must be a burden to the spirit of every member of that profession in Cambridge. All our friends have left Cambridge as though before a scourge of locusts. Not only must each physician individually fill his house full to overflowing with his friends and relations, but he must feel his share of the responsibility of making the whole "800 to 3,000" comfortable and happy.

'The new arrival *must* be Sir James Paget.[1] He and Dr. Paget have just issued forth, and a careful study of their backs puts the fraternal relationship beyond doubt. They are two of the ablest physicians in Great Britain. . . .

'On Wednesday we are all asked to see the Museum lit up for the Conversazione with electrical light. Mrs. Brownlow asked me yesterday what she should wear. I told her if we consulted our best interests, we should all wrap our faces up in some kind of head covering and look out on the world with one eye. Nothing more frightfully unbecoming than the glare of electricity having ever been discovered. . . .

'It is hard to realize you are on the verge of becoming a grand-mother, that we are all so rapidly approaching the age called old by those pushing behind us. Well, I for one have had my share of what was going at each age, and have no reason to complain. . . .

'P.S. I can't keep my eyes off the doctors who come in couples, in groups, and alone to call on Dr. Paget. They are all so *intensely* respectable looking!'

Cambridge, Sept. 7th, 1880

'My dear Sister,

I have no gossip, no news, no anything to write about from this deserted village. One by one the people have been dropping in to say goodbye. "I suppose for another half year, Mrs. Jebb," for the last fortnight. And now they have all gone cheerfully away to their own places, mostly of amusement. It really reminds me of the chapter in the Bible. One man must go home to see his mother's maid married; another to Normandy, his people were so very dull and discontented, and so on. You would think they all, for their own sakes, would *prefer* to stay in Cambridge for September,

[1] Sir James Paget, 1814–99. Surgeon Extraordinary to Queen Victoria.

grinding over their books, but that it behooved a man not to be too selfish.

'And, indeed, to go away now is to lose something. The air and weather generally never are so nice in Cambridge as during this month. One could dance in delight getting out into these big solitary college gardens, with such a sky overhead, such clear sunshine, still trees and beautiful colours. The absence of almost everybody else has made me turn to my next door neighbours. These morning readings of German have made us very well acquainted, and now I get a good deal of companionship and pleasure out of their society.

'Tuesday. Dick came in as I was writing to say it was time to start, and your letter had to be put by. To our joy we found the Sidgwicks still staying on at Six Mile Bottom, where the Halls live. The Crosses, visiting there, might have been too much for us in their new felicity.

'George Eliot, old as she is, and ugly, really looked very sweet and winning in spite of both. She was dressed in a short dark soft satin walking dress with a lace wrap half shading the body, a costume most artistically designed to show her slenderness, yet hiding the squareness of age. I thought of what Mrs. Lionel had told me, how George Eliot had been seen at all the fashionable milliners and dressmakers in London, choosing her trousseau. Whatever money and taste could do, to make her look not too unsuitable a bride for a man of forty, had been done.

'In the evening she made me feel sad for her. There was not a person in the drawing-room, Mr. Cross included, whose mother she might not have been, and I thought she herself felt depressed at the knowledge that nothing could make her young again; to her we were all young of a later generation. She adores her husband, and it seemed to me it hurt her a little to have him talk so much to me. It made her, in her pain, slightly irritated and snappish, which I did not mind, feeling that what troubled her was beyond remedy. He may forget the twenty years difference between them, but she never can.

'I feel myself, sometimes, when with a lot of young people, a vague sadness at the knowledge that they are increasing and I am decreasing, that they are just beginning a life almost over for me, which I found and still find very pleasant. It must be a hundred times worse for George Eliot, who cares about success of all kinds a good deal more than I ever could. You can see by her books how much strength of intellect she devotes to showing the emptiness and heartlessness of beauty; and it is said by her friends that she never has heartily liked a pretty woman.

'If ever she did wrong in her life, I am afraid she will suffer enough now to make atonement. Not that Mr. Cross is apparently not devoted to her, but such a marriage is against nature. She will never be happy when she sees him talking to other people, and she will constantly realize that no power on earth can make her a suitable wife for him. If power *could* do it, she would succeed. She has always cared much more for men than for women, and has cultivated every art to make herself attractive, feeling bitterly all the time what a struggle it was, without beauty, whose influence she exaggerates as do all ugly people.

'Mr. Cross I liked very much. He is tall, fine looking, a good talker, altogether an exceptionally interesting man.'

Glasgow, Dec. 9th, 1880

'My dear Sister,
    . . . Heneage and Geraldine [Jebb] have been visiting us and are now at Desmond, perfectly happy at having finished with the law forever. I doubt if he will really like the church any better, since no position can be found without some crumpled rose leaves, but experience may teach him this, and at least after thirty he can't change again. He is really nice in every way, and I like him immensely, only what are people to do who expect the impossible of life?

'His wife, with the true Irish mind, was counting over what income they would eventually have, even if he did nothing. They all think that once he has taken orders and after a year's curacy, the family ought to have sufficient influence to get him a living. Luckily, he and Geraldine have no children, so things might have been worse. I am more than ever of the mind that no people could have been brought up worse, considering the small fortune they have to look forward to, than my mother-in-law's children. Tiny has married a rich man, and Dick has energy and ability that no training could spoil, but Heneage and Bobby are ruined. . . .

'No news from Polly this week. . . . How old we are all getting, who were only children the other day!'

Glasgow, Jan. 11th, 1881

'My dear Sister,

After two years of being ill at Christmas-time, I went over this year with Dick to Ireland, and was rewarded by the great kindness everybody showed to me, and by Dick's mother especially who thanked me for making her son so much happier than she had ever seen him. I suppose he used to be morbid and wretched most of the time, for he is not exactly what I should call a shining example of brilliant spirits now.

'We all gave each other little presents and everything was as pleasant as the New Year time ever can be after one has passed thirty. . . .

'Bret Harte[1] came here on Saturday, and made Dick's hair stand on end through most of dinner. He may be a genius, but he is certainly no gentleman. With Principal Caird on one side of me, I was kept in constant anxiety for fear my countryman might say something *too* broad for a clergyman's ears, let alone mine.

'He insisted on smoking, which nobody ever does here, until after they have finally parted from the ladies, because of the odour, I suppose. Dick offered a cigarette, he said, "No, I never smoke anything but a cigar." And finally Dick had to take him down to the study, where, alas, no cigars were to be found! Jane had apparently distrusted the waiters and had hidden the box behind the sofa. He had to take a cigarette after all, and smoke the pipe of solitary reflection; Dick told him he was sorry but he must join the other guests.

'He did tell some very good stories at dinner, and talked without ceasing. I happened to have a sick headache, which just at dinner began to make me almost too stupid to speak or understand. I hoped champagne would correct it, and not wishing to be thought an idiot, told Bret Harte, while the man was filling my glass, that I hoped the wine might cure my headache.

[1] Francis Bret Harte, 1836–1902. American author, appointed U.S. Consul at Glasgow in 1880.

' "You are like the Scotchman," said he, "who sat down at table, drew everything within reach on both sides into his immediate neighbourhood, simply remarking in explanation to the people around him, "I'm not very weel."

'He amused me very much, if only he had not been such a responsibility; but the people in steady Glasgow are not going to stand him socially. He has begun by flirting outrageously with a Mrs. MacLier, a fast woman known to me and most people by sight, but not in any other way, and Glasgow does not approve of that sort of frivolity. Altogether he is too coarse for cultivated society.

'George Eliot is not to be buried in Westminster Abbey. Mrs. Sidgwick said her friends gave up pressing it, foreseeing that there would be on the part of both moral and religious people, the strongest opposition. She had been ailing for a good while, though her death in the end was very sudden. Dr. Simpson said there must have been previous disease, when she died of pericarditis.'

Glasgow, March, 1881

'My dear Sister,

We have been to so many dinner parties, but I find few are really worth going to. For people who like good eating, dinner parties are worth having, and I suppose a fair proportion must possess this taste, since they continue to be the favorite entertainment. I, who do not care about eating which only gives me indigestion, enjoyed an evening reception at Mrs. Lee's ten times more. A party which Mrs. Nichol said she admired Mrs. Lee's courage for giving! She asked about sixty people and gave them excellent music, but nothing to eat except cakes, ices and sherry.

'It was rather ridiculous to march us all down into the dining-room two by two to see the meagerness of the big table, looking like an expanse of ocean with a tiny island dotted here and there. I should have had tea and coffee in addition which almost everybody takes in the evening; and then not have used the dining-room at all, but have had the refreshments in the square hall outside of the drawing-room. The sight of the dining-room was too suggestive of good cheer. Yet the party was much more amusing

166

than a dinner party, just because one could move about and have such a large choice of people with whom to talk.

'On Tuesday we are going to a big Launch. The new Cunard steamer, *Servia*, the biggest ship they have ever tried, is to be launched on the 1st and we are asked to the luncheon on board, given by the company to a select number. . . .

'Did I tell you about the new house we have taken at Cambridge? It will cost us in rent and rates £200 a year, and we shall have to keep a gardener, but we have money enough, fortunately. We shall have a lawn tennis ground, kitchen garden, hot beds, and a conservatory, and every belonging of a house in the country; and all side by side with the College Gardens. At "the Backs", the very best situation in Cambridge. Far better than building a house for ourselves.[1]

'Dick must make Heneage an allowance until he gets a living, which will be rather a pull. After being married for eighteen months, without any sign of a family, what does Geraldine do, but take this very time when they are penniless to give hopes of an increase to come off next September. Meanwhile, Heneage is taking his studies with a good deal of ease, Irish fashion, and feeling that somebody will look after him. Just now he is on a visit to the Aunties, then he means to come back, he says, and really settle down at Desmond. . . .

'On Thursday I persuaded Dick to write a note of excuse for me to the Macarthurs' party, and to go on this festive occasion by himself; which he did with much grumbling. He found a pleasanter affair than usual, he said, a reward to him for playing the man! (You know Cranmer's remark to his fellow sufferer at the stake, "Play the man, Master Ridley." Dick considers that in spite of Cranmer's encouragement, this must, under the circumstances, have been hard to do. It is one of his favorite addresses to himself, when he feels the occasion requires, such as a dinner party, or any gathering where the fellow creature has to be encountered. Yet he never will let me refuse an invitation, and now we are committed to two balls in the near future!)'

---

[1] This was their beloved 'Springfield' the lease of which they later purchased; it was to be her home as long as she lived in England.

'My dear Sister,

Last week we went to a musical evening, among other evenings of entertainment, which was most pleasant. I should like to have devoted my whole attention to the choral singing, but I defy anybody to sit in the chair that was given to me, without giving a good share of thought to keeping in position. Just as surely as I lost myself in the music, I found myself sliding slowly to the floor, and had to pull up and settle again into a very obtuse angle.

'Then, the woman in front of me had on a most distracting dress, which might have been cotton print, what Whistler would call "a nocturne in white and black", or white silk under black figured lace. It stared me in the face, stretched across a wide expanse of back, and would not cease from asking "What am I?" And I don't know yet!

'Our hosts were Mr. and Mrs. Mirrlees, very rich people, who went to America at the time of the Centennial. He had one of his railway locomotives on exhibition, a splendid thing, which they sold on the spot to some Cuban planter. They have twenty-five acres of land right in the best neighbourhood in Glasgow. It makes me shudder to think what taxes he must pay. . . .'

CHAPTER XII

—————⟫❈⟪—————

Glasgow, Jan., 1882

'My dear Sister,

Tomorrow my dressmaker finishes her engagement with me and I hope my satin dress. I couldn't have believed a dyed dress could have turned out so well; I cheerfully bear witness to Miss Watson's wisdom, upon which I am happy to say I acted at the time. Just before she called four years ago, I had been looking at a dress length of splendid new black satin sent home from the shop. "Why didn't you buy it white first, and get the good of a white satin?" she asked. "You could so easily have dyed it black." Happy thought! They consented to change it for me at the shop, it did admirably as a white dinner dress, then, dyed a pretty red; and now it comes out once more ever beautiful and new, black! Even the way it was made at first, very full princesse with a set in train, suits for the present panier style. . . .

'At a dinner party the other evening, Lord Ailsa, a shy young man, sat by me the whole evening, while I ransacked heaven and earth to find something to talk to him about. At length "Chickens" succeeded with me. He said if I had ever started my chicken farm in America, I should have had to import French workmen, nobody else understood chickens. An English fowl sold in London for 3/6 while a French one brought fifteen francs. There is a fact for you! I liked the little man, and feel proud that eventually I did succeed in putting him at his ease and making him talk. . . .

'Write me a long letter about all the children, which is what never fails to interest me. Tell me Maud's experiences in Washington. And, oh, ask Nellie if she would like to come and pay me a visit? It is so long since I have seen any of you, that I should enjoy having her. I see no chance of my coming over next summer. If you think well of it, I will buy her a return ticket, you could put her under the care of the Captain, always the best protection, and Heneage would take her off the steamer at Liverpool. I should like her to come as early in April as possible, to get here by the 1st, perhaps, and then spend the summer with us in Cambridge. What do you think of my suggestion?'

Nellie accepted the invitation immediately, and after much correspondence as to details of the trip and what clothes to bring, she arrived in Glasgow in early April, offering new opportunities for her Aunt Cara's match-making abilities.

Glasgow, April 8th, 1882

'My dear Sister,

... Nellie has arrived safely.... You need not think I should be disappointed in her. I did not expect her to be pretty, but she is nice looking, and she has what is worth a great deal more than mere beauty, she has gentleness and self-possession, without a shade of pertness, which give her an air of good breeding. Her sweet voice is a great gift. By the aid of it all her Americanisms, and she has so many that they make me laugh, only sound sweet and attractive. I am really delighted with her. Her absolute freedom from affectation or any desire to make an impression gives a great charm to her manner.

'Tonight six young people are coming to dinner, and I am going to give her the handsomest and nicest of the young men to take her in, a Mr. Crailsheim, half German, but very rich, who will amuse her, or rather interest her for the evening. I gather that the voyage was made pleasant by the unremitting attentions of two young gentlemen.

'Later. Nellie and I have spent the morning trying on dresses. My blue plush jacket is lovely on her and has at once been made over formally to her, only, worse luck, she cannot wear it here. A sage green cashmere Greek sort of robe delighted her more than anything. She said how Maud would have raved over the colour, and she means to wear it tonight for dinner. She looked so nicely in a new hat of straw and velvet and white feathers that I have just made it over to her. I am going to get her a new spring suit next week from you, and a ball dress, a present from me, and then I think she will do.

'Maud's letter was interesting about Washington. I remember General Sherman perfectly, red hair and all. In my day he had not a loud voice, and his manner was simple and perfectly free from self-consciousness. It must be a great treat to Maud to meet the variety of people to be found in Washington; my favorite resort was the Capitol and the House. When she gets to know some of the Senators and Representatives she will find going to the debates very amusing. I am sure Polly will never forget our assisting at the trial of Andrew Johnson.'[1]

When Nellie first arrived, Dick was visiting in Ireland, and wrote one of his typical little notes to Cara,

'My own pet wifie,
I just write a line to say that my plans remain as announced yesterday, i.e., ARRIVAL, 12 midnight on TUESDAY, TO BE CALLED ON WEDNESDAY at *seven*, with a view to renewed toils for you. As to the provision of any bodily refection or little comforts for the wearied traveller, arriving in the gloom and silence of the mid-night hours, it may be enough to observe that the views of such an ascetic would be met by anything in the nature of cold viands. With regard to the appeasing of thirst, the quarter to which we should be disposed to look for appropriate means would be Eastern France, rather than to such towns of the Central region as adorn the banks of the Loire, Samur, for an example. . . .

'Today is a glorious day, I have been sitting for hours in the garden, enjoying the view of the sea while I write. I am looking forward so much to meeting Nellie.
　　　　　　　　　　　Ever your GOOD'
　　　　　　　[There is no signature, but a picture of a
　　　　　　　stick man with outstretched arms towards
　　　　　　　a woman and a cat.]

　　　　　　　　　　　　　　　Glasgow, April, 1882
'My dear Sister,
　　We were so late at Nellie's first ball last night that I feel good

[1] Andrew Johnson, President of the U.S. after Lincoln, was impeached un-fairly.

171

for nothing this morning. Neither Dick nor Nellie have shown any symptom of waking to life. My energy reaches just far enough to have taken my breakfast in bed and now to try in a feeble way to give you a short account of things. This last has been a very busy, very gay week, busy with the dressmaker, gay with many dinner parties.

'I have made Nellie a present of her first ball dress, and flowers to wear with it. You should have seen her when we came home from town yesterday and found her dress spread out by Jane for inspection on my bed. She could do nothing but stand for half an hour and look at it. It is white tulle over white silk with long sprays of perfect French flowers on the skirt, a wreath of smaller round the throat and round the short sleeves, a spray on the left breast and another for the hair made altogether a delight for the eyes to see.

'Nellie looked extremely well in it, was indeed lovely with the excitement of such novel experiences. It was delightful to see her enjoyment all through the evening. She danced every dance till we came away and was a success in every way. Lady Thomson told me she was delighted with her.

'Of course she is an untrained girl, too young yet not to be capable of much improvement, but she has the first elements of great attractiveness. I want greatly to try to teach her to carry herself more gracefully, without hurting her feelings or making her self-conscious. And also to get her into the way of laughing less. So many young girls giggle when they are either shy or excited, and a worse habit could not exist. I have indirectly suggested this mistake by praising to Nellie one or two girls whose manners are good, I can't say with much success so far. It occurs to me that girls in Philadelphia *do* giggle a good deal. People laugh out of mere good nature, but I have always thought it a mistake and that you can look just as kindly and pleasant by smiling.

'I wish I had you here to make these hints to Nellie. I am determined that she shall be happy and have a good time more than anything, and I don't like to give her the impression that I am critical. Alone with me her manners are perfect, and I suppose it is more than human nature can expect to have her just as simple and unaffected with strangers.'

In May, Nellie went to Italy with her aunt and uncle, from which place Cara wrote.

Florence, May 14th, 1882

'My dear Sister,

I doubt if Nellie enjoys this part of her visit quite as much as the month of new people in Glasgow, at least not while it is going on; she will afterwards when time has been given to digest it all. We are taking the sights rather slowly but are going over a good deal of ground.

'Gerald Balfour has been of immense use to us in sightseeing. Living here in his villa he has got to speak Italian perfectly, and he knows everything in art that is worth seeing, a knowledge invaluable to us, who would be killed by the labor of hunting out everything for ourselves.

'Both he and Dick think Nellie very pretty! I doubt if you do her beauty justice at home. She has beautiful eyes and hair, and a clear white complexion. . . . G.B. is trying hard to improve Nellie's taste in music, by lending her Beethoven and classical things, not with striking success so far. She says Beethoven is hard, and not having heard yet much good music, I doubt if she quite feels his great superiority. I know I don't, but I never was musical.

'Our intention now is to leave here on the 29th of May. This new bill permitting Fellows of Colleges to marry makes a great matrimonial rush among those beings. I hear that thirty weddings are expected to come off among Cambridge men this summer. I only hope it won't quite spoil the charm of the place by filling it with semi-paupers.'

Florence, May 21st, 1882

'My dear Sister,

We are all fairly tired of Florence by this time, for one thing the weather has got so hot that the bare idea of going out in this sun sightseeing makes us shrink, and we are counting the days until we can start for home. Besides, three weeks in lodgings with nothing but sightseeing to do is quite enough. The mind gets full of so many new impressions that it wants leisure to digest them all.

'Now for a piece of news that will interest you all. Nellie has an admirer who would very easily be a lover if she felt any drawing towards him herself. I have known well a good variety of people in my life, but I have never known anyone quite his equal. *If* Nellie could love him, she would have for a husband the most superior man I ever met. For this reason she may not be able to love him, she is so young, so little accustomed to the intellectual range where his thoughts dwell.

'He is extremely attracted by her and thinks her very lovely and lovable, but says he would never think of marrying a girl who did not really love him. He has been a great friend of both Dick and mine ever since I came to England. Don't fancy from this that he must be in the sere and yellow leaf. Gerald Balfour was just twenty-nine a month ago, and with his slender figure and slight mustache is generally taken for five or six years younger. It strikes me you know all about him already that he belongs to the English highest class; can call cousins with half the nobility of England; is own nephew to the Marquess of Salisbury. For fortune he has about £26,000 ($125,000) which is all safely invested and yields him an income which I am sure he understates at £1,000 ($5,000) a year.

'He is not deeply in love with Nellie yet, but he has talked it over with me, and says the only thing that keeps him from so being is the utter absence of response from her. It is too funny! In London almost any girl would love him, and think herself blessed to have his love. It seems as hard for Nellie to establish any meeting ground of sympathy between her and him as it would be if he were a wild Indian. It is, then, as hard to love up as to love down. By *up* I don't mean socially, I don't care two straws about that, but morally and intellectually. He is very full of earnest purposes in life, and that Nellie seems to have none of these he puts down to her extreme youth. What attracts him is her perfect simplicity of character and her sweet ways, which I prophesy will win her many lovers. I used always to say, you know, that Maud would be the beauty of the family, but that Nellie would have the gift which makes people fall in love with her.

'I doubt myself if she ought to marry G.B. Of course she enjoys his admiration, but I don't think she is ever at home with him. She thinks him very handsome, though too *thin*. The presumptuous

174

young woman! Seven years ago he was voted the most beautiful youth in England; he had a divinely beautiful face, now a bit thinner, I must admit. As a youth he was called in Trinity the B.V.M. because of his perfect purity of beauty. (Blessed Virgin Mary, those initials meant. He never knew of this till I amused him by the telling last year.) Now he looks more like Dr. Schell than anyone else you know, though with features the Dr. never had, a large firm perfectly beautiful mouth, and fine large eyes. The two men are alike in having very sweet deep dimples which soften the severity of their faces when they smile, rather prominent chins, and thick wavy hair.

'But to go back to Nellie. She says she is no more in love with him than "with that candle", but still she does not want him to stop paying her attentions. I think she is trying to fall in love with him, but she says she doesn't want to marry him unless she loves him. Meanwhile the situation is becoming somewhat strained as he knows she knows he is trying to win her affection, and she knows that he knows it. (There is a sentence worthy of *Punch*!)

'Did you ever think Nellie's hands beautiful? He considers them the most beautiful he ever saw. Reserved as he is, he managed to overcome nature so far as to tell her how beautifully she used her fingers, in my presence, too! He thinks her eyes and eyebrows beautiful, and the shape of her head and hair. He says he knows plenty of girls far more beautiful than she is, but the essential thing is that a girl should attract a man, she attracts him and they don't. Her power of looking lovely every five minutes is far more charming than any steady beauty.

'We leave here for Cambridge on Friday night, none too soon! I don't want Nellie to give the slightest encouragement until she has had time to settle her impressions. I confess that her being so impassive was at first a great surprise to me, he is so attractive. Tomorrow morning we all start at five o'clock (oh, dear!) for Vallombrosa, the place of leaves, you know. We shall take poetry with us, G.B. reads aloud beautifully, and cards, have our luncheon in the woods under the trees, and come back to a late supper at home. This is our last expedition, and then nothing remains but to pack and leave.

'Dick is very busy collating at the library; it is for him now we are having to wait. I am eager to get back to Springfield, and to the garden especially.'

Nellie later said that Gerald Balfour was the most conceited man she ever met. What a blow for Cara who had always declared no woman could ever refuse him!

'My dear Polly,   *Cambridge, June 22nd, 1882*
    . . . Nellie has as yet no new admirers. The men come to play tennis day after day, not the same ones of course, they are very civil and nice, but I can't say one of them shows any signs of special interest; nor does she in them. Some are good specimens of the race, too.

'Young Stephen, who has just taken his degree, is expected by all the men of his year to come to the front in law and politics. People prophesy that he will be the head man of his generation in England. I agree with them. He has a splendid head and everything about him shows power, force and intellect. He comes of a very able family. His grandfather, Sir James Stephen, was Chancellor of England, or Chief Justice, I believe it was; his father is now one of the leading Judges, Sir James Fitzjames Stephen, author of *Liberty, Equality, Fraternity*, and I know not how many books; his uncle Leslie Stephen, who married Thackeray's daughter, writes delightfully.

'I believe nobody ever heard of a Stephen who was stupid or a failure. This youth is expected to surpass all the rest. Already in the Tripos here, he took his degree a year ago and is now twenty-three, he stood head and shoulders above the second man. Well, if I were Nellie, I should be very much attracted by him, and I should think him worth winning. I don't say she doesn't; she has only met him twice and she liked playing tennis with him extremely. He would be difficult to impress, but nobody is deterred by that. To win what is difficult gives a double pleasure.[1]

[1] James Kenneth Stephen, 1859–92, was a most outstanding young barrister. He was also a Fellow of King's and a lecturer. He wrote *Lapsus Calami*, a book of parodies and humorous verse, still well-known. He had many friends in Cambridge, but unfortunately went out of his mind in 1886 and died six years later, at thirty-three.

'Frank Balfour is the most charming of men, and Nellie, like everybody else, likes him, only he is more than difficult, he is impossible.[1] I don't think in all the thirty years of his life he has ever been in love with anyone. Now that Darwin is gone, he stands first in natural science. His thoughts are so taken up with his own work that he has none to spare for his personal happiness. Mr. Colvin said it was almost wicked for him to go about the world with that sweet look of blessing on his face, himself untouched by any emotion. He has been here twice to play tennis, comes again on Saturday, and then I fear he will vanish entirely from our view during Nellie's stay. He goes off to climb mountains in Switzerland on the 10th of July, to return only for a day or two at a time to Cambridge until the October term.

'Gerald comes to England next week. Whether Nellie likes him now or he continues to be attracted by her, I can't tell. Unless she shows a good deal of responsiveness, his nascent passion will probably come to a very quick end. Meanwhile, I shall decline to talk much about either of them to the other, and certainly I shall not be so silly as to try to influence Nellie to like him. Never again in her life will she have an equal chance, I feel sure. . . .

'George Darwin, my other intimate friend, has not taken any fancy to her, nor she to him. He thinks her a nice girl, easy to get on with, but not the least pretty. She takes exactly the same view of him. He has gone down for three weeks.'

Nellie wrote to her sister Maud in June, 1882.

'Aunt Cara's house is very pretty especially the drawing-room; the carpet has a soft yellow ground that I know you would admire and the furniture nearly all Chippendale, very pretty to look at but exceedingly uncomfortable, I mean the chairs, of course. Then she has velvet portiers of a blue green color and the wood of the room is painted to match; it is really a very pretty room, she used to have yellow Indian curtains, but they were so unbecoming she couldn't stand them and they were taken down. . . .

'The other night we were invited to a dinner party to meet Dr.

[1] Francis Maitland Balfour, 1851–82. Biologist of European reputation, and Professor of Animal Morphology at Cambridge University.

Tyng of New York, and of all the American accents I ever heard, his was the worst. He was quite overpowered by Aunt Cara's brilliancy, and remarked to the lady next to him that she was an ornament for *any* college. The English idea of an American is one who chatters straight along, without saying anything in the end, so several times I have been taken for a young Englishwoman, which I think not the highest compliment that could be paid, though they do, I suppose. . . .'

Cambridge, June 29th, 1882

'My dear Sister,

You read my letter over again and you will see there is nothing to be anxious about. Nellie did *not* fall in love with G.B. at Florence, and she is not likely to do so here where she meets so many jollier youths. He came back on Saturday and his return was anything but a success. I think he was surprised to find how little he cared whether she liked him or not. If Nellie had responded to his fancy at first, of course it would have been different.

'She is not a girl to lose a man's affection. She is very lovable as G.B. said, and though certainly not intellectual, there is great good sense. She never says silly things, nor does she prose along as great talkers often do with pointless remarks. She lets other people talk to her, an attractive thing to the men over here, these being in the habit of leading in the conversation. I never saw a race so impatient of twaddle, nor one so little incommoded by silence. They don't demand that talk shall be continuous. Our two countries do not at all agree in this respect.

'A Professor Goodwin from Harvard called on Sunday; I went to see his new-made wife on Monday, and they both prosed on steadily about their own experiences in a way that wearied me extremely. Not a bright or amusing thing the whole time, just *talk* like the parts one always skips in books.

'Not only is Nellie liked here, but she will find this social life of use to her. She has never been taught to be unselfish apparently. You can be as selfish as you like in essential, but society will not permit the exercise of that quality in minor things. You *must* sit at table after you have finished, till the dinner or meal is over, you *must* stay in the drawing-room in the evening when you would like to take a book and go off. In a hundred little ways politeness requires that you pay consideration to others. I tell Nellie that nothing is so foolish as to show selfishness in small matters, that even unselfishness itself finds its reward in apparent thoughtfulness for others.'

Cambridge, July 20th, 1882

'My dear Sister,

I think Nellie really does like Frank Balfour, now. But then, why wouldn't she? Gerald has a certain decision and authority of manner which makes him not always so much liked, but Frank is the sweetest human soul the earth has ever held.

'Lady Rayleigh, his sister, told me a day or two ago that she did not think Frank had ever felt an emotion of romantic love in his life. He has said that if one of Burne-Jones' women would step down from the canvas, he would adore her. He is so sweet a nature, if he does marry, his wife will be the most enviable of women. Gerald says *how* he would love her, if he ever gets into that relation. If you knew him, you would be glad to have any daughter of yours married to him if she had to live in Africa. But he has gone away, not to be back in Cambridge till September, and I can't say that he showed the least sign of being more taken with Nellie than with anybody else. He is always so gentle and courteous in manner to everybody.'

While Cara was writing these lines, Frank Balfour lay dead on a mountain-side in the Alps, whither he had gone for a climbing expedition with his brother Gerald, as he had done for many summers before. Both he and his guide somehow fell and were killed on July 19th. Nellie wrote on July 25th,

'My dear Mama,

Nothing else is talked of here but Frank Balfour's accident, and scarcely anything else thought of, even. I never knew anyone who was so loved by everyone and who was so perfect. We are both so glad that we had seen so much of him the very night before he went away. He and Gerald came to dine with us and we had such a pleasant evening. Frank was saying how much he would have to

179

tell us about his trip when he came back in August, and then we all sat around the piano and sang hymns which he had not done since he was a boy, and though he sang frightfully out of tune, he was blissfully unconscious of the fact, and enjoyed himself so much that it was as much as poor sleepy Gerald could do to get him away. We are both very glad that just before he left he had his picture taken and had promised us each one when he came back. We intend to claim them, though he will never give them to us himself. I can't realize that he is dead at all, it seems as if he would turn up any minute for a game of tennis.

'Tonight we are to dine out again though little do we feel like it. Lord and Lady Rayleigh[1] were both to be there, but now of course, they won't. . . . We expect George Darwin to come in this afternoon and tell us if there is any other news.'

According to an address by Professor Arthur Gamgee, reported in *The Times* of August 25th, 1882, 'Francis Maitland Balfour, whose sudden death has so recently cast a gloom over us all, was a man who appeared destined to advance our knowledge of animal development more than it had been advanced by the labours of anyone of his predecessors. . . . The great text-book of comparative embryology is the real monument of Balfour's fame. It is impossible to convey an idea of the merits of this little book. . . . Those of my hearers who had not followed Balfour's scientific labours, but who merely knew him as one of the most respected workers in the field of biology, will, I trust, even from my brief sketch, have formed some idea of the activity and originality of his mind, and will understand how his death has occasioned a feeling almost akin to despair, in that he occupied a place which it appears to us now impossible to fill. "How are the mighty fallen and the weapons of war perished!" '

'My dear Sister,
Cambridge, Aug. 4th, 1882

People are getting over the shock of Frank Balfour's death, but those who half loved him, of whom I am one, feel that Cambridge

---

[1] John William Strutt, Lord Rayleigh, 1842–1919. Cavendish Professor of Experimental Physics at Cambridge, 1879–84. Married Evelyn Balfour, sister of Frank and Gerald.

will never be quite the same place again. Michael Foster, his old chief in science here, and loving friend, wrote a beautiful letter about him to the *British Medical Journal*. After telling all that Frank was in science, he went on: "But to those who knew him well, their wonder at his genius was lost in their love for the man. His gentle courtesy, sound judgment, unswerving faithfulness, gay affectionateness, his bright intellect made life seem easier when he was near."

'It is quite true. The thought of seeing him again was always one of the pleasant things in coming back to Cambridge, and in September the place never seemed quite deserted because he stayed up to work in that quiet time, and I could always count on his coming to tennis two or three times a week. It is impossible to realize that bright beautiful unselfish life has come to a full stop. George Darwin says he could have spared better any of his own brothers; he is almost heart-broken. He brought a letter from Gerald to Arthur B. which the latter had forwarded to him, for us to read.

'Death must have been instantaneous for both Frank and his guide. The guide's skull was crushed in and Frank's neck broken. They were half buried in snow on Sunday morning, the accident having happened on the Wednesday preceding. The bodies were so difficult to get at that it was not till the next Wednesday, just a week from the death on the 19th, that they were brought in. Gerald had his brother's body embalmed and is now coming home with the coffin. He hopes to be in London tomorrow and at their place in Scotland in time to have the funeral there, at Whittinghame, at noon on Saturday. We are to have a service in Trinity Chapel at the same time.

'I think I told you that Mrs. Darwin, the widow of the great Darwin, has taken our Springfield for six months. . . .'

Nellie wrote to her mother on August 10th,

'. . . I have given names to several of our intimate friends, so that when we speak of them strangers will not know whom we mean and it makes it very amusing sometimes. There is an old maid here who runs after Aunt Cara all the time and tells her all her confidences, she imagines that she has many lovers and in fact is very much like Aunt Emma. I have named her Aunt Cara's Beloved and she always goes by that name now, although the other evening when Mr. Darwin was here he said if he weren't careful, she would be *his* beloved soon, and it is true she really thinks that he is in love with her. Little does he know that he, too, has a name: the Constant One, he is so called because he is here so much and is so constant. We have named Mr. Stephen the Willing One, because he always accepts invitations so cheerfully and is always so ready to do or go anywhere, and so they are marked and named without their knowledge, poor things.

'There is no repelling Miss Maine if she makes up her mind she likes you, there is no help for you. Aunt Cara receives long letters eight and ten pages long which "her Beloved" calls notes, and begins them with "Cara Mia". "That fool of a woman", as George Darwin says. It is really too funny.'

Nellie wrote again the next week.

'The people are now beginning to leave Cambridge till the October term, when they all come back again. Mr. Darwin left on Thursday, but he thinks he will be back in September. We have seen a great deal of him lately and he is the kind of man, the more you see of him, the more you like him, he is such a perfect gentleman. He is the most popular man in Trinity, now that Frank Balfour has gone.

'Dick came home from Greece on Wednesday. While he was away we had been having people come in the evenings, American fashion, and it was delightful. One night Mr. Shaw and Mr. Heape came to play whist, and most of the other evenings Mr. Darwin would drop in and we would play go-bang. But now that Dick has come back of course all of that is stopped, as he likes a quiet *English* evening, among the "domestic circle" as he calls us. . . .'

Cambridge, Aug., 1882

'My dear Sister,

. . . Next week we are going to town for the day, and then on to Aldworth, Tennyson's home, to dine and sleep. I hesitated a good

182

deal about accepting, but have decided to go on Nellie's account. She may never have another chance to see the poet. Talking to him is always anxious work, he is so morbidly sensitive and so greedy of praise, and for my own part I get out of going there whenever I can. However, this time we shall only stay over one evening. . . .

'Nellie says she is not sorry she lost her chance of G.B., and as his fancy proved so very short lived, she is quite right. I don't myself think she would have suited him. George Darwin is another matter. I won't say what answer he would get, and I am quite sure he would make her happy. . . .'

It was only a few weeks later that George Darwin did propose to Nellie, but she refused him, sailed for home, and remained single the rest of her life.

Glasgow, Nov. 30th, 1882

'My dear Sister,
    You ask me about George Darwin's religious opinions and I can only say I know nothing whatever about them. If you ask me if he is a man of truth and honour, of good character and life, what he *is*, I can answer. What he believes on a matter so inner as religion is, as Mr. Gore says in *Democracy*, between him and his maker, not a thing to talk about.

'But when you call Charles Darwin an infidel, it sounds like a breath out of another century. You can't have read anything written about him in newspaper or magazine for the last twenty years, or any of his own writings. I wonder what you think of Galileo, by the way? He was put in prison for saying that the earth moved, when revealed religion had declared it to be the centre and the sun the thing that rose and set.

'Darwin lies buried in Westminster Abbey, where half of the clergymen of England met to do him honour on the day of his funeral. A more lovely life no man ever lived, full of sweetness towards all connected with him, so good a husband that his widow seems half to have lost her own life in losing him. She has never been well since, and looks, her son says, ten years older than she did a year ago.

'But there is no use in telling you what he *was*, and if you don't read general literature nor his own books, you can't know what he thought or what was thought about him. No man ever did so much work with such health. He told George that he couldn't imagine a greater curse than enforced idleness. I wonder if you had known Frank Balfour what you would have thought of him? . . .'

Glasgow, Jan. 1st, 1883

'My dear Sister,

. . . I don't see how strength can come if I pass most of the day in bed. Dr. A. is giving me Ma's favorite medicament, quinine, to great benefit, I think. At first I was told I must go south to the Pyrenees as soon as I was strong enough to travel; but now, though I can go if I want, the Doctor says it would do me a world of good, still he does not positively command it.

'I don't like to desert Dick who is totally dependent on me for company, he won't go anywhere except from social duty, *never* with the idea of enjoyment. I asked him what he would do if I were to depart altogether. "I don't know, I suppose I should sink into hopeless despondency," he replied. He has always suffered from depressed spirits since he came to man's estate, and nobody but me has any power to lift him out of them. I have the great blessing of being born cheerful. . . .

'A letter has just come from George Darwin who is staying at the Tennysons'. Hallam gave him a general invitation when they met at the Greek play, *Ajax*, performance at Cambridge in December, to make them a visit. G.D. took this seriously, as is the custom of Englishmen, proposed himself for last Saturday to stay till Monday, and when he heard that on Monday the Master of Balliol was expected, he made up his own mind, if asked, to remain till Wednesday.

'His first reception was in the poet's gruff manner. G.D. said it was very kind of them to let him propose himself in this way. "H'm! I suppose Hallam asked you," responded his host. Later on, he got to think Mr. Tennyson extremely nice, and most amusing and interesting. They are not in the place we visited, but at their winter home on the Isle of Wight, the poet's favorite residence.

'A Lady Sophy Selborne was also of the party, apparently not attractive, or especially gracious to George, for he says nothing else about her. She may be there on Hallam's account, his father wishing him to marry (*well*, of course). Hallam once said he thought the title "Mrs." was very ugly, whereupon Dick responded he would, to avoid it for his wife, have to marry a Lady M. or N. The idea struck Hallam very favorably. I shouldn't wonder if he were to confine his attentions to young ladies who under no circumstances would ever be reduced to the "Mrs."....'[1]

Cara decided after all to go south for her health, and accompanied Mr. and Mrs. Blackburn and their daughter to Pau, France.

Pau, Feb. 8th, 1883

'My dear Sister,

If paper could speak this sheet would tell you that it comes out of the midst of summer. I never saw such a delicious winter climate as here. I can't wear coat or cloak; I really *sleep* in a manner worth calling so with my window open; sit about on benches to rest without the slightest chill; and yet feel not the least sign of relaxation. On the contrary my appetite is a wonder, if everybody else did not eat as much I should be ashamed. We all seem able to go conscientiously through the table d'hôte bill of fare without an effort.

'I see, now, that the cold weather is the cause pure and simple of all my difficulties. My nervous system does not like it, and the cold hands and nose, familiar to your memory, are signs of depressed vitality. The change of climate has worked like magic.

'Pau is one of the most beautiful spots on the earth's surface. I can hardly dress or write or do anything steadily in my room with that most perfect view stretched outside my window. My room faces south towards the Pyrenees, snow-capped and brilliant at this season. I never felt such a perfect climate.

'To be sure, being with the Blackburns is a good deal like wearing a hair shirt. They are so determined to assert their own knowledge and your ignorance, as is the nature of egotists, but I don't mind. When the prickles grow uncomfortable I take

[1] Hallam Tennyson did not marry a Lady, but a Miss Audrey Boyle.

refuge in my own room and sit looking out of my window far off until my feelings get soothed again. I know they are really kind and they don't mean to be prickly, only soft pleasantness is not in them.

'Here is an instance of the sort of thing that goes on. In London Edith told me I should come in for the Carnival, which strange to say has its celebration in Pau on Ash Wednesday. I thought this queer, but supposed as she had lived here years and years, she probably knew. It seems that at the intensely Protestant time, this celebration on Ash Wednesday was meant as an insult to the Catholic feeling. Well, I told this to Mrs. B. who dismissed it at once as not credible. "Shrove Tuesday is the day of course, it never could be Ash Wednesday." It *was* Ash Wednesday, all the same.

'Well, this goes on about everything. Mrs. B. can't believe in the smallest information *you* volunteer. The daughter is constantly snubbing her, which would be more than a sufficient revenge, supposing I wanted any. We get on beautifully for it never enters their heads that *I* have any feelings, and I dislike wrangling too much to stand up for my own intelligence, if it can't be seen without.

'Mrs. B. is very amusing in her self-deceptions. She fancies she talks very little, and all the time her tongue is never still; goes straight on through any little thing you may want to tell; never gives you the slightest notice in the way of a response. This drives the daughter wild. If the mother would leave her a fair share of the company, she wouldn't mind, but the old lady has a great interest in young men; will hang back, ask a question, in some way draw any stray one in reach into her own clutches. As Miss B. remarks, it *is* too bad.

'The daughter is now thirty, a fact which increases her bitterness, whenever it occurs to her, to have been ten years eclipsed by her more interesting parent. Mr. B. is kindly, able, luckily without a shadow of self-assertion in him. He is a dear old gentleman with the sweetest face and the shabbiest clothes.

'We take what amusements come in our way. On Monday we hired a pair of horses and drove beyond Morlaas to see the "meet", a very gay and merry scene. They let a fox out of a bag a few hours before to make sure there would be one in the woods, and at the appointed time, people drove out in carriages, etc., to see the hounds thrown off.

'The man of chief interest to our party was Lord Rowton, Lord Beaconsfield's private secretary and devoted friend. Mrs. B. had met him ten years ago, and was quite determined to claim acquaintance again. Of course she managed it, she is one of those plucky little women who do whatever they want. I was very much amused to see how!

'In this sort of thing, carriages keep moving about according to the people's idea of the best point of view to watch the hunt, and over and over again we passed him. She contrived to give him a square full bow, which brought him out of his seat at least. The other man in his phaeton knew us all, and I suspected him of having had his memory of Mrs. B. refreshed by this friend.

'He said he must come and see her and have a talk about Egypt; I believe it was there that she had met him. Whereupon she instantly tried to get him to fix a time. This was taking his politeness a little more seriously than he meant. He covered up his determination not to bind himself by an excess of extreme volubility and escaped, no doubt congratulating himself on having got off so well.'

Glasgow, April 10th, 1883

'My dear Sister,

Dick came back from Ireland this morning, firmly persuaded that his mother will not live out the year. He had not meant to go to Ireland till the 1st of May, but was about to go on a fishing excursion with Dr. Lee to Lochleven. When he wrote this home, his mother said, "He little knows it is his last chance to see me. I shall be gone before May." They telegraphed him, Dick threw up his fishing at once and went to her, to find her very much as usual.

'They had two doctors consulting over his mother while he was there, only to say again that there was no local disease whatever, her heart was as sound as their own! I don't see under these circumstances why she should die next year any more than any other person of seventy. If ever there was a warning of the danger one incurs from dwelling too much on oneself, encouraging all one's fancies and notions, she is one.

'Have you seen Mrs. Carlyle's *Letters*? Three big volumes they are, but I mean to borrow and read them all. She had a hard time, yet no doubt she took a good deal of comfort in complaining; and she got much genuine affections and sympathy outside the domestic circle. I can't help thinking Froude must have slipped in a thing or two unmarked by Carlyle for publication; one can hardly credit a man of his own free will furnishing quite so much gratification to curiosity and capering in exactly that dress before the public.

'Would I have mended his trousers while he was off amusing himself with Lady Harriet Baring? I would not. She must really have enjoyed the thrifty managing part of her life, or one can hardly imagine with her sense that she would have given in to Carlyle's demands upon her in this direction. And as to his going away when painters and paperers were in the house, you may be sure she was glad to get rid of him. I never think of such a thing as cumbering the house with Dick when work of that kind is to be done. Unless a man has a gift for moving, he is only in the way and I don't blame him for not having the gift. Dick is ready to hire a company of men, and I daresay it was Mrs. C.'s own economy, not his, that put so much of the burden of manual labour on her.

'Did I tell you that Heneage Jebb has had a small living presented to him already? A piece of great good luck, his curacy was to have ended this spring. Lady Kenmore, Aunty Fan's devoted friend, asked the Duke of Bedford to give it to Heneage. Only the first fruits, she says, she will make him give a much better one when such falls vacant. . . .'

Nellie was still debating in a rather half-hearted way whether to accept George Darwin or not. In a letter to her in early May, her Aunt Cara advised,

'George Darwin is so kind and nice, so really generous in big things, so companionable and amusing, that if only you had been five years older, I think you might have liked him. He is wonderfully improvable, already he has thrown off entirely the little thoughtless ways that used to strike one. I laughed at him about talking instead of waiting on the tea table, and now he says the mere sight of a teapot brings him to his feet in an instant, and he hands cups and cakes without intermission. . . .

'I had a delightful week in London. An old friend turned up in the shape of Arnold Morley[1] (you would have fallen in love with *him* at once if you had the chance, and no good, for I doubt if he thinks of marrying, he is too much taken up with law and politics). I am going to ask him down for Sunday when Dick gets back and I can arrange things. I dined with his people in a splendid house in London, went with his sister to look on at a political banquet and hear Gladstone and others speak, with him to the House of Commons, and altogether had a great deal of amusement at his hands. I never shopped once! Just gave myself up to the pleasure of going about and seeing people. George Darwin, he, Edith and I dined at his own rooms one evening and went afterwards to the theatre, to a box, always the pleasantest. . . .'

[1] Cara's former beau, Arnold Morley, 1849–1916, was a barrister, later Chief Liberal whip, 1886–92, Postmaster General, etc. Married widow of Daniel Runyon of New York, 1911.

CHAPTER XIII

Now it was Nellie's older sister Maud's turn to visit her aunt. Before she left home Cara requested that she bring the following things with her to Cambridge.

'I should like Polly to pack an extra box with a dozen tins of Oysters, the Erie kind, a couple of dozen tins of Tomatoes, a dozen muffin rings, and, if you could get it, a waffle iron. And would you please instruct Maud how to make waffles your way, for I shall want her to teach me. And if you can possibly get one, will you send me over a root or two of the Madeira vine, to plant in my greenhouse? I bought one for ten cents at the Nursery garden on Locust Street.'

'My dear Sister,   *Cambridge, July 7th, 1883*

... Maud is a very nice girl, the more I see of her the better I like her. As always with people I like, the wish arises very strongly in me to help to make her happier. I see these young men will not do. In none of their minds has matrimony any place, and Maud is not a girl to surprise anyone into matrimony. I wonder why? In many things she is like her mother, who always had plenty of genuine lovers, and she is often very pretty.

'I am inclined to believe that a man like Mr. Cartmell, only he is so old, might make her happy. Inveterate match-maker that I am! They have only once met each other. I suppose I think of him because I know him well enough to get at his ideas, and to put ideas into his head. Handsome he is, and good and very accomplished, and ten years ago for about a month I had a great fancy for him myself. His being a clergyman put him out of the running for me, and I can't say that the fancy would have lasted in any case. . . . But he is just short of forty, I fear, come to think of it, too old.

'Gerald Balfour seems to have given up all idea of matrimony. The ones who admired Nellie would not naturally be struck in the same way by Maud, the two girls are so different. Nellie's sense of humour and ready drollery, when she speaks at all, give promise of something more interesting behind, and people who are taken by that sort of thing feel a charm in her want of self-consciousness. Gerald says Maud is nice, gentle and refined, but I can see he is not interested.'

Part of a letter of Maud's to her mother, June 3rd, said,

'I never saw Aunt Cara look better in my life. She really does not look over thirty. It is wonderful to see how people love to listen to her; the minute she comes in they all turn and gaze at her with delight and brighten imperceptibly when they hear her converse.'

And to Mary Spencer, her sister, two weeks later,

'Gerald Balfour said he would come down for Saturday until Monday. You know that G.B. at one time had a passing fancy for Eleanor Butcher, a fancy that lasted *two days*. . . . English girls are so awfully susceptible. If a man speaks to them, almost, they instantly imagine he is desperately in love with them. So it is with Eleanor and she has never gotten over her fancy for Gerald. She refused George Darwin and a Mr. Leaf telling them that she "loved another man". In consequence she takes every opportunity of meeting him and trying to make an impression. . . .

'After Aunt Cara tried once to make the match and found that G.B. did not respond she simply does not throw them together and will not make opportunities for them to meet. So when she expected Gerald she did not know exactly how to keep Eleanor away. She invited Harry Cust[1] and his sister and George Darwin's

[1] Henry John Cockayne Cust, 1861–1917. Editor of the *Pall Mall Gazette* and M.P. A great diner-out and man about town; belonged to the Souls, Margot Asquith's society of wits.

brother, Mr. and Mrs. Horace Darwin, to tennis and tea on Saturday. They are all great friends of Gerald's. Late on Friday Eleanor dropped in and among much chatter told us that Mr. Langley had invited them and a few others to take a long row the next afternoon. Aunt Cara, finding that she was so engaged that she could not come to see Gerald, thought the best plan would be to say outright that he was coming, and added that he wished to be quiet so she had only invited a very few intimate friends to meet him.

We both noticed a change come over Eleanor's face when she heard the news. I said to Aunt Cara afterwards that I would be willing to make a bet that Eleanor would appear the next afternoon. Aunt Cara replied, "Eleanor would not have the rudeness to come uninvited, or show so plainly that she was running after Gerald."

'The next afternoon I was playing with Harry Cust against Aunt Cara and Gerald, when, glancing up, I saw Fanny and Eleanor approaching. I was so amused, and Aunt Cara angry. Eleanor did not look pretty and did her best to win Gerald's attention, but he only chatted a minute and then turned aside to the others. Fanny made many apologies saying she saw we were playing tennis and so came in, but Aunt Cara, without being rude, was not very gracious. They had thrown up the boating party saying it was too cold to go!'

The next letter is from Cara.

Cambridge, Aug. 18th, 1883

'My dearest Nellie,

Who shall be the hero of my tale? Writing about people is always so much more interesting than about things. Mr. Goodhart[1] has come into our daily life lately. He would do if, alas, he had not most ungratefully taken flight to Scotland a week ago, to be seen no more until October. Maud always said he was not in the least serious in his attentions, but still his coming was an interest to both of us. And he liked her even if he did not mean anything. Dick did not believe he "would a-wooing go" to anyone, but

[1] Harry Goodhart, 1858–95, Fellow of Trinity. Tutor to the Duke of Clarence who was best man at his wedding to Rose Rendel, 1886. Professor of Latin at Edinburgh University until he died at thirty-seven.

thought he liked being tame about the house. It was the old question, was my conversation or the *beaux yeux* of Maud the attraction? That last week which I am convinced he stayed over for the sake of being with us, he was here every day and all day. . . .

'He is not handsome, he does not talk much, it is that he gives an idea of power and helpfulness and significance. The undergraduates of Trinity make a sort of hero of him, he does everything so well. One of the best football players in England, unmatched at lawn tennis, splendid in cricket, an unerring shot, and withal able and intellectual, he is just the stuff out of which to make a hero. It would have been a pretty tale; alas, I wish something had been in it.

'Maud seems to be enjoying her summer in a quiet way. Not that she throws the vitality into things that you and I do, which makes us always get a great deal of enjoyment out of life. She could not have had the same fun as you are having in Virginia. Your rides and adventures there remind me so much of my own in Florida long ago, when I took rides in lovely scenery by moonlight, and was for the time in heaven. I can bring up now a lovely road by the side of a beautiful lake, where I rode with people I liked, thought and quoted poetry, until my very soul felt satisfied. I had to come down to earth as one always does, in this case literally, for mooning along, my horse took fright at a shadow, shied aside, and off I went. You were luckier than I in escaping with so few mishaps. I have been thrown in every part of the world almost, six times I counted, and I don't know how many times after I stopped counting.

'Gerald is still here, leaves for good on Friday. I have very good talks with him occasionally. I asked if he saw you again and you were more interested in him now that you were older, did he think the old feeling would come back? Not likely, he thought, that was past history. I do not agree with him. I read him bits of your letters and he is always very much interested, and I notice that he likes to talk about you, and to have me talk. I continue to wonder that you failed to be impressed by him. To me he will always be the divine youth, the most attractive to imagination. Maud sees his eminence over others at once. He is not so handsome as he was, but his air of distinction will always draw all eyes to him in any group, and make other men look commonplace.

'George Darwin is here every day as usual. Gerald says he has the sweetest most unspoiled nature. I agree with him. Do you know, I almost believe Eleanor Butcher would give him a different answer if he proposed now? He is, come to think about it, not only the most significant but the most attractive man she has had in her offer. One is in the habit of considering her a great success, and yet she has never had a handsome man among her following, to mean anything.

'Mr. Leaf[1] is *very* plain, short and disproportioned. He is as good and able as gold, of which he has such plenty, but his exterior would please no girl's fancy. Mr. Nettleship, who has been staying at the Protheros' and is freshly in my view, is also short, not so good looking as George Darwin in face, with the great disadvantage of legs very much bowed. Once Maud called my attention to these I never see any other part of him!

'George has by nature the straightest of lines, a very well proportioned figure, and a really beautiful forehead. Nobody would ever call him, as they would the other two, ugly. These make up the list of Eleanor's admirers. But in mentioning her the other day to George he said he was very glad she had not accepted him for he felt the life here with him would never have satisfied her, and that married to a wife so devoted to excitement he should only have been miserable. She *is* selfish, there is no doubt; yet she is the cleverest girl I know in England. I wonder she has not had more success. G.D. says it is her self-consciousness that stands in the way, nothing repels so much. . . . '

Cambridge, Oct. 4th, 1883

'My dear Nellie,

Maud's affairs just now are so exciting, I can't give my mind to anything else. She only left at noon the day before yesterday for London, and already I have heard from her twice, and have written to her twice.

[1] Walter Leaf, 1852–1927. Banker. A man of extraordinary erudition. Translated the *Iliad* in co-operation with Andrew Lang. Married Charlotte Symonds, 1894.

'You will just remember H. M. Taylor,[1] the man who dined here the day of Edith's visit, and would not be measured. About ten days ago we both "guessed" that he really meant something. He called the day after our return from Scotland and then, though he talked exactly as usual, I saw he *wanted* us to see his meaning in coming. Unluckily for his peace of mind, Mr. Goodhart came at the same moment, and all the afternoon Maud devoted herself to him and would not look at H.M.T.

'Mr. Goodhart struck me as decidedly devoted. I am sure no Englishman would single a girl out in the way he does Maud unless his intentions were serious. And now I am beginning to be frightened! In Cambridge he plays tennis so well, is so much liked by the undergraduates and everybody that one is tempted to give him undue prominence. Away from Cambridge he is nobody in particular, and has, at the outside, only £500 a year from his fellowship and lectureship. Then, he just does not become the ordinary garb of men. He is handsome enough in his tennis shirt and loose trousers. *Why* is there something always queer about the legs of these attractive creatures, which straightway catches the eyes of the indifferent and makes them think *our* heroes common?

'Maud likes him now, and I believe would accept him, but I am not sure she could not in the end get to like H.M.T. who would be a far better match. He is very manly, a good shot, Alpine climber, tennis player, has an income of, I fancy, about £2,000 a year, and money enough besides to pay £3,500 down for Mr. Eaden's house next door to us. I fancy he could settle at least £10,000 on his wife to secure her future. I have not tried to influence Maud in the least, have only sympathized with her, and tried to make her see her own mind clearly.

'My great fear is that Mr. Goodhart may be her Mr. Cartmell. Even when I had a fancy for that being (and he *was* both handsome and attractive a dozen years ago, you incredulous young things!) I knew he would never do, and that I should become bored to death with him. And oh, how inferior he is now to Dick, who

[1] Henry Martyn Taylor, 1842–1927. Barrister, Fellow of Trinity and lecturer. Became blind, 1897. First University Mayor of Cambridge, 1900–1. Lived next door to Springfield on the Backs from 1883 till his death.

goes on becoming greater as well as more devoted to me every day. You hardly knew Dick, but Maud has grown not only very fond of him, but perfectly at her ease with him, being so much together. He likes her, too, extremely, and takes the keenest interest in all her affairs.

'But oh, dear, I wish I knew more about Mr. Goodhart's family. His father has some educational appointment in Brighton, his only sister is engaged to some not very rich individual, since they can't marry for a year, and his brother is a sailor. Now, though some gentlemen go into the Mercantile Navy, not many do; it is hardly a profession one expects people of much social consideration to choose.

'If only George Darwin were back, I could consult him. He has got to like Maud extremely, is on terms of almost brotherly intimacy with her. The day before she left they had a little confidential talk, when he told her not to think too much about Goodhart's coming to Rome. She said she had not lost her heart at all, and G.D. must not think she had. In telling me how nice he was about it, she told me she rather wondered at you for not liking him.

'I suppose Maud has told you of H.M.T.'s second letter? She sent it down to me this morning. He admires her frankness and candour. (I wrote the letter myself!) and he thinks her answer encouraging! May he come to see her in town? Will take the next train to suit any time she appoints. Heaven save the mark! Can't a man understood a "NO" unless it is shouted at him? The answer to this second letter can't be misunderstood. Still, I don't believe he will give it up, unless Maud becomes engaged to some one else. Englishmen are given to take these things more seriously than Americans, and now the ground is broken, he will pay attention more vigorously. "If only he were taller," Maud says. His *legs* are perfectly straight, which is so much to the good, and his head and shoulders are fine.

'Dick favours H.M.T. because of his position in the college, "a man of influence," but he agrees with me that nineteen years difference between them is too much, and that Maud must not marry any man unless she really loves him. . . . I have got very fond of her, especially in this last month or two. I miss her very much.'

Maud, about to spend the winter travelling on the continent with her American Aunt Emma, felt the same affection for her Aunt Cara. She wrote to her mother, October 7th,

'Aunt Cara came to London yesterday, and I was perfectly delighted to see her. She is a wonderful woman. . . . I do love her very much and I do not at all wonder why so many men did the same thing. . . .'

The first refusal Maud sent H.M.T. after his proposal, ghost-written by Cara, said,

'My dear Mr. Taylor,
    Your letter has deeply moved me. I am touched by its trust and manliness and I feel how great is the honor you do me. I should like to prove to you that the trust, if circumstances were different, would not have been a mistaken one. But I want to answer you as simply and frankly as you have written to me. I like you so much that I have been searching my own heart to see if in time I might not come to love you.
    'At first I thought I would ask you to let me know you better, and then see. But when I think of the dear family at home I know that the emotion must be strong, indeed almost irresistible, that would make me wish to live so far away from them. I am so sorry, dear Mr. Taylor, so very sorry that I cannot give you a different answer. "No" is so harsh a word. And there is so little time and I feel my letter so inadequate. I must write it now for it would be unfair to keep you in doubt a moment after my own mind is clear. Please believe how grateful I am for the belief you have shown in me. How glad I shall always be if you will accept my friendship and
        Believe me,
                Ever yours sincerely,
                        M. DuPuy'

The second was more to the point.

'Dear Mr. Taylor,
    I am sorry that my last letter was so vague and undecided as to give you a wrong impression. "No" seems to me the hardest word

197

a girl can ever have to say and yet the more I think about it, the more sure I feel that she must never say "Yes" unless she not only likes but loves the man she says it to. I was so afraid to appear hard and ungrateful in answering your letter, which was a great surprise to me, that I seem to have blundered inexcusably.

'For on questioning my own heart, I find that though I like you as I like many in Cambridge who were kind to me, I do not love you. Please believe that though I am very, very grateful to you for a preference which does me so much honor and though I express myself so stupidly, what I really mean is that feeling as I do, I cannot marry you. My answer must be "No". Under these circumstances would not a meeting between us be painful?

'Yours very sincerely,

MAUD DuPuy'

About this time George Darwin wrote a letter to Cara, a thought-provoking paragraph in which follows. It calls up a picture of ships stranded on sandbars all along the coast of India!

'Oh, dear, I've made a tiny little mistake in my great Tidal work and I find that the people in India have been acting on it and have printed a numerical table based on the false formula. Well, last night I couldn't sleep a wink and at 1:30 I got paper and pencil and began working the thing out and satisfied myself of what it ought to be. . . .'

Greenock, Dec. 22nd, 1883

'My dear Sister,

See what malign fate has done in making us stupid, that is. You should think by this time we knew the route to Ireland, and yet here we are stranded for exactly twenty-four hours. Dick meant to enquire what station in Glasgow was the right one to leave from, for the Belfast boat; he bought the tickets and engaged a stateroom for me, and quite forgot the important question. When we came on to Greenock, the boat had gone, so we came back to this hotel, and here we are. The rain is falling in torrents, the sea was calm last night and bids fair to be this, and there is nothing to do preferable to staying here.

'Dick has been realizing the advantages of science since break-

198

fast. He started out to send telegrams to Ireland, and then to proceed to Glasgow to get our tickets changed, and secure berths. He found the office had a *telephone* on the pier, and that he could relate his misfortunes quite comfortably from that spot. The first time he has ever used a telephone. He is absorbed in admiration and wonder still, and has talked of nothing else since he came in. . . .

'Last week I visited the Storys, and it seemed like spring at Roseneath. I happened to go because Mrs. Story had asked me to dine and sleep to meet Eustace and Lady Frances Balfour. I was very glad of the chance to meet Lady Frances,[1] and I suspect she was curious to see me. She is a simply delightful character, with a bright active imagination, full of go and eager interest in whatever she does, interested in politics, literature, poetry. I never met anyone I should like more to have for a friend. I can understand and sympathise in her way of viewing things and I feel sure she would understand me. It is with a pang I feel the hope is impossible as our lives are too far apart for us ever to be thrown much together.

'Eustace I don't care for.[2] He talks a great deal, and never suspects himself of being rather commonplace and shallow-brained. He has a sweet disposition and a perfectly imperturbable temper, which last is not always an indication of quick perception and lively understanding. I could see that his self-satisfied platitudes were a good deal of a trial to his cleverer wife. What a fate there is in marriage. She fell genuinely in love with Eustace, he being tall and dark, and she short and fair, when nineteen years old. They are the best of friends now, but if she had the choice over again, she would not marry him. She would be exactly the wife for her brother-in-law Gerald. He is able enough to make her look up to him, and her bright chattiness would always be a delight to him. Eustace irritates her, as he would me, and then she is sorry and tries to be kind to him to make up for the feeling, which he, bless

---

[1] Lady Frances Balfour, 1858–1951. Daughter of the eighth Duke of Argyll. Became a leader of the Suffrage Movement. She was also author of several biographies.

[2] Colonel Eustace Balfour, 1854–1911. Fellow of the Royal Institute of British Architects.

him, never even perceives. They have one little girl, a bright unaffected little thing, a great joy to them both. It will be a pity if there are no more children.'[1]

Glasgow, Jan. 8th, 1884

'My dear Nellie,

No letter has come from Maud since the first one from Rome. ... I don't mind telling you home people in confidence what I daresay you think yourselves, that after six months of married life, Maud would be devoted to any man like Mr. Taylor, and quite happy and settled in her life. Her interests lie in practical directions; with a good husband, a nice house to manage, all the better if the house is big and handsome, a settled position in society, she would feel herself very fortunate, and be a very busy active woman. He *is* too old for her, and with Mr. Goodhart she would have had the two or three years of romance, and just as good a husband as H.M.T. But he did not fall in love with her, and so that ends the matter.

'I have just had a note from him saying that he will be playing football in Edinburgh and will be happy to come to Glasgow to see us if we can take him next Sunday. I have said we would be delighted, and have pictured the only amusements in store for him on a Glasgow Sabbath! He can go to Church with me in the morning; he can take a walk in the afternoon if he looks like an attendant at afternoon service, and walks with the serious step of such. Nobody will he meet at dinner, for I doubt if even Prof. Veitch will be allowed by Mrs. V. to come on that evening, she is sure to have a Church or something. But he can have a game of chess with me quietly in the strict privacy of the drawing-room. These and these only are the delights in store for him.

'Chess has grown to be the permitted Sunday game in all country houses and that I know he does not object to, for he and Maud played last summer. I ought to add that first she searched the Bible from cover to cover, before she allowed herself to play. Not a line could she find against amusement after one had begun

[1] They had four more. The little girl was Blanche, later Mrs. Edgar Dugdale. She was Head of Intelligence Dept. of League of Nations Union. Wrote the *Life of Arthur James Balfour*, 1936.

the day by going to Church. Much was commanded against labour or causing others to labour, but not a syllable against play. I often wonder where the Puritans first got that idea of sinfulness. The sabbath was so plainly made for a day of rest and recreation after six days of labour, for a people whose taskmasters so evidently needed the strongest commandment to keep them from claiming work on the whole seven days. Lambs that play all the week play on Sunday, too. The word holy means simply something apart. . . .

'But this is an old argument, and he who hopes to change the opinion of another wastes his breath. Far be it for me to want to, except that the people who make long faces think themselves justified in judging everyone who acts not after their pattern. When Emma Jebb said she thought it was wrong for people to use their minds in religious matters, that faith was what was required and not reason, she did not guess she was using the great Roman Catholic dictum; and that if religious people had believed with her, Luther would have deserved only burning and that she herself had no right to be a Protestant. I never dreamt of contradicting her.

'Aunty Fan has told me all about her will, and how in the matter of inheritance we are to have the least of everything. Do well by yourself, and you will relieve your family of that responsibility, seems to be the ground for action among Dick's relations. Dick is to have the family miniatures, the portrait of Bishop Horsley, the small amount of plate left by the thieves, and a large dinner service with the Horsley crest, this last because his grandfather left it to him long ago in his will. All the money, only £6,000, is to be divided between Heneage and Bob. We are not to have the Jebb forks and spoons because they forsooth must go to them, with the money. I don't care a bit to inherit the money, but I should have liked Dick to get his share of the family silver. It is splendidly heavy and all marked with the Jebb crest. . . .'

Glasgow, Jan. 24th, 1884

'My dear Sister,

Some weeks ago Professor Crosswell wrote in the name of the Phi Betta Kappa Society of Harvard asking Dick to deliver the annual speech at the end of June. Dick turned the idea over and asked what I thought. I wasn't troubled of thinking anything, feeling sure he wouldn't go. He played with the notion, not really giving it serious consideration. Now, today, comes another letter from Professor White urging our coming with the urgency of eight pages, explaining the importance of the occasion, sending Charles Francis Adams'[1] speech of last year, saying how glad everybody will be to see us, and asking us to stay at his house.

'Dick seriously inclines to go, and I seriously incline to go with him. He dislikes the loss of time from his *Sophocles*,[2] I dread unspeakably the torments of the voyage, yet in spite of both serious drawbacks, I feel that the chances are very much in favour of our coming. Dick says, "I'm very much more in sympathy with the Americans than you think." "If you mean you don't like anyone to be above you, you are," say I, in tones of perfect conviction. But if he thinks his views in general are shared by that excellent people, he will have to change his mind. He likes seclusion, can't bear to dine at a table d'hôte, no power hitherto has ever got him into a tramcar, and as to his laundresses' bills, I dread to think what sums he will have to pay. He never puts on a shirt twice, and always changes that garment before dinner. Fancy a certainty of 14 shirts a week! Well, two months travelling even in America where cabs do not exist, can't ruin us. . . .

'George Darwin writes that he is going to stop for a few days or a week both at Rome and Florence. I told him to write directly to Maud from Tunis as she might have left Rome before his visit at Tunis was over, and as he will also be in Naples, he might come across her there. Maud was to be presented to the Pope almost directly.'

Cara had to go through several agonizing weeks of uncertainty before she knew how his visit to Italy turned out. In February, George stopped at a small town, Castellammare, where Maud was staying for several weeks with her Aunt Emma.

[1] Charles Francis Adams, 1807–86. American diplomat, son of President John Quincy Adams.

[2] The great work of his life, in seven volumes, 'the most completely satisfactory commentary on a classical author written in the English language' (D.N.B).

'Dearest Maud,

Some occult influence makes you and George Darwin always write by the same post. Letters from each of you were brought by that erratic conveyance last evening, though I had no hope of hearing before this morning. I have given up understanding the Italian post and cheerfully take my letters when I get them.

'Well, dear, you probably know by this time that it is all right. George writes that he thinks he will go to Florence on Wednesday, yesterday, and he would not dare to do that if he had not fallen in love with you and did not mean to ask you to be his wife.

'Until you *are* engaged, do not go out with him at all without a chaperone. You can sit and talk to him in the hotel drawing-room, at his motion, of course. I think I should show a tendency to withdraw from behaving to him as if he were a cousin, since he isn't. You know even in Philadelphia you would use judgment in giving a man your society, and you would take care not to be seen so much with him as to make people talk. In Florence you must be very particular. Besides, a man thinks none the worse of a girl for being a little particular. I have told George that your going with him so freely at Castellammare was exceptional, you had got to know him so well at Cambridge, that in his case you felt you might allow yourself to enjoy the benefit of his companionship without the fear that he would misunderstand you.

'Still, it is now high time to make a change, and besides, all is very well that ends well. In Florence you are in the world again, and will want to make a good impression. Nobody in the world has less inclination to be fast than you. Tell George that now you prefer not to become the subject of comment, that he knows what an English girl would do, and not to ask you to go anywhere or do anything he would not ask of an English girl.

'And don't forget that a man always expects a girl to have instincts quite independent of country or convention, where delicacy is concerned. You are so really delicate in mind that no one who knew you well could ever for a moment feel a doubt, and I am happy to say that George has never felt or hinted at one. Still, I am sure he will rather admire in you a determination not to become the subject of comment.

'Once you are engaged to him, do exactly as your own instincts dictate. I wonder if the telegram will come today. I wish he would let me choose the engagement ring, or you when you come to London. I fancy those things are frightfully dear in Florence. Still, of course, in things of this kind you must let him take the initiative.

'I feel so happy for you, dearest Maud. He is so sweet-tempered, so thoroughly sound at heart, and kind, besides being so very able, that in spite of his ill-health I feel you have drawn one of the big prizes in the lottery. You will grow very fond of him, and in things where you need improvement you will improve each other as two well-meaning people always do.

'Be sure in writing to him to see that the spelling is correct. I would, if I were you, make a list of every word about which a mistake is possible. To start with, you might begin with "stayed" which I notice you always spell as if it were the adjective "staid". And if I were you, I would not use the word "blue" unless I meant the colour, nor the "blues". It is so easy to say "out of spirits". Spelling and punctuation are more important than they seem, because they are often the only indication people get of the kind of education you have received. Language again shows the class of society in which you have been placed. Unless you are quite sure of a custom, it is better to use a word in its obvious meaning. If you want to say a man is unsophisticated or innocent, say so, don't call him "green". The more you read the less tendency you will feel to do this, and your language will not suffer in being less spirited.

'Will your engagement make any change in your plans? Command me in any way you like, you both know that. You can join me in London or Cambridge or wherever I happen to be after the middle of April. Mrs. Darwin will perhaps ask you to make her a visit in order that she may become acquainted with her son's wife. Oh, what a difference between his family and H.M.T.'s and how differently you will feel towards them. Oh, if you could only have had the house next door! No hope of that; H.M.T. will think a wife easier to find than another house so exactly to his mind. . . . Every time the bell rings I wonder if it is a telegram from you.

'Let me sum up all these hastily written counsels by one last word. You lose nothing, on the contrary gain a great deal, by an outward care for conventions. And in Florence a town full of English and Americans you can't be too careful. Castellammare did not matter, though even there I never dreamt George would stay so long or single you out so markedly. I meant you to get really to know each other, and to do what was best fitted to bring that about. He stayed longer than I meant him to, or thought he himself would think desirable. As he meant to propose, it explains itself, and is all right. He must call me Cara, not Aunt. I can't stand that from a man so near my own age.'

'My dear Sister,

After being sure you were to have an English son-in-law, I am thrown back by the progress of events into great uncertainty. Maud has left Castellammare, and as yet George has not, as far as I know to date, gone to Florence. That he liked her extremely I am sure, for he has so written to me. But nothing in his letters or in hers show me that either has got beyond liking. If he joins her in Florence it will mean that he at any rate has made up his mind he would like to go on with the affair to the happiest conclusion. Of course he must take his chance of what Maud will say. It is not my affair at all, and he can judge a great deal better than anybody not on the spot, from her manner towards him what her sentiments are.

'Well, anything may happen. If he were a younger man I should be sure he would want to go on, or if he were of a less doubting and anxious mind. He makes the greatest mistake of his life if he loses this chance. Maud would be a splendid wife for him, and once the thing was settled, would grow extremely fond of him. His talk would interest her, his ability and knowledge would impress her; and her quiet determination would make her influence over him very great. His strongest point in character is that he has a very warm heart, and next to this a very sweet unsensitive temper. Maud and he are very companionable, he talking and she listening, and I believe if they had stayed in the same place a week longer, the die would have been cast in a way to ensure them both a happy future.

'His first intention was to leave Rome on Thursday. A letter just come from him this morning makes me very doubtful whether he has not decided to stay there a few days longer. That nothing decisive has happened I know, because, whether accepted or refused, the first opportunity after he had proposed he would send me a telegram.

'But after feeling quite sure something would come of it all, a reaction has set in, and this morning the air is very full of the smoke it seems all to have ended in. I shall keep this letter open till the last moment before the post hour, in case a telegram should come.

'I have been so full of Maud's affairs lately my own have gone out of sight. It occurs to me, now that the first days of spring have come, that I have nothing to wear. Black is very tiresome and unbecoming, and when for a change I put on my grey cloth of last year, Dick could not express sufficient delight at the change. He does mourn his mother deeply, but that makes him see no reason why he shouldn't, for instance, go to balls.

'I entirely refused to accept an invitation to a fancy ball for this month. "How can we go to a ball in fancy dress," I asked him, "when we are using the deepest of black-edged paper and cards?" He doesn't mind black-edged paper at all, since it is neither unbecoming nor troublesome. I refused to accept the Bachelors' Ball for the 1st of April unless he bought narrower edges, convincing even him that to answer a ball invitation on that paper savoured of the ridiculous. He wanted very much to go to the ball, about which I don't care a farthing, so I gained my point as to the paper.

'We are deep in everybody's debt as usually happens in Glasgow where Dick is too busy to have any spare energy. I never knew anyone whose mental demon drives him to work so hard. Now in his walks his *amusement* is to translate the satires of Juvenal into English verse. It takes his mind off the other kind of work, he says. And the result will in the end be another book. Juvenal is so extremely difficult that thus far he has never been adequately translated, even in prose. He has just finished twenty pages on *Troja* which will come out in the April *Fortnightly*; and an article on Olympia for the new volume of the Encyclopaedia Britannica.

'All this writing involves an immense amount of reading in many languages, search and comparison of authorities, etc., and this in addition to his University work here, considered by most of the Professors hard enough by itself. I do well to call his peculiar genius a demon when it drives him to such incessant toil. . . . Coming to America will be a splendid rest for him.

'12 noon. No telegram yet. If none comes today I shall be nearly sure George has found his liking for Maud is of the nature of Will Spencer's, not the kind to marry on. Well, he is not exactly the man to fall desperately in love and I feel not the slightest anxiety that his decision will make Maud the least unhappy. The only consequence of any importance is that she asked me to write to H.M.T. to tell him *not* to come to Florence in April.

'4 p.m. No telegram.

'With dearest love to Ma and Polly and Charlie and all,
from your loving sister CAROLINE

'Later. Telegram this moment come. He has proposed and been accepted!'

Cara wrote to George, March 13th, 1884.

'How I should like to have a good talk with you both. Such a nice letter has come to me this moment from your mother. She says she only yet knows Maud's "sweet looks", and she shall so like to know her better. Dick says it is a charming letter. I think it especially pleased him because he was afraid your family might think this a match of my making. And it wasn't a bit, mind that! You were both a thousand miles away from any influence of mine and words can't say how thankful I am. If there is a suspicion of my being a matchmaker, I utterly and entirely repudiate it. . . .'

Glasgow, April 3rd, 1884

'My dear Nellie,
. . . I wish, by the way, you would all help George in his wish to have a quiet and early wedding. He ought to go on being with Maud more or less until they are married, as this is not as we all know exactly a case on either side of love at first sight. He gets fonder and fonder of her every day, but if there comes a long break of being together *at her desire*, it will take away a good deal of his happiness. I cannot see why your mother and father insist on their waiting a year and a half.

207

'What makes him love her, and be so happy with her, is his belief that she adores him. To a lonely man of 38 whom no woman has ever loved in that way before, it is infinitely sweet to have been capable of inspiring such a love. If Maud only has sense, such as her mother would have had, she can make him perfectly worship her. Already he yields to every whim of hers, to give her pleasure; buys her box after box of sugar plums which to his dyspeptic mind are rank poison, and even goes to church with her every Sunday, though sitting in church to a man of his restless temperament is a species of torture. "She shall be happy, and have what she wants," he writes constantly. . . .'

In preparing to visit America again, Cara received a charming letter from James Russell Lowell, the American poet, essayist and American Ambassador in London, to introduce 'Mr. and Mrs. Jebb' to Oliver Wendell Holmes.

10, Lowndes Square, S.W.
June 6th, 1884

'Dear Wendell,

Mrs. Jebb is an American and Mr. Jebb deserves to be and perhaps will be in that other world that redresses the balance of this. *Him* of course you will meet (for I hope you are still President of the Phi Beta Kappa,) but *her* I wish you also to meet for she is— but as this is an open letter she will be sure to read it (eh, Mrs. Jebb?) and so I will leave her to speak for herself. I will only say that I am doing both of you a great kindness in bringing you acquainted [*sic*].

'Did you know that you owe me a letter? I can't call it a little debt when I think what yours always are to me. I am a bad correspondent but I always answer *you*. I needn't tell you how pleased I was with what the *Saturday* said of you t'other day, only I should have pitched it higher. Whom have they to compare with you, marry come up?

'Charles Norton is just coming in and I must only say again that I am always,

'Affectionately yours,

J. R. LOWELL'

In June the Jebbs arrived in America for Dick's lecture at Harvard and Maud's wedding in August. Cara described the visit in a letter to the bridegroom's mother, Mrs. Charles Darwin.

'My dear Mrs. Darwin,

It was so nice to get your pleasant letter yesterday. If, in the midst of such talk and exchange of ideas as one always finds when large families come together after an absence, the art of letter writing had not entirely vanished from me, I should have written to you long ago. I never wrote so few letters in my life as since we landed, because I suppose all one's energies are used up in talking.

'We *have* been busy. At Cambridge, Massachusetts, we were in a whirl of engagements which took away my breath. Everything delights Mr. Jebb. He often has said to me he was a good deal more in sympathy with Americans than I thought. I think he must have made up his mind not to dislike one thing on this side of the water. He likes getting up early, he approves early dinners, "in this climate", thinks tea and ice water and no wine agree with him "here", makes friends wherever he goes, and is altogether a great success. You can imagine how this delights me.

'After Cambridge, we went to stay at Newport for a week, where still the same press of engagements continued. It was all very flattering and very enjoyable but no words can tell how glad I was when at last the time came I had fixed as the end of *my* visit to New England, when I could turn my steps straight towards the home people.

'Now for the wedding. Why the date was changed from the seventeenth to the twenty-second I don't yet know, and neither does George. We both got somewhat tired of the endless discussion of details (they do talk a great deal about things over here) and we made up our minds not to question or reason. Whether the ceremony should be in church or in the house was a moot point for a fortnight, and if in church, who should be allowed to come? Everybody had a reason for his opinion, and everyone, down to the children, had an opinion.

'This family, being strongly Episcopalian, suspected that the

Spencer family, being strong Presbyterians, did not want to give such a victory to the former sect. "They might even go so far as to ask the Presbyterian clergyman to visit at the house!" said my brother, whose church principles are "high". George preferred the house from strictly personal motives, fewer could be there, and Maud because, not having arranged for much show and circumstance, she feared her wedding would be condemned as plain. I did not take a side, but am now of the opinion that the house party was wise. There is no time to cry, and much less solemnity in a marriage in a drawing-room, and I don't see why people should not, as much as they can, escape being tearful and solemn.

'Maud looked really beautiful; her colour brilliant, her eyes shining, her figure shrouded in a veil, tall and graceful. She is much prettier this summer than you have ever seen her. It does not suit her to be fat, and the whole stone and more of weight she has lost, is a great improvement.

'Directly the ceremony was over, and oh, dear, it takes one's breath away to think how much destiny for two lives can be fixed in that short eight minutes, George went about talking to the people and in the interests of conversation, entirely forgot, I suspected, the interesting position he occupied. Never in my life saw I a bridegroom act with such an absence of self-consciousness. He whispered to me that being married made a man ravenously hungry, when did I think they would have supper? He watched the door with perfect singleness of mind, and picked up Maud and marched her in with an expression of interest quite independent of the occasion.

'They started for Buffalo at eight-thirty, the ceremony had been at six, while the rest of us stayed behind and played merry games with the children, sang songs, etc. "Not a tear was shed, not a funereal note." My sister would have liked to give the occasion its due, but the healthy matter-of-factness of her bevy of daughters was too much for her. The real parting will come when Maud sails in September, but everybody is too happy and content for even that to be very mournful.

'George is not as delighted with the habits and customs of the people and climate as I should like to see him. He doesn't like what they give him to eat, he thinks the sun is hot, the railway carriages different from the English, the arrangements in general much inferior to those of his dear native land. He will only be thoroughly and entirely happy when he can bring his bride back to you at Down.'

CHAPTER XIV

On board steamer to England
Sept. 14th, 1884

'Dear Polly,

Our voyage is nearly over, and so I suppose I may count on an end to my sickness. . . . It seems a dream to me that my longed-for visit to America is over. Dick cannot say enough of his delight with everything American. He never enjoyed a holiday so much, and he is depressed at returning from "that bright country" to this. He said he felt disgust at the sound of none but English voices when he first came on the steamer. (Some true American ones have refreshed his ear since. We have the Bishop of Fond du Lac on board who has all the proper intonations, strong.)

'It would not be at all difficult to get Dick to live in America altogether. He says the Professorship of Greek at Columbia College, New-York, is worth $7,500 a year, and that he could get this if he wanted it, when a vacancy occurs. Wouldn't it be strange if after all my wide wanderings, they took another turn and I came back to live and die in America? I should like New-York, with that assured social position, very much. But these are all dreams with which I like to comfort myself in the sadness of my recent parting from you all.

'I wouldn't have lost that week with Ellen for anything. Seeing her there in the midst of her family, I was struck afresh with her wonderful sweetness of temper, and the quiet ability with which she makes everyone comfortable around her. It was a very happy week with mother and her and you, taking me back to my old family feeling. Dick says I must not forget to give you all his love, evidently he suspects the necessity of emphasis.

'I don't say anything about our passengers for the reason that I have been too sick to bother about strangers. The Bishop is a lean and slippered pantaloon, at least in his old clerical garments which he thinks good enough for the sea. Clothes have much to do with an appearance of dignity. For the most part I gather we are commercial. Everybody I speak to seems to live at Nottingham or Sheffield, and I don't wonder *that* English accent is not sweet in Dick's ears. . . .'

Maud's American cousin, Ella DuPuy, decided to come over to Cambridge to enjoy its society, and to stay with the newly-married couple. George and Maud had decided to live in the Jebbs' house, Springfield, until their own house, Newnham Grange, close by, at the end of 'the Backs', was ready.

Glasgow, Dec., 1884

'My dear Sister,

Maud and Ella have had a happy month together. . . . Never was matchmaker more eager than Maud, and I don't wonder, with such a prize as Ella to secure for a neighbour. She would have liked Gerald, but saw that was no use. He never mentioned her name in his letter to me. Henry Butcher thinks he is seriously taken with Laura Tennant. He could talk of nothing but her the night he passed with them on his way through Edinburgh. And his letter to me a week later showed the impression still strong. . . . Maud has her eye on Mr. Dew Smith for Ella.

'On Monday morning the paper told of the death of a good friend of ours, whom we had met at dinner at the Butchers' house only the Saturday before: Sir Alexander Grant, Principal of Edinburgh University. He seemed apparently perfectly well, then, except that his face was very red, and his eyes not clear looking. Perhaps at fifty-eight one has no right to expect clear eyes! Last Saturday he dined out again, sat up reading for three hours on returning home, did not feel sleepy, so had recourse to a remedy he often found useful: at two a.m. he got into his cold bath! Did anyone ever hear of anything so wild, and on a cold December night! He was struck with paralysis stiff from the head down, could not move a muscle. They rolled him in a blanket and there he lay till assistance came. His mind seems to have lived longest; he did not become unconscious till noon the next day, when what they called a stroke of apoplexy struck him, from which he never recovered. . . .'

Paris, Jan. 5th, 1885

'Dear Polly,

. . . I came up to London last Monday, met George and Maud there and on the first of January crossed the channel and came on here. Crossing perfectly calm and uneventful, neither Maud nor I in the least ill. George is very much devoted, very anxious lest Maud should tire herself or take cold. That is going to be a very happy marriage, and each is going to improve the other. Maud would have been wretched if she had had to economize in life; she has no more idea of the value of money than have the lilies of the field. She likes the best things, and she likes to feel herself among bright clever people.

'Maud is not made of the sterner stuff for whom adversity is good. Prosperity develops the sweet grace of humility in her, makes her grateful to Providence, and anxious to give of her abundance to others. She is really kind and generous and as hospitable as her mother, with a delicate and lady-like mind. She is not in the least clever, but she has great good sense and tact.

'Ella says one of Maud's strongest points has been that she always reached up. Now she loves George with all her heart and is very proud of the place he takes in science. He shows to much more advantage in his customary surroundings than he did in America. He is more comfortable here; when he is uncomfortable he is at his worst. . . .'

Cambridge, June 4th, 1885

'Dear Polly,

Well, I had a very pleasant Saturday and Sunday at Oxford; Phillips Brooks talked a great deal, and was altogether nice and simple.[1] He has a great deal of frank humour; and oh, how he ought to bless his stars that *I* was there to be amused and interested, instead of being thrown entirely on the mercies of people who, if they ever are either one, have taken a vow not to show it. The

[1] Phillips Brooks, 1835–93. Eminent American clergyman.

214

other people staying there were respectable in their several callings, but certainly not brilliant.

'Sir Arthur Hobhouse, a London barrister, was good to look at, tall, thin, deaf as a post. He was particularly struck with the badness of Mr. Brooks' delivery, and as he said nothing of the sermon I don't believe he heard a single sentence. Lady Hobhouse is an aunt of Ida Darwin and a very nice woman when one has her alone. In general society she feels no call to do anything but listen. Then, we had Mr. and Mrs. Waterhouse, he a well-known architect and she a pretty old lady, but neither of them particularly interesting.

'Phillips Brooks reminds me very much of Charlie, and made me wonder if the latter would not have found the Church a congenial profession. The heads of both slope down in the same way at the back, their foreheads are somewhat alike, they have bright large eyes, which smile easily and always look open and frank, and they both require big hats. Mr. Brooks tried on three or four college caps, and ended by wearing his own tall one with the borrowed gown made necessary by convention.

'I asked the great man to stay with us, when he comes to preach his Cambridge sermon on the 13th. He was already engaged to the Vice Chancellor, but he wanted so much to go with us down to the boats, that I wrote to invite the whole Ferrers party, with the result that they decline, but give me him, for the boats and supper. On Monday he comes over to us to dine and sleep. Arnold Morley and Miss Morley are to be our visitors from Saturday till Monday, so that I shall be a good deal occupied.

'Maud, I think, will be ready to take Ella to sleep and be there altogether. Ella's visit has taught me that my day for having young ladies of the family with me is past. Naturally, young people prefer each other's company; but as hostess I don't so much enjoy a guest who is so little with me, and whose interest is not with me at all. Ella can't help feeling most at home with Maud, and it will be the same with Nellie and Carrie. . . .'

Cambridge, Aug. 8th, 1885

'My dear Sister,

The chief event of the last week is Mr. Potts' death on Tuesday. He had been ailing for the last two years, but always refused to give in, and really died of self-will in the end. A swelling came on his hip and the doctors said it ought to be opened; he would not consent, and died from weakness and blood poisoning. He might have died from weakness anyhow, as he was eighty-three years old.

'I have a very kindly feeling towards his memory, and confess to a good deal of shock at the state of mind in which I found Jeannette when I went to see her the morning after his death. She was so much excited that she could not conceal her feelings, and it was a very unlovely spectacle. He had done the best thing by dying, but had he arranged things satisfactorily about money? Her talk was of his tyranny and meanness, mingled with a history of efforts to get a satisfactory will signed. She should not have told anyone as it is not her business to manufacture witnesses against herself. In one breath she told me of Mr. Potts' ravings, and then asserted that he was perfectly sane when he signed the will.

'A week or two before he had signed a deed giving all his property to two trustees, to be held for the benefit of St. Paul's Hostel, subject to an annuity of £250 a year to Jeannette. She told him that, not being witnessed, the deed was illegal, whether the truth or not I can't say, and that if he meant her not to go to the Poor House, he must make a will. She says she distinctly made no promises, but heaven knows what the old man thought she said, for against the repeatedly expressed intention of his lifetime, he signed a will leaving everything he had to her.

'I think for safety she went too far. Whether he was coerced or whether he signed the will thinking in his feebleness that it was something else, (he could not read, it had to be read over to him) will probably not be known. Jeannette's only danger is from the heir-at-law, Neville Williams, Mr. Potts' nephew. The sister came to stay as soon as she heard of his danger, and, towards the end, she telegraphed for Neville. They may oppose the will, and if they do I think they can surely break it. . . .

'Jeannette thinks she will have about £600 a year when all is settled. With true Jeannettian touch, she went on to tell me the things she had ordered, not only crepe mourning now, but a black dinner dress trimmed with jet, and a sealskin coat! "But why so much at once?" said I; "you won't want the dinner dress for three or four months anyhow?" "Because the trustees are bound to pay for my mourning anyway, if the deed holds, and the will is void," she answered with a chuckle. "I always wanted a sealskin and now the poor little old dear *must* pay for it." Verily the children of light are wise in their generation. The idea would not have occurred to me. . . .

'When I went into Mr. Potts' house, swept and clean, I could not help the tears coming at the thought of the kindly little hospitable man whose heart was warm in spite of all his oddities. Jeannette was dry-eyed, and not even my tears made her for an instant soften. Superficial tears don't amount to much, but they would have shown more softness than not to be able even to shed one tear.

'Now I think of it, I have heard Jeannette complain often, but I never in my life saw her shed a tear, or even look tearful. She is always kind and hospitable in a general way, good to the poor, and genuinely religious, but she belongs to the class to whom self-preservation is so strong an instinct that it excludes the possibility of self-sacrifice. . . .

'And now, to please Polly's matchmaking soul, I think, I *think* Ella has an admirer. I took her to a little dinner at the E. C. Clark's on Monday, and there she met Professor Thomson.[1] He took her in to dinner, and afterwards walked straight to Ella and sat by her until we came away. She wore her white satin in which she looks lovely, and was that night in her best looks. One evening's attentions are not much, you will say. True, but everything must have a beginning and this is the first beginning even that any one has made. No one has singled her out for even ten minutes talk until now.

'Professor Thomson may also be supposed to be looking out for a wife. He is a friend and admirer of George's, and has had the great good luck to be elected Professor of something mathematical, at the age of twenty-five or six. In strictest confidence I told Mrs. Adams that I thought he admired Ella. She regretted to

[1] Later Sir J. J. Thomson, 1856–1940. Famous Cavendish Professor of Experimental Physics, 1884. Married a daughter of Dr. Paget, Cara's neighbour in St. Peter's Terrace. Master of Trinity, 1918.

say that he had a way of *singling out girls*. Well, we shall soon see. Maud has had him in her eye as an eligible, and before Ella met him last Monday, she had invited him for next Saturday to row them to the boats. It occurs to me that George said he was one of those incapables who couldn't row, but anyhow I think he is to come there to supper. . . .'

Cambridge, Sept. 12th, 1885

'Dear Polly,

The great news of the day is Dew Smith's attentions. Every day now since his return he has had some communication with Ella. Twice he has sent her a big basket of grapes and roses, he does things in a princely manner; and almost daily he has been to see her. Yesterday he did not come because George happened in at the shop[1] on purpose to tell him in a casual way that Ella was not very well and was keeping her room for the day. It is her principle not to see people she likes to please when she is not up to the mark. She says it does harm instead of good. The day before she was not feeling well, and was arranged on the sofa in the drawing-room with patterns of beautiful stuffs and Japanese embroideries around her, when Dew came in. She looked very picturesque, George said.

'Here lies her fault, or does to me who never went in for that sort of thing. The suspicion of an arranged effect irritates instead of pleases. One evening when George was away I ran across, to find Ella seated in a becoming light in a picturesque attitude with her guitar on her knee. It may have been entirely accidental, she may have been playing to Maud who was writing letters; but she looked exactly as if she were sitting for her photograph. No sound of music had caught my ear, while waiting for the door to open. Her attitude suggested to me a thought I should not otherwise have had: she thought my ring was that of Dew. But I am not an artist. Things that annoy me may please artistic people. Dew may feel

[1] 'The Shop' was the Cambridge Scientific Instrument Company, founded by Horace Darwin, George's brother. Albert George Dew Smith, 1848-1903, co-operated with Darwin in colour photography at the Shop; he was a noted amateur photographer. Though not a Fellow, he had rooms in Trinity until his marriage to Alice Lloyd. R. L. Stevenson knew him and depicted him as Attwater in *The Ebb-Tide*. Ella DuPuy never married.

gratitude at the compliment paid to his taste. He is not a simple nature himself, likes effects and grouping, may think arranged attitudes more pleasing than absence of thought about such things.

'George is very fond of his wife, keenly interested in the baby Gwen, and very proud of his house. He has a more than ordinary pleasure in possessions. The house takes the shape of property which can be seen as well as thought of. They were talking one day about the delight of ownership. George and Ella felt this keenly, while Maud said she didn't. George gave a sort of groan. What she lost! But I agree with Maud, I like security and independence, but I look at a thing for what it is, it gains no glory for being mine. Dick is the other way: whatever anybody else has, seems to him nicer than his own. Except where his warm heart is concerned. He thinks that although in general a most unlucky man, his one tremendous piece of luck was in meeting his wife.

'Jeannette came in yesterday morning; she certainly has the sweetest disposition. I never go there and never of late years ask her to dinner or anything (I couldn't make her mix with my set and had to give it up) and yet she comes to me with all her affairs, feeling sure of my interest. She shows insight, for I would really do anything I could to help her.

'She had to take an oath to administer Mr. Potts' affairs according to his wishes. She had never kissed the book in doing so before, and it gave her conscience a great shock. She could not rest until she had written, offering to put every penny of Mr. Potts' money into the hands of the trustees selected by him for his abortive Hostel, since it must fall for want of sufficient endowment. The Hostel was to have made a home for the children of Indian Officers, sent to England to be educated.

'Jeannette came home after taking the oath, went into Mr. Potts' study, sat down on her old seat, and the first thing her eye fell on was his Bible. She opened it, and at once her eye fell on a text, marked by him, which she never had noticed in her readings before, something to this effect: "Since thy purposes are mine, thine enemy shall not prevail." She took this as an omen that she was doing right. Certainly a good conscience agrees with her. She looked fresher and prettier than you can conceive, a different woman from what she was the morning I saw her after Mr. Potts' death. Then she was excited and full of all sorts of plans and imaginings, which made you think she might have done anything. Her lawyer is very much afraid of her in the witness box. "I *am* so muddleheaded," she says. But you can only get out of people what is in them, and her real goodness must show, side by side with her natural anxiety and her silliness. And I gather that the sister, who proposes to contest the will, is quite as inconsequent, and will betray the real thing against her side, that Mr. Potts never meant to leave her a penny.

'Either she or Jeannette would tear up a deed or a will, in the instinct of self-preservation (their strongest) without a moment's hesitation, but they would both feel afraid to tell a lie under oath. This is not inconsistent. They think if they said "so help me God" and then consciously denied the truth, He would *not* help them. But it shows a genuine faith, anyway.

'I am very sorry there is to be opposition to the probate of the will and hope the Judge may not think sufficient evidence exists to let the thing come to a trial. . . .'

Unfortunately none of Cara's later letters mention what the outcome was. But the files at Somerset House in London show that the will did stand and Jeannette got all his money, so triumphing over his sister!

Cara's next letter has no heading and was marked that the first part must be burned.

'Yes, I do see the *Century*, and do read the war articles with absorbing interest. Of course if I had a diary I could manage to make a decent article about Fort Pickens, and indeed a book about those early Army experiences. Not having a diary, I cannot remember dates or names or many of the facts which would be the bones so to speak of the animal.

'My personal reminiscences are to myself of thrilling interest, and with a good deal of fun and adventure about them; but then I don't particularly care to tell *them*. Though there never was any real harm in anything I did, there was a good deal of harum scarum and the utter recklessness and thoughtlessness that goes with plenty of courage in one's youth; that was, at any rate, a part

Nellie DuPuy in same gown as portrait,
Philadelphia, about 1883

Richard Claverhouse Jebb, August, 1882

Gerald Balfour

George Darwin

Maud DuPuy

Maud and George Darwin with Ella DuPuy holding her 'guitar', Newnham Grange. Photographed by Dew Smith

Portrait of Caroline Jebb by Sir William Blake Richmond, about 1888. Owned by the author

At the Cambridge May-week races, June, 1887? Nellie DuPuy, centre top, in leg-of-mutton sleeves. Carrie DuPuy is seated at her feet and to her right

Richard C. Jebb, M.P., 1895

of *me*. I smile now as I think of the way I used to manage to get amusement out of situations and adventures.

'I am like the man who repented of nothing on his deathbed, or rather, thoughtfully answered that he did not think he had anything to repent of; he had never lost a chance to *enjoy* himself in his life. Now, in my sober middle age, I rather like the thought of the gaiety of my morning of life. If our sins are the steps that lead us to heaven, our early experiences are perhaps what give us breadth and sympathy and growth of character. After all, to develop is perhaps the best way to become capable of being of use to others. If *I* don't write, (and I never had the least vanity in that direction, even if I had the capacity, of which I am not at all sure) I keep up Dick's spirits and enable him to write. And I get praise enough in my home to satisfy any woman. . . .'

London, April, 1886

'Dear Polly,

. . . Poor Lionel Tennyson is dead, a strong tall young man of thirty-two, who was born to live as long and be as vigorous as his father. He caught the jungle fever in India where he and Mrs. Lionel went to make a visit to Lord Dufferin, and died on the steamer at Aden. His mother will be broken-hearted.

'Another sad death is that of young Laura Tennant, Mrs. Alfred Lyttelton. Her baby was born on the 17th after three days of suffering. She had been expecting it for weeks and I fancy its delay in coming was what cost her her life. The child was unusually large and a boy which is supposed to make a confinement more difficult. After the birth the haemorrhage was bad, but they got that under control and on the following Wednesday she was supposed to be doing well. On Thursday she was permitted to see her mother and brother and was conscious and hopeful. Fever came, and after intense suffering, she died on Easter Eve.

'I feel very sorry for her. She had everything to make life happy, including a sunny temper and a brilliant mind, and *having sense*, she was improving in character with every hour. Old Mr. Veitch told Dick he never had known a sweeter or more generous character. She did not know what it was to think ill or evil of anyone. She was too adaptable in my opinion to have sincere convictions about anything. For the moment she thought in sympathy with her company whoever the company might be. Of course this made her, with her bright witty mind, a delightful friend. She would have grown in depth as she thought more, and had more experience; charity covers a multitude of sins, and she was genuinely charitable.

'I had a brief note from Gerald forwarded from Glasgow saying how sorry he felt for poor Alfred, who had been a proud and adoring and perfectly happy husband. These lines of Lowell's at the end of the "Bigelow Papers" where he writes about the young killed in battle, come back to me when I think of these two deaths. I haven't time to quote all of them. They are the finest Lowell ever wrote, I think, and the part begins, "Rat-tat-tattle through the streets. . . ." '

Still another American niece, Carrie DuPuy, came over to visit England, and sent home reports of the gaieties of May Week. She wrote,

Newnham Grange
Cambridge, June 13th, 1886

'. . . I go out with Aunt Cara a good deal, since Maud gets so easily tired, and Aunt Cara is not so easily fatigued. We went to the cricket match on Wednesday, and then I went with a party to the boat-races. They were most exciting and I will say for Nellie's benefit that Trinity Hall bumped Jesus, which has been at the head of the river for ten years. . . .

'Oliver Wendell Holmes is in Cambridge just now. George breakfasted in Hall with him this morning. He told some very good stories and was altogether a genial autocrat. He is to be given a degree on Thursday, and we shall probably go. The Trinity Ball is to be on Wednesday, I did not at first care to go, but Aunt C. and Maud have aroused my interest in it. Prof. Hughes and Mrs. Hughes have asked me to dine with them and then go to the Ball with some other young guests. He is one of the stewards of the Ball, so it is the nicest way to go. . . .

'Well, I went to the Ball and had as nice a time as it was possible for anyone to have. . . . We went home during the last dance at half-past four. The next day at twelve Oliver Wendell Holmes received his degree of LL.D. I think I would rather have missed the Ball than that. The undergraduates in the galleries cheered tremendously, and while he was receiving the degree, one of them called out "Holmes Sweet Holmes". There was a long Latin speech made to him and we could see his shoulders shaking with laughter. Imagine how *The Autocrat of the Breakfast Table* would sound when translated into Latin! . . .'

When the fall came, Carrie became a student at Newnham College. She was evidently rather lazy and not applying herself to her studies, for her Aunt Cara wrote,

Glasgow, Jan. 30th, 1887

'Dear Carrie,

Whose vocation is work, you say? Well, Milton's was, for one. He hoped "by *hard work*, which I take to be my portion in this life, to do something the world will not willingly let die". For another, George Eliot. Nothing struck me so much in reading that not altogether attractive *Life* by Mr. Cross, as her enormous mental industry. She felt every moment precious and *owed* to her own improvement. To read about her work took my breath away. She could not be at peace unless time was used to its utmost second. When she took exercise, the active brain was still at its own work. She and Lewes would talk Spanish or Italian, or whatever language she was at the moment called upon to use for her studies, *and* they would talk metaphysics or philosophy in that.

'I believe hard work is the vocation of everyone who makes the most of himself and makes a mark on his generation. It never was my vocation, mind you, so when I say it is not yours, I only mean that I don't yet see in you any signs of membership in the small army to which Dick belongs. He is sometimes idle, but he is always then restless and ill at ease, his conscience disturbed. He is only really content when he is working hard.

'And mind you, work and play are not the same. Work in which you can take no pleasure or interest is *slave* work, but I have yet to see the work in which, if I have to do it, I can take no interest

223

at all. The sense of accomplishing something is itself a pleasure, and then the feeling that you have overcome inertia and have grappled successfully with a task or a duty is sweeter than any you get in mere play. Play is good, too, indeed I should like to write an article on its uses, but I don't need to preach that side to either you or me.

'Oh, Mr. Cartmell is engaged to be married, I almost forgot to tell you. The lady is fair and tall, he thinks I must have noticed her and him talking to her at the Newnham party last October! I didn't, of course, having other interests besides noticing his doings. She is one of the most high-toned, noble-minded women he has ever met, is very well read, and knows French, German and Italian well. He is very happy and I am very glad his future looks so fair. All he wants is a sensible wife to make him as nice as he used to be. He was growing prosy through the want of a little affectionate criticism. . . .

'Why do you object to romance? It is a natural quality in the young, and the longer life lets it linger the luckier for its possessor. The boy or girl who thinks love of chief importance has the pull over young people with whom material things are the only essential. Have reason above all things, and the more you have of it the more you will value warmth of heart in those you have to do with.

'But I don't put feeling first on my list of human qualities. Reason and justice are the best for the race and for the individual, and truth. To see things exactly in their clear light without any bias from prejudice or self-interest is to have a delight in freedom hard to get from the passions, which are binding. All the same, it is splendid now and then to be carried off your feet by a great wave of noble passion, as when slavery was put down, for instance. . . . The moral of all this sententiousness is: Have as much sense as you can, and also as much feeling.'

Glasgow, March 24th, 1887

'Dear Maud,

Mrs. Butcher wrote me a letter to tell me of the breaking off of May Sellars' engagement. The man she was engaged to has behaved abominably. She and her mother were in London a month choosing her trousseau. They came back on the nineteenth, and the wedding was to be the fourteenth of April. Mr. Grey had even had the loan of a friend's house promised him for use after the marriage until they could furnish and settle in their own.

'Well, last Sunday morning she had her usual affectionate letter from him, and on the same afternoon, like a bolt out of the clear sky, came a telegram saying he was miserable; he would come to Edinburgh by the night train. He arrived on Monday in what seems to have been an abject state of misery and irresolution. He said he found that there was not enough sympathy between them and that he had come to the conclusion everything must be at an end. Just fancy how terrible this must have been to poor May, who, rather cold at first, had grown since their engagement to love him devotedly.

'Then, all the wedding presents were given, the trousseau ready, the invitations for the wedding out! No man's personal happiness is worth such a sacrifice of his duty to another, and his own honour. Besides, you never can be sure whether a particular course will make you happy or not, but you can be sure when you do right. . . .'

'Dear Polly, *Cambridge, Sept., 1887*

I am alone for a couple of days, and though I don't want my solitude to last long, you don't know how I enjoy it. If you do not bore yourself, solitude is a great treat. You feel that nobody is wanting your company, and you do just what you like. Dick has gone to Brighton till Monday, and I couldn't go too because I had to see the builder about fireplaces and mantelpieces for the new rooms.

'Mrs. Parkinson must have watched Dick drive away from her steadily occupied signal station on Thursday, for about an hour after he had gone came a note formally asking us both to dine on Friday, yesterday, to eat some venison.[1] If Mr. Jebb were away, would I come? I don't know why I am always thought fit and worthy to share these gastronomic treats. This is the second time I have been asked when the other guests were few and celebrated gourmands. The Porters and Parkinsons are known to make their

[1] Mrs. Parkinson, later Mrs. Cobb, lived at the Hermitage, almost opposite Springfield.

tables their highest interest. Well, I went and a splendid dinner for six we had.

'You should have seen the surprised and grieved way in which Dr. Porter[1] turned full round on his chair to look at me with his benignant spectacles when I declined venison. "Don't you *like* venison?" was all he said, very much as if I had declined a peerage. I must be a greater humbug than I think, for in spite of my sin towards the venison, the kind man asked me to dine at his Lodge tonight to meet exactly the same party. I have noticed that people who are fond of eating are generally kindly and happy. They can attain their aspirations, unlike the idealists, and are thus not disappointed beings.

'Dr. Porter had a slight grudge against J. W. Clark[2] because when he and Mrs. Porter were in Paris, J.W. told him of a place where he could get an excellent dinner for four francs. The price was all right, but the dinner was not excellent and the poor Master felt, as he said indeed, that he had lost a day. "When you go to Paris for only a few days the *price* of your dinner is not what you care about," he added regretfully. Nobody can help liking Dr. Porter and his wife, and I like dining there in spite of the strictly limited nature of the talk. . . .

'Gerald Balfour is much stronger, apparently having got strong as rapidly as he ran down, when once he gave up the bad air and late hours of the House. Mrs. Sidgwick says he is deeply happy, and as for Lady Betty,[3] he fell in love with her at once. Miss Lushington who knows her told me she was a very rare woman. "She is so gentle," she said, with a little burst of enthusiasm; "and I am sure she looks upon life as a sort of paradise."

'Gerald and she have not been parted a day since the engagement. Up till now he has stayed at Knebworth Park, Lord Lytton's place, and now they are both going to Whittinghame where Alice Balfour will be their hostess, and on for a visit to Inverary Castle. . . .

[1] Dr. James Porter, 1827–1900. Master of Peterhouse, 1876–1900.

[2] John Willis Clark, 1833–1910. Fellow of Trinity, Registrary of University, 1891–1910.

[3] Lady Betty Lytton, the eldest daughter of Lord Lytton, 'Owen Meredith', the poet and diplomatist; and grand-daughter of Bulwer-Lytton, the novelist.

'George came in while I was contemplating my carved oak mantelpiece. "Ah," said he, "you have chosen one like Maud's." (Only like in the fact that it is carved oak of which there are some hundred thousand in the United Kingdom!) "Did you go to Maud's place for it?" Considering that I took Maud and Ella to *my* place, as far as the best known warehouse in London can be called anybody's place, this was rather good. When I get rugs sewn together for my new stair carpet, George will certainly say, "Ah, you have adopted Maud's idea!" When it has been my own from the beginning, adopted from Mrs. Henry Butcher.

'George is as good as gold, but he manages to rub you the wrong way with almost every other sentence. Nellie feels it as much as I do, and we laughed together this afternoon over our individual experiences. He is sound in essentials but he has no more tact than an owl.'

'My dear Polly, *Glasgow, Nov., 1887*

The cablegram that came ought to be a relief; and I daresay as soon as I get a little used to the knowledge that I have no longer a mother in the world, I shall think only with thankfulness that her sufferings are ended. I have been very anxious for you, too, dear. You had taught her to look for such constant thoughtfulness and attention at your hands, that you almost went beyond the limits of human strength in your eagerness to give her ease. I shall be anxious till I hear that you are well in mind and body. Thank God, it is well with her. . . . I wrote a little note to John's wife just now, I tore up last night's, which I enclose. I meant to write to Ellen, too, but when I began to write to you I broke down so often that I find I have been four hours at this.'

'Dear Polly, *Glasgow, Dec. 16th, 1887*

It makes my heart ache in sympathy for you to read of your lonely evening when all was over, even the funeral, and you came back to the empty house. Dick says you must come and live with us, that I am to tell you so in a way to make you know he means it.

'My husband has grown with every year more and more precious to me, but he is necessarily a good deal occupied and I am often conscious of what a difference it would make if I had you to be with me. I hate to go out for a solitary walk, I always did; and that is just the thing Dick enjoys most. I cannot keep his pace, and if he is to get the good of exercise, so necessary for him, I must not hamper his walks by my lagging steps. If you were here it would be splendid, and I think we should both like to grow old together, as we were children together. . . .

'I think you will feel being alone more than almost anyone, for you have never been alone in your life. Mother was always there, as is not even a husband. I am afraid that after your busy life you will be a little dull over here, but you can have plenty of books to read, and there is a very good church with a good preacher nearby. I like the Presbyterians best for preaching myself.

'If I can find the notice of Gerald Balfour's wedding in the *Queen* I will enclose it. Lady Frances, whom I saw here the day before I went away, was just fresh from the wedding. Nobody but the immediate family and the Salisburys were present. Lady Betty looked her very best and was brilliantly happy. Lady Frances does not take a hopeful view of Gerald's health, is afraid that he is delicate and that a breakdown of the lungs will be the outcome. It will make a tremendous difference to her little boy if Gerald has children who live.[1]

'Lady Frances seemed to have enjoyed her visit to Cambridge. She thinks Gwen Darwin[2] a little American baby, not at all like an English child. Certainly she is not made after the same plan as little Blanche Balfour. Also, she considers Gwen the image of Maud, wherein I differ from her. I wish she were, she would then have a chance of being prettier than any of the Darwins ever were before.'

After much writing back and forth, Polly arrived for a long visit in Glasgow.

Glasgow, Jan., 1888

'My dear Sister,
Polly and I have had a grand day's shopping. How you would have enjoyed being with us. "Only you would never have got

[1] He and Lady Betty had five daughters and one son.
[2] Gwen Darwin, later Mrs. Jacques Raverat, 1885–1957. Wood-engraver and artist. Author of *Period Piece*.

Ellen away," said Polly, with decision. I had to keep an engagement at two o'clock and Polly reluctantly followed me, having still ribbed woolen stockings and combinations on her mind, and indeed on her tongue. Polly's most crying need was a bonnet, and fortunately her purse strings had not unloosed for a year to pay for any head covering, so that such a purchase struck her as most fit and proper. She was in great good luck. We found an extremely handsome French pattern bonnet, black straw with beads and bows, marked down to 16 shillings ($4.00). It suited Polly exactly, and there she was in five minutes set up for the winter. Her old black straw and that hideous square shawl she wore over it, may be locked away for the winter. "All the fashion at home, Caroline," she says, regretfully, "cost two dollars and a half; just new, too."

'Polly and I have glorious times together. She is greater fun than ever and the voyage and change have done her all the good in the world. The freedom to go where she chooses, to own her own time, cannot help but be enjoyable. For years she scarcely left Mother for an hour without fretting to get back, knowing Mother would be wearying for her. To have Mother back again strong and well, she would give up anything, but as that cannot be, she takes the good of the present hour. I am quite sure she has not been homesick a single hour since we have been together. She thinks this climate *far* pleasanter than Erie, not knowing how specially just now we are favoured with delightful weather.

'Twice yesterday she trotted off to Church without me; (I was not well enough yet to go out) and both services and sermons had her good word. Already we have hit on a way for her to do her hair which is very becoming. We discarded instantly the central turret she used to build, which was always wobbling and settling to one side. Now she wears no other hair than what grows on her head, turned up very high and made to look a mass of waves and ringlets. The shape of her head and the way her ears are set on the head look very well indeed, now. The turret was dear to her heart, but she was meek and now she feels rewarded. I don't believe she will ever keep house again. She really likes boarding, and if she does not take lodgings at Cambridge will probably gravitate back to West Philadelphia and board. She means to spend a year with me before she makes up her mind to do anything. . . .

'Lonely or unhappy she will never be, with her love of reading, her interest in things in general, and her great sense of humour. You see she makes few personal demands on life, and it is the unsatisfied personal claims about which people fret.'

Cambridge, June 16th, 1888

'My dear Nellie,

. . . Dick is wonderfully happy this spring in every direction, and I really think his attacks of depression are things of the past, having more to do with the liver than we guessed. At least with better health have come almost boyish light-heartedness and good spirits.

'He has won Polly's affections forever by always being so nice to her. It amuses me to see how eagerly she reads any bits about the Bologna functions in the papers in the hope that his name may be mentioned, sometimes when I myself have forgotten. I am happy to say he is one of the five English and Americans who were honoured with the Arts Degree in Bologna: James Russell Lowell, Max Müller,[1] etc., being the others. . . .

'Miss Duckworth,[2] Maud's young guest at present, is quiet, but I find her extremely good company. She is full of quiet intelligence and quick to appreciate the least touch of drollery or humour in talk. And oh, she is such a beautiful creature. Mr. Colvin says her family have always been rarely beautiful. The grandmother still is a delight to look at, and her mother, now Mrs. Leslie Stephen, was a famous beauty. At first view she looked old and as if she *had* been a beauty. I have only seen her once, but I daresay I should see her beauty now once the impression of age was got over. With intimate association beauty always comes out, if it is there.

'I am going to stay with the Leslie Stephens from Tuesday till Thursday next week, when I daresay I shall come to agree with

[1] Friedrich Max Müller, 1823–1900. Eminent German philologist and Orientalist. Professor of Modern Languages at Oxford.

[2] Stella Duckworth, Virginia (Stephen) Woolf's half-sister.

Jim Stephen who says, "My aunt *is* beautiful, not was!" Burne-Jones is to be at dinner then. . . .'

Cambridge, Autumn, 1888

'My dear Sister,

Richmond[1] is coming to paint my portrait on the twenty-fifth. May it be a success. I have put on a lovely blue plush tea-gown faced with pink, just for Dick to see how I look in colours. I have had black so long, he wanted to see if colour made a difference. And oh, how it does! He says I have not looked so well for a year. Richmond must see what he thinks of this gorgeous robe. Unluckily all my other coloured dresses are left in Scotland. I knew I should wear mourning till January, and not need them, and I never thought of the portrait. I think I shall probably be painted in black velvet. The dress is pretty low in the neck, and the white lace frill keeps the black away from my face. The Princesse shape looks more like the fashion of all time than most dresses, and I look thinner in this than in anything.

'Maggie and Jane stay on steadily, but just now there is a good deal of excitement in the air. They have made the acquaintance of the head gardener in the Botanic Gardens, a great catch in their rank of life. Jane asked to go out on Thursday, and it turned out that she and Maggie in their very best bonnets had gone to inspect the Botanic Gardens. Which is ahead I don't know, and if Maggie thinks the match good enough for herself, I wouldn't give much for Jane's chances, nor for the peace of the household, if Jane should happen to pull ahead. Maud's servants are on the qui vive with the same interest. They gave an evening, out of their board wages, some time ago, when the head-gardener was the chief attraction. . . .

'Incidently, Margot Tennant[2] is moving heaven and earth to catch Arthur Balfour, rumour says with some hope of success. He was staying at their place, and she was at Whittinghame in the

---

[1] (Sir) William Blake Richmond, R.A., 1842–1921. Son of George Richmond, R.A.

[2] Margot Tennant (Lady Oxford), married, 1894, H. H. Asquith, later Prime Minister. She was a younger sister of Laura, Mrs. Alfred Lyttelton, whose death Cara described.

autumn. Eleanor Butcher now means to marry as she thinks she is getting to a suitable time of life, twenty-eight. She said she could not make up her mind, though, the rich men she knew she *could* not live with, and the nice boys, though attractive, she would tire of in a month. She almost gave me to understand that she would take Mr. Leaf in time, because she liked him from long acquaintance. She is handsomer than ever, and if you see a new picture of Dante and Beatrice, by Hedley, the Beatrice is Eleanor. She was the artist's model.

'Dick was yesterday elected an Honorary Fellow of Trinity College for distinction and world-wide reputation, the Master writes. . . .

'No news from Polly for a week. She is on her way back now from Paris and Italy and will forget that a postcard would travel faster than herself. She has seen a great deal for a marvellously small cost in money. Americans beat the world in economizing when they try. Her party have addresses all over Europe of cheap and nice pensions, they carry their change of linen in a shawl strap, they *walk* to all the points of interest unless the distance is so great as to make them treat themselves to an omnibus, and I really think they enjoy the fun of travelling more because of their makeshifts.

'Polly washes her own handkerchiefs and flannels in a wash basin, and lets the air dry them for her while she sleeps. There is a natural pleasure in fitting things in that extravagant people miss. I look for her arrival daily now, and, dear old Polly, how glad I shall be to see her again.'

CHAPTER XV

In April, 1889, Dr. Kennedy, Regius Professor of Greek at Cambridge, died at last, and to quote from Cara's *Life of R.C.J.*, 'This time there was no doubt in Jebb's mind as to the course he should take; none the less the wrench would be great in leaving Glasgow. We had lived there fourteen winters, had been warmly welcomed by its people, had shared its interests and been given a part in its duties. The position at Cambridge was far more favourable to literary work, but he was doing good service in Glasgow which it was hard to abandon. The pecuniary sacrifice would be great; but money never entered into his considerations. Indeed to take care of it was one of his difficulties all through life. . . .'[1]

On the 27th of May Dick was elected to the Greek chair at Cambridge and shortly afterwards to a Professorial Fellowship at Trinity College. In May he also became President of the Hellenic Society in succession to the Bishop of Durham.

In October, Dick wrote an interesting letter to his brother, Heneage, from Brighton.

'We came on here after a very pleasant visit to the Tennysons. The poet, who was eighty in August, is wonderfully well; I had two walks with him, and he seems to be as regular as ever in taking exercise. He recollects the elder Hallam[2] as having a broad brow and large luminous eyes, a contentious man. Sydney Smith said of him, "There is Hallam, with his mouth full of

---

[1] C. Jebb, op. cit., p. 266.

[2] Henry Hallam, 1777–1859, historian, and father of Tennyson's close friend, Arthur Henry Hallam, whose death at twenty-two inspired Tennyson's *In Memoriam*.

cabbage and contradiction." Tennyson is going to bring out a volume of poems next year. It will interest you to know that one of them, *Demeter*, is dedicated to me in three stanzas alluding to my Pindaric Ode written for Bologna last year.'[1]

'TO PROFESSOR JEBB

(Addressed to Richard Claverhouse Jebb, Professor of Greek at St. Andrews, [*sic*] Scotland and afterwards at Cambridge, England, one of the most eminent Hellenists of our day.)

> *Fair things are slow to fade away,*
> *Bear witness you, that yesterday*
>   *From out the Ghost of Pindar in you*
> *Roll'd an Olympian; and they say*
>
> *That here the torpid mummy wheat*
> *Of Egypt bore a grain as sweet*
>   *As that which gilds the glebe of England,*
> *Sunn'd with a summer of milder heat.*
>
> *So may this legend for awhile*
> *If greeted by your classic smile,*
>   *Tho' dead in its Trinacrian Enna*
> *Blossom again on a colder isle.'*[2]

Tennyson's son Hallam edited the works of his father, and added this note to the poem, 'First published in 1889. My father met Jebb at Cambridge for the first time in 1872. He gave him the following Sapphic in English with the Greek cadence, because Jebb admired it:

> *"Faded ev'ry violet, all the roses;*
> *Gone the glorious promise; and the victim,*
> *Broken in this anger of Aphrodite,*
>   *Yields to the victor."* '[3]

[1] C. Jebb, op. cit., p. 274.

[2] *The Poetic and Dramatic Works of Alfred, Lord Tennyson*, Houghton, Mifflin, c. 1898, p. 598.

[3] Hallam, Lord Tennyson, *The Works of Tennyson*, N.Y., Macmillan, 1932, p. 783.

Cara continued, 'When October came, we both confessed it a great relief not to have to make the usual move to Scotland. Jebb quickly fell into the old ways of work at Cambridge, the morning lectures, the habit of Syndicate meetings, of scholarship examinations. . . . Then at the Christmas vacation, six weeks instead of two, what a delightful change to be able to go to Rome and Naples, to cheat the English winter of its darkest month!

'In April, 1891, he received an Honorary degree from Glasgow University, and in June, Oxford conferred upon him her Honorary D.C.L. in company with a group of very distinguished men, an honour highly valued. It seemed now as if no new distinction remained for him; that he might for the rest of his life devote himself to work; write books; give addresses on education and scholastic projects; take his share in University business and peacefully grow old. But fortune had still other offerings in store.

'We were sitting quietly at breakfast one morning at the Lyth when the post brought him in a letter. . . . He looked thoughtful but said nothing till breakfast was over, when he asked his wife to come out on the terrace. It was one of the many little rules he made for himself that she must always be told first anything that concerned him. It was now a question of a new departure which would greatly interfere with literary work. . . .' He had been asked if he would be a candidate to fill the vacancy of the representative to Parliament from Cambridge University. 'After a few minutes deliberation, he exclaimed, "Upon my word, Cara, I think I'll accept it. After all, it's not a life sentence. I can come out when I like."

'The nomination was made on the 6th of October, and on the 10th Jebb was returned unopposed. . . . Small time was there now for his own literary work. It was only by the most strenuous effort that another volume of his edition of Sophocles was finished. Claims of every kind were made upon him, and he always gave his best, if possible, which meant some thought, some time devoted to each occasion.

'It was our habit to take a house in London for three months after Easter, and then for him to pair when possible during the remainder of the session, keeping himself free to vote on any important measure. He could also, by arrangement with the

Whips, stay down unpaired. Cambridge is so near London that it was easy for him, when summoned by telegraph, to be at the House in time to vote the same evening.'[1]

London, Feb. 3rd, 1893

'My dear Polly,

It always amuses me to be here with Dick, and receive every night his account of the day's proceedings in the House. Tonight will be especially interesting. He hopes to have a chance to speak on the Uganda business, and I am keeping awake till he comes home to hear how he sped. He gave a very good speech on the subject by request at a "Uganda" meeting in Cambridge in November. He scarcely knew the place existed when he was asked to speak at the meeting, but one of his talents is his ability to learn anything very quickly. If the chance does come tonight it will be great luck and no trouble therefore.

'Everybody wants to speak so much that an ordinary member has difficulty in seizing an opportunity. Poor Sir George Stokes went to the House three times with "a nice" little speech in his pocket, but somehow could never manage to catch the Speaker's eye. He is a modest *little* man, and in that crowd inches tell. You know two or three men stand up at once and the speaker names the one he sees, who then has the floor.

'Dick is a little man, too, as well as a modest one, but he lets two or three people know he means to speak on a subject before-hand, and I fancy the Speaker has a hint. All the *big* speeches, like Chamberlain's[2] and Morley's[3] of today are even mentioned in the papers as coming. These men take up most of the time and it is very hard for new members.

'One letter came tonight for Dick that pleases me. Edmund Gosse[4] writes to suggest that Dick shall bring in a motion that some public honour shall be done by the Nation to Tennyson's memory. Dick has not seen the letter yet, and he may think it

[1] C. Jebb, op. cit., pp. 278, 284.

[2] Joseph Chamberlain, 1836–1914. Famous politician, Colonial Secretary, 1895.

[3] John Morley, 1838–1923. Statesman, radical thinker and man of letters.

[4] Edmund Gosse, 1849–1928. Distinguished man of letters, Librarian to the House of Lords.

impossible in such a busy and exciting session to arrange to do this.

'One thing I see is settled: there is to be no Poet Laureate. Gladstone said today no appointment was in contemplation. Swinburne is the only poet of great genius, and he won't do. His appointment would offend too many, not to say that the Queen would scarcely have a Laureate who had praised the murder of the Russian Emperor. (Something of that kind is the subject of one of his poems, I forget exactly what.) William Morris, the next best name, is a pronounced socialist; so for the present her Majesty must go without a Court Bard. . . .'

Cambridge, Nov., 1894

'My dear Polly,

This has been the busiest term; we have already given seven dinner parties, and on Monday I must send out invitations for a final one. We had Mr.[1] and Mrs. Birrell, he M.P., she the former Mrs. Lionel Tennyson, to stay from Saturday till Monday. They are an absolutely delightful couple. His talk is always strong and sensible and above all humourous. You read his *Obiter Dicta* if you want to see what I mean. Humour dominates him almost too much.

'Mrs. Lionel is a changed being. She used to flirt tremendously during Lionel's life and after it, but now she is absorbed, and is absolutely devoted to her rather plain brusque husband. She told me that after five years of marriage, she felt a sort of excitement still at having his society for a whole afternoon to herself. It was striking to see how different she is. When she and Lionel stayed with us, she did exactly what she pleased, and he went his own way. Now, Mr. Birrell has but to say a thing for her to want to do it. She says he is such a perfect stepfather to her three Tennyson children who all worship him. I don't wonder. Nobody could help but feel here is a strong good man in whom reliance can be placed.

'She told me her first marriage was unhappy, because she never could understand Lionel. She could not feel that he cared for her or the children, and sympathy and affection are the food she lives

[1] Augustine Birrell, 1850–1933. Essayist and later a Cabinet Minister.

237

on. She is a high-bred, delightful creature, polite to the heart, frank and forthcoming, generous, for in both marriages the settled money was all hers. I asked Mr. Haldane if Mr. Birrell was as much in love with her as she was with him. "He has a good steady affection for her," he said, "but too much humour to be desperate about anything. Of course he is a bigger creature than she is."

'On the 11th came another party from London, Mr. and Mrs. Paul, she was Miss Ritchie, Miss Thackeray's cousin and also sister-in-law, and Mr. Haldane. The Pauls are nice enough, but Mr. Haldane was a joy. Oh, how delightfully that man talked, and how able and interesting he is. When only five years at the bar, he became Queen's Counsel. No one ever got on faster, and no wonder, for he is able beyond most. He is M.P. for somewhere and the rising politician on his side. And lately he has become the favorite of a clever ladies' circle in town. Mrs. Harry White[1] is a great friend of his.

'I never knew a man such good company in a tête-à-tête. He took to me, too, and when I said I hoped he would come again he said he would come whenever I asked him. You know when the company suits me, I can generally be good company too. That man will be Lord Chancellor to a certainty some day. He is all round the ablest man I have yet met on this side. Dick liked him, too.'[2]

'My dear Polly,   *Cambridge, Jan. 15th, 1895*

Sir John Seeley died on Sunday night of cancer of the throat, and other ailments.[3] The throat has been operated on repeatedly, each time the knife going deeper. Six months ago the last operation took place. The doctors told him another would be impossible, but he seemed so well when I saw him a fortnight ago, and so very sweet, that his death comes as a shock. All worldliness and ambition had quite faded out of what was always a fine character, and latterly he was most lovable.

'If you get a chance to read the *Times* of today, read the long

[1] Wife of the American Ambassador.

[2] Cara prophesied correctly about Richard Burdon Haldane, first Viscount. He became Lord Chancellor in 1912.

[3] Sir John Seeley, 1834–95. Professor of History at Cambridge University.

notice of him. He long ago expressly declared himself to be a Christian in the Biblical sense of the word; and clergymen have come to consider his *Ecce Homo* a remarkably moral book. I don't like Lady Seeley, who I fear was, in the patience she demanded, one of his stepping stones to heaven; but his daughter was a great comfort to him so that in her he had some domestic happiness. . . .'

London, March 30th, 1895

'My dear Polly,

. . . Tonight we dine with the Leckeys, they always have nice dinners and I am looking forward to a pleasant evening. On Monday I go back to my chickens and Daisy and Zoë (Melbourne is my most interesting Cambridge correspondent) after exactly four weeks in town.[1]

'On Thursday I come up again to go to a dinner at Mrs. Tennant's when I am to meet Mark Twain. Nothing less attractive would have brought me up so soon. Dick has to stay in town till Friday, and looking after his packing (he packs and I see what he forgets when he thinks he has finished) is another inducement to me to come up for the night before.

'Did I tell you that Augusta Butcher is to be married at Easter? She has accepted a Mr. Crawley, a great friend of Frank Darwin's, a barrister, and apparently a very nice man. All her friends are delighted, for her life was very lonely after Eleanor's death.[2] I fancy Mr. Crawley has been her suitor for some time. He is about forty-four years old, so she, although thirty-eight, is considerably his junior. People marry so much later than they used. The marriage is to be at Henry Butcher's in Edinburgh. I am to see her here this afternoon and hear all about it.[3]

'I must go now to a private view of Sir John Tenniel's drawings, and must then drive about and leave cards, so goodbye and much love. . . .'

[1] Cara loved animals, especially Daisy, her cat, and Zoë, the chestnut mare. Melbourne was her gardener-coachman.

[2] Soon after her engagement to the painter, Charles Furse, Eleanor Butcher had died suddenly.

[3] Tragedy seemed to follow the Butcher family. Augusta and Charles Crawley were both drowned in a boating accident on the Wye in 1899, leaving two small children.

London, May, 1895

'No, Miss Polly,

There must be no making copy out of my letters, or the character of those letters will change completely. They will become bare and infrequent records of my health and the state of the temperature. People whose business it is to write give the world quite sufficient details of a personal character about those in whom it takes an interest. What I write to you is the tale of my own doings simply, and if occasionally these are connected with great people, the point of view remains the same. So, no extracts, please, for any purpose. . . .[1]

'Dick and I both enjoy London now that we know so many people. The crushes are very amusing. You only stay an hour or two and you have nice little talks with lots of people. Sir John Lubbock[2] asked to be introduced to me at the Leonard Courtneys' on Friday night, and I had a delightful talk with him. Mr. Courtney[3] himself is very able and not without wit, and he and I always get on. But if it isn't one, it is another, and I always enjoy this touch with a bigger world. Cambridge is a little heavy and learned, and these nimble London wits and tongues stir up one's own. . . .

'Did I ever tell you of Mr. Goodhart's death? Very sad it was, just when he was doing such good work, and he always seemed such a strong man.

'And now another shock has come in the sudden death of Mrs. Leslie Stephen. I will cut out the notice of her death from this morning's *Times*. I nearly called there the very day she died, should have done so if I had not been out so long as to want to get home again. What the family will do now she has gone one can't tell. She the very heart and centre of them all! I never felt quite sure of the attitude of the Duckworth children towards the little ones, and their own step-father. I should not be surprised if they were to part company and make two households.

[1] It is sad to realize that Polly destroyed almost all Cara's letters to her.

[2] Sir John Lubbock, 1834–1913. Later Lord Avebury. Scientist, author and M.P. He was responsible for the institution of Bank Holidays.

[3] Leonard Courtney, first Baron, 1832–1918. Secretary of State, and a Privy Councillor.

'Tuesday. Have just come back with my Republicanism strengthened, not that it needed strengthening, by a sight of the little Queen of Holland.[1] She, with her mother the Queen Regent and small suite are staying at Brown's Hotel just opposite our Club windows. Her footman is splendid. Such calves and knee breeches, such an imposing figure and bearing, fit to get him a footman's place on any spot on this globe, such a fine manner! He is perfect because *he* has been selected for his duties.

'But the poor young Queen of fifteen is simply a plain badly dressed little girl. She had on a grey shapeless dress, fair hair hanging straight down her back, a plain little hat. Why should that human being be put over all the other human beings in her kingdom? So that nothing short of a revolution can put her in a position to find her natural lead. . . .

'I thought I told you about Mark Twain. He is a gentle unpolished creature with thick gray hair standing out about four inches all over his head. He talks steadily, and he likes very well to stand up and tell rather prolix stories to the whole assemblage. I found the party at which he was very pleasant. . . .'

Several authors have given descriptions of Cara and Dick at about this time. Gwen Raverat, Maud's daughter, wrote in *Period Piece*, 'If *we* had no carriage, my great-aunt Mrs. Jebb had one, and my mother drove out with her nearly every day. Springfield, where the Jebbs lived, stood across the road, behind the crossing-sweeper's corner; it was a dull, plate-glass-windowed, white-brick-and-slate Victorian house. But though it was even uglier than the Hermitage, it was a very different affair; quite as comfortable and much more amusing and less formal.

'Aunt Cara was an exceedingly beautiful woman. Rembrandt's painting of "Bathsheba" at the Louvre is a pretty good portrait of her. I once saw her in much the same costume, and she looked quite lovely. She had auburn hair—real auburn, not red—a charming Rubenesque complexion, and a deep rich voice, like red velvet. She was quite unselfconscious about her appearance, as you can afford to be if you are beautiful enough. I have seen her playing tennis in a ridiculous little black nose-bag, tied on with

---

[1] Wilhelmina I.

elastic, to keep the sunburn from her nose. Her amusing American turn of conversation, complete lack of inhibitions, and great personality, gave her a unique position in Cambridge society. . . .

'It was no wonder people liked talking to her; her conversation was amusing, even witty; and she was well-read. There is a pleasant story of how she once set a Jebb niece to read *Paradise Lost* aloud to herself and her sister Aunt Polly, in order to improve Aunt Polly's mind. The poor old lady was terribly bored and was nearly asleep, when Aunt Cara woke her up, by saying sternly: "Listen, now, Polly; it's Satan speaking."

'The Springfield household consisted of: first Aunt Cara's Prime Minister and confidant, Melbourne, the groom-gardener; a perfectly round little man, a "reg'lar Norfolk dumpling" as he justly called himself. Next in the hierarchy came Zoë, the pretty yellow mare; then Glen, the collie dog, given her by Andrew Carnegie; then Darius, the cat; then the three maids, who stayed for ever; and last of all, or so we thought, poor Uncle Dick. . . .

'After lunch, Melbourne would go out to Queen's Green, and catch Zoë and harness her to a kind of low, rather shabby but elegantly built Victoria, squeeze himself into his navy-blue coat, put on his top-hat, take up Aunt Cara and my mother, and drive them off to the delightful duty of paying calls. As they bowled gaily along, Melbourne drove with his head turned over his shoulder, for he took a principal part in the conversation. He knew all there was to know about the current events of the Cambridge world, and gave Aunt Cara much valuable information.'[1]

Mrs. Keynes remembered this same scene and wrote about it in her book, *Gathering Up the Threads*. 'It was a joy to see Lady Jebb, "Aunt Cara" to the Darwin children, in her elegant lightly-built victoria, a beautiful Victorian lady with long ostrich feathers swirling round her hat. The driver of the horse sat on a small dickey in front and received a poke from his mistress' parasol when she wished to give him any directions. This usually resulted in an argument in which the coachman not infrequently had the last word.'[2]

[1] Gwen Raverat, op. cit., pp. 86–93.
[2] Florence Ada Keynes, *Gathering up the Threads*, Cambridge, W. Heffer, 1950, p. 51.

And about Dick, his friend Oscar Browning said, 'At Cambridge I was certain to find him in the afternoon in his spacious library, writing his edition of Sophocles, always with a pencil, the portrait of his beautiful wife looking down upon him with encouragement. He took great pains with his lectures. When I knew him, they were prepared so that they might be published, with a complete translation, critical, exegetical and illustrative notes all arranged in separate columns. . . .'[1]

Cara unintentionally gave an amusing picture of themselves in her next letter to Carrie DuPuy.

Cambridge, Feb. 8th, 1898

'Dear Carrie,

Perhaps you may be surprised to hear that on Saturday your aunt and Sir John Gorst on bicycles, accompanied by R. C. Jebb on his tricycle, went up the towing path as far as Baitsbite. . . .

'On Tuesday the Sidgwicks, the Bertie Russells,[2] (Miss Smith, daughter of Mrs. Pearsall Smith) and Lord Lytton came to dinner. Mrs. Bertie Russell[3] was here on Friday, and what another caller later said of her is quite true. She said she really was not at all clever, the cleverest thing she had done was marrying Bertie Russell, who, besides being Earl Russell's[4] brother, *is* extraordinarily able. The marriage strikes me as not being without risks. He is now only twenty-five and she is thirty-one. Very sweet and gracious, perhaps you saw her, and decidedly pretty; which qualities are better for winning with than for keeping the thing won. She rather bored me than not, on Friday. . . .'

In 1898 Cara's sister Ellen died and we have no more letters to relatives in America. But whenever she was away from Cambridge, she wrote to her niece, Maud Darwin.

[1] Oscar Browning, op. cit., p. 44.

[2] Bertrand Russell, b. 1872, now Lord Russell. Famous philosopher and mathematician.

[3] The first Mrs. Bertrand Russell was Alys, younger daughter of Mr. and Mrs. Pearsall Smith, American Quakers and Evangelical Revivalists. Her brother was Logan Pearsall Smith, author of *Trivia*, etc.

[4] This Earl Russell was famous because he was tried for bigamy in the House of Lords.

'My Dear Maud,

To begin at the beginning: humane precautions made us have a very decent crossing. It was certainly the case for an exhibition of chloral. The ship was bobbing up and down so much at Dover one could hardly get on board. But the chloral did not fail. I was not happy, but neither was I sick. A cup of coffee at Calais made me as fit as ever, and we rolled on comfortably to get our sleeping carriage at Paris.

'Dick's Parliamentary acquaintance as usual turned up. This time it was Sir William Walrond on his way to San Remo. I heard the usual talk going on in the passage of the sleeping carriage, showing good fellowship at small mental expense. "Will be a quiet session, probably." "Very indiscreet speech of Monson's." "What rot the French do put in their papers about the English." And so on, till they both thought the time had come to turn in.

'All the next day the sunshine and the sea were heavenly. Everybody welcomed us here, we had our old rooms, Dick ordered tea, and afterwards we settled down to unpack. The dinner was delightful, a change of cooking is part of the general beneficent change, and then I took my *Via Crucis*[1] to early bed, while Dick, tired as he was, went down to the evening concert. When his mind is free, he really loves music, and his education in it makes his enjoyment intelligent. Only two of our old friends have as yet arrived. One of them has lent me *Khartum*,[2] so you need not keep that book for me.

'I haven't played [gambling] at all yet, and don't feel inclined. I find it amusing to watch Mr. Dawson and as he generally loses a little every time I look on, I say "Better him than me". Then I stake in imagination and it doesn't come up, and I am pleased to think the solid coin remains in my pocket. You get more amusement out of the game by looking on, I find, than when you are in danger of losing at each stroke. I have found some one to play chess which I like much better.

[1] By Marion Crawford.
[2] *With Kitchener to Khartum* by George W. Steevens, London, 1899.

'My chief occupations here are reading, walking, playing chess. Dick considers the rest heavenly. No syndicates, no bores constantly dropping in on their own business (friends dropping in for a chat are a different thing), no work of any kind. He means to let his brain lie quite fallow for a month. Tomorrow we are going in to Nice to see if a tricycle is to be had, which does not propel itself. If he can hire one what delicious rides we shall have over these smooth roads.

'Dick is gently suggesting it is time for his walk. We walk by the clock for exactly an hour from twelve till one every day. Then we come in for luncheon. At two we proceed down to the concert and reading rooms. You ought to see the skirts, not a wave of fullness anywhere, but such round proportions as these French women show! No artificial tournures required. The dress is held tightly with one hand across the lower back to keep the slight train off the ground, and the sight is one for gods and men. I indulge a constant grin. . . .'

CHAPTER XVI

———————

By this time Jebb had accumulated quite a list of well-deserved honours. He had been given the Gold Cross of the Saviour by the King of Greece for his great work in interesting England in the appreciation of the study of ancient life in its bearing on the classics. In 1898 he had been made Honorary Professor of Ancient History at the Royal Academy of Arts, rendered vacant by the death of Gladstone. There were only four such honorary members at a time. He had been President of the Hellenic Society, which group he had helped to form. He was sought by innumerable groups to speak, debate, write poems, letters to royalty, insignias, and to help write the Latin inscriptions for current coins.

In 1897 he had declined a knighthood, for reasons of his own, but when he realized that friends thought the Cambridge representative should be distinguished by this honour, he accepted when it was offered to him again in 1900. Cara no doubt got great pleasure from being Lady Jebb.

Jebb was also a Trustee of the British Museum and was one of the founders of the British Academy for the Promotion of Historical, Philosophical and Philological Studies, which was granted a charter by King Edward in 1902.

In June, 1905, the King gave him the Order of Merit 'in recognition of the great services you have rendered to literature'. He was particularly pleased about this because he had had no hint of it beforehand. When he asked John Morley if he hadn't suggested his name to the King, he denied it and said on the contrary the King had mentioned Dick's name to him for this honour.

The next month Dick was invited to go to South Africa as

President of the Education Section of the British Association. Cara, dreading the sea voyage, stayed at home.

A 'Letter for Women' printed in a Natal newspaper, August 21st, 1905, said,

'We are all agog over the coming of the British Association. A literary and scientific treat indeed. May their visit be a veritable gulf stream of enthusiasm to warm and quicken the ocean of our dullness and ineptitude for all but the littlenesses of life! I know quite a number of the people coming, and only wish I could charter an hotel to take them all in. It is such an opportunity, and so many people are missing it with intent.

'But to return to the people I know: Sir Richard Jebb, one of the most finished Greek scholars of the day and a charming man. Unfortunately, his wife does not accompany him. She is quite the most beautiful and fascinating woman I ever knew. An American woman of culture and breeding is, to my mind, the queen of the sex. Mrs. Darwin is a niece of Lady Jebb's, and also very witty and charming. . . .' The rest of the clipping is cut off so that the author is unknown.

Dick wrote almost daily letters to Cara during this exhausting tour. One he ended by saying, 'It has all been pleasant and most interesting, but the pace! It has been very tiring; no rest from travelling and sightseeing; it would have killed you.'

Oscar Browning, who also went on this trip, said, 'The Governor was very hospitable, asked us to dinner and enquired about our plans. He said that we proposed to do far too much, and that to carry out our plans would kill some of us. This proved to be the case. At least two died and several others caught diseases which led to their death. In the long journey sketched for us, there were only two days rest. At other times we were working hard during the day and travelling at night.

'Our President was George Darwin, whose chief duty, besides giving the opening address, was to inaugurate the bridge over the Zambesi [at the Victoria Falls], a great and important work. Sir Richard Jebb's address was looked forward to more than anything else. . . .'[1] In fact it was so successful that Dick had to repeat it at Johannesburg.

[1] Oscar Browning, *Memories of Later Years*, 1923, p. 105.

When Dick finally returned home in October after a long delay at the Suez Canal, he was very ill, with a high fever, and soon took to his bed, too exhausted and ill even to tell Cara anything about the trip. She wrote in her diary:

'November, 1905.

'19, Sunday, 22nd after Trinity. Dick no better. Fever at night. Still it does not seem more than a feverish cold.

'21, Tuesday. Signs of pleurisy. Pain in side. Nurse Pearce came.

'22, Wednesday. Pain in side: Poultices: he said if it were not for me he would not care to live. . . .

'3, December. Ah, so ill, my darling. . . .

'5, Tuesday. So ill. Was operated on for abscess of liver on adjacent tissues. Successful. . . .

'7, Thursday. Hiccoughs all day long with very short breath. Alas, my dearest. . . .

'9, Saturday. My dearest and best passed quietly away at 2:45 p.m. The dignity of the end was remarkable. His mind the last to die. I sat with him the hour before. He did not speak but he has been singularly quiet through the whole illness. The nurse gave him a little milk at 1:45. . . . He was a long time taking the 2 oz. He held the glass himself, but I noticed it lay aslant in the fingers of his left hand, his right hand lost strength first.

'Suddenly as I sat by him these words rose into my consciousness. "This our brother is delivered from the miseries of this sinful world." I believe at that moment he became unconscious of discomfort. I ran out to call his brother and sister to pray. He was still breathing short, very short, gasps. Heneage said afterwards he had never seen such a dignified death. His head looked so noble and beautiful propped up on the pillow. There was no sign to any of us, only the quiet glazing of unseeing eyes. No agony of death. His going out was more peaceful than any falling to sleep. A great spirit fell back to God.

'All through the illness the dignity and reserve of the coming change seemed about him. He talked very little, wished not to be talked to almost from the first, would listen to no letters.

'10, Sunday. Tye, Heneage, and I had a peaceful sorrowful day together, talking of him.

'11, Monday. Letters, telegrams in masses. So honoured is my dead. I ought to be lifted out of selfish grief.

'12, Tuesday. They are planning a funeral for him such as has never been seen in Cambridge.

'13, Wednesday. Funeral. Sunshine through a veil of mist. We carried him, surrounded by representative pall-bearers, to his resting place by Adams and Luard. Ah, my dearest.'

Cara described the funeral in her *Life of R.C.J.* He 'was buried in St. Giles' Cemetery. . . . The funeral *cortège* met in Trinity College at 2:30 p.m., and the first part of the service was held in the chapel. . . . It was a most touching moment in the ceremony when, after the service in chapel, his body passed for the last time through the Great Gate of Trinity. A pause was made, while the choir sang the *Nunc Dimittis* and the Master and Fellows, ranged on each side of the long gate-way, seemed to bid a last good-bye from the great College to her son.'[1]

So once again Cara was left a widow, but this time she mourned her husband deeply and sincerely. Her friends and relatives tried to help her in her loneliness, but his place was never to be adequately filled. She kept a diary sporadically, and in March, 1906, entered in it, after a gap of twenty-three years:

'What eventful years have passed since this book was opened; years of success, years of ever increasing happiness together, years of growing fame for him. . . . Alas, alas, shall I ever see the beautiful south again, and not have all its brightness turned to dark because he is not there to share in appreciation of its beauty? I went to San Remo in the winter but could not look at the beauty of its mountains, its skies, its seas, without an aching of the heart. Never again could we delight in them together. I knew what he was to me but I did not guess how his shadow would come between me and the sun, would make all beauty of nature so full of sorrow for me.

'It is hard to believe that others feel as I feel, have the same heartache, the same loneliness. Their dear ones could not have had his variety, his lovableness, his sweetness, his boyish freshness of spirit, all intensified by the great mental powers which were his

[1] C. Jebb, op. cit., p. 425.

249

endowment. The pain of the loss *must* be in proportion to the value of the gift. Rare as were his intellectual gifts, his was a still finer, rarer nature. How delightful it was to have his morning greeting, always with something to say filled with quick perception. Never knew I such loyalty of soul to love, to duty.'

Cara had already set to work gathering the material for her husband's biography, and in October, 1907, the Cambridge University Press published '*The Life and Letters of Sir Richard Claverhouse Jebb, O.M., Litt.D.* by his wife, Caroline Jebb; with a Chapter on Sir Richard Jebb as scholar and critic by Dr. A. W. Verrall'. *The Times Literary Supplement* said that the book had been written 'with delicacy and discretion by Lady Jebb herself, who has once more triumphantly refuted the common opinion, as Mrs. Creighton, for example, had refuted it before her, that a man's life should never be written by one very near to him and least of all by his wife. It is true that Lady Jebb has left her husband very largely to depict himself in his intimate letters to members of his family and a few of his closest friends, in his still more intimate letters to herself, many written before their marriage and, as it appears, before their formal engagement; in his private diaries, and other memoranda, and partly at least, though sparingly, as was becoming in a man of Jebb's fastidious reserve, in some of his public utterances.

'But to do this with the delicacy and discretion we have indicated, to add the continuous yet slender thread of narrative which turns a mere collection of documents into an articulate biography, to indicate with admirable self-restraint and yet never unduly to disclose the perfect sympathy and affection which bound husband and wife together, all these achievements betoken a rare skill in the biographer and attest the verisimilitude of the portrait. . . .

'Jebb's real nature, as is abundantly shown in these familiar letters, was thoroughly human, deeply loving, intensely sympathetic, and eager for sympathy in return, playful, kindly, tender, genial, humorous, never bitter, though sometimes severe in his judgment. . . . His friends knew all this long ago. His mere acquaintances and the world at large never could have known it but for the happy inspiration which has induced Lady Jebb to tell it them. She has written the biography of her illustrious husband in his own spirit.

'Those who only knew him from his works will find much of the highest interest in this admirable biography. It is a worthy tribute to a great memory, and Lady Jebb, has, in writing it, displayed everywhere a remarkable discretion of judgment. There is no excess in it. The narrative is simple, clear and never over-burdened with useless matter, while above all there is never a word of ostentation or overpraise.'[1]

Cara again wrote in her diary, July 24th, 1908. 'Three years ago this week he left me to go to South Africa. From that visit he returned ill and suffering. I would give all the years of my life to come if only I could live those last weeks we were together once again. So many things I would have told him, such love and worship I would have shown him. Now he cannot see, he cannot feel or hear, though I spend my days in trying to reach him.'

[1] *The Times Literary Supplement*, Oct. 10th, 1907.

CHAPTER XVII

Cara found her solace in travel and spent many winters in Southern France, California and Washington, D.C., where her nieces Nellie and Carrie DuPuy lived. Each summer she would return to stay once more at Springfield to be near Maud[1] and her friends in Cambridge. But in 1917, her favourite niece, Nellie, at last persuaded her to come and live near her. Perhaps Cara had been finding life in war-time Cambridge difficult and drab. She later said that Springfield was altogether too big for only one person to live in. However it came about, she sold the lease of Springfield[2] and settled down permanently in Washington, whence she proceeded to write monthly letters to Maud.

The Brighton, Washington
Jan. 23rd, 1917

'My dear Maud,
Somebody ought to write to you this steamer and it seems to be me. Carrie has left her guest, Clara Atlee from Philadelphia, in our charge and apparently gone to bed. After impetuously showing her about Washington regardless of the lives of both, Carrie is completely prostrated, and cross! She makes even Clara laugh. Carrie has the art of being natural and therefore amusing in every mood. We should be often old and dull without her moods to make a sparkle.

'Well, social life goes on demanding. Mrs. Stanley Matthews, widow of celebrated Supreme Court Judge, gave a big luncheon for me yesterday. Such splendour! Gold plates, gold dishes, gold

[1] Sir George Darwin died in 1912.
[2] The freehold of the land on which Springfield was built belongs to Caius College.

forks, gold spoons, splendid *signed* pictures on the wall. A nice old thing. Calls you "Dearest, dearie, dearheart", anything dear that comes handy. "Now, dearie," she said, "don't you go when the others do. (24 of them) I want to take you to leave cards on some of the Supreme Court ladies." Very glad I was to go and get it done so comfortably. It was the day "at home" for the Court which made four about as many as we could do. Mrs. Holmes, Mrs. Lamar, Mrs. Lurton and Mrs. Hughes.

'I am to go with Mrs. Matthew to a huge dinner on Friday to meet the Japanese author of *Bushido*. A really remarkable man with a fat American wife. (If we aren't in the thick of things! Like the old woman who lost her petticoat, I wonder "Can this be I?" My light step has come back, I walk, I talk, I get tired, but not *that* tired. Rest comes with resting and off I start.)

'We lunched with the Harry Whites on Sunday. . . .'

Washington, Oct. 30th, 1917

'My dear Maud,

Today I am feeling the turn towards health, after a severe cold, and indeed last night had Nellie and Carrie here with Frances to play bridge with me. Carrie would keep saying how close it was. The lace curtains were blowing out into the room all the time and I was wrapped in furs! But she never seems able to get air enough. Still, her peculiarities are greatly modified and, when she can remember, she does try to spare Nellie in many ways.

'Also, on Sunday, I permitted myself to keep a luncheon engagement at Mrs. Shaler's. I wanted to meet Mr. Vanderlip who was to be there. He is the millionaire who is working for the government at a dollar a year. He gave $100,000. last year to the first loan and he has just given the same amount this year.

'It was amusing, rather, to have lost my way by a street, to stop to look at the number on a house just as a plainish looking man halted with the same purpose. He walked on and I followed him. "I believe that man is going to the Shaler's, too," was my inward comment. We were *both* late, which was sweet to me who hate to keep a party waiting. He strode so fast I could only pant after him reaching the front steps as he rang the bell. We stood together and I couldn't help telling him how glad I was to see

him, for the above reason. It was Mr. Vanderlip. He has promised
to come and see me (for we made friends at once) and to bring his
wife when she establishes herself here. . . .

'This climate makes my digestion much better. The sun floods
my rooms all day long. Louisa as "slavey" is doing splendidly.[1]
I am giving her American wages, $30. a month, and she is costing
me no more than the three did in Cambridge. She cooks what I
require very well, does out the flat and keeps it in beautiful order.
I wish you could see this apartment now. My carpets and pictures
and the pretty furniture I was able to collect make all the rooms
charming. . . .'

'My dear Maud,
 . . . I am very gay for me just now. I am going to luncheon at
the Spring-Rices[2] in an hour, and am having four ladies to tea
when I come back. Tonight is the invitation to hear the yearly
lecture at the Institution, to be followed by a conversazione and
ices. Tomorrow I am dining with Mrs. Biddle Porter and Saturday
is the Gillette-Hill daughter's marriage. Every day this week there
has been some engagement.

'I will keep this letter open and tell you whether the Embassy
luncheon was a success. The Duchess of Devonshire has been
staying there a fortnight, being in Washington to settle her
daughter into a house the latter's husband has taken. He is joining
the British Embassy here. I hope these great ones may be out at
this house to luncheon. I used to notice that the Duchess liked to
lead the conversation when talking to a Commoner. They are not
all good at it. I used to startle them by an amiable effort to put
them at their ease. The present Duke is in Canada. I met him once
at Willy Buckler's[3] at tea, but did not find him much better than
his uncle who was the wettest of blankets.

[1] Louisa was one of her maids she had brought over from Cambridge. She
later married and stayed in Washington.

[2] Sir Cecil Spring-Rice, 1859–1918. British Ambassador at Washington,
1913–18. He was also a poet, and a nephew of Iddie Butcher (Lady Monteagle)
of whom Cara wrote.

[3] William Hepburn Buckler, 1867–1952. American lawyer and archaeologist,
special agent at U.S. Embassy, London 1914–19. Educated partly at Cambridge,
married an English wife, lived latterly at Oxford.

'It made me laugh to read in Sunday's paper about Lady Salisbury. I can remember her holding out her hand to the announced guest and going on talking to someone she knew on the other side of her. The whole article is amusing, and is signed "Ex attaché".

'Stocks and all American investments are down, down, down, each day lower. Yours are probably the same.

'Later. It was very pleasant at the Embassy but not thrilling. The Ducal party not in evidence. Sir Cecil very nice but no more interested in me, or any of the others in fact, than if we were so many graven images. Lady Spring-Rice quiet and nice and very tired. The other guests were the Swedish Ambassador and Mrs. Mardvelt, Senator Lodge, Mr. Mitchell, a dramatist, a very superior man who had known Sir Cecil at Oxford, Lord Percy and another young attaché. I liked it enough, but suspect the feeling of "being done" pervaded us all a little too much.

'I am "at home" every other Sunday, and see many people, but I like my own Cambridge and my own old friends the best. I hardly realized how many friends I had grown fond of until I miss them here. And I haven't had a game of chess since you and I played together. I miss those late afternoon hours more than anything else. . . .'

Washington, Jan. 16th, 1918

'My dear Maud,

Your letters are always very interesting to me and you really are *very* nice in writing often. My eyes in this far away place turn towards Cambridge as a Jew's used to turn towards Jerusalem. . . .

'Caroline has gone off to New York for a week. She was one of my small trials for she would come in every day bringing a sort of hurricane with her. She wants to be kind, poor thing, and she doesn't know how the sick want to be quiet more than anything. But she really is very kind in offering to do things and having one on her mind. She forgets the things, but that doesn't matter. . . .

'I wonder if your Billy lost his books because he was with that lot who were bathing and breakfasting, never dreaming the Germans were near, when the General was surprised in his pyjamas! And the English lost more than half what General Byng had won. I actually cried when I read the account in our paper. No sentries, no outposts, Germans strolling towards them through the villages! It was bitter news to read.

'Of course nobody was censured. I am not sure somebody wasn't as usual given a peerage as a solution. General Byng ought to have been made Commander in Chief.'

Washington, April 15th, 1918

'My dear brother John,

... 'I went to the reception at the Corcoran Galleries for the Archbishop of York last week and quite enjoyed myself. I hadn't meant to go but when Admiral Capps and his wife came in the afternoon to call and he asked me to go with them, that made it a different proposition.

'Harry White, late Ambassador abroad whom I knew when I was in England, was chairman of the reception committee, and was as always very kind to me. After I had met the Archbishop, he asked me, "Now, what can I do for you? Would you like to be presented to Lord Reading?"[1] "Very much indeed," said I. Lord and Lady Reading were standing by one of the open doors. When my name was mentioned, Lord Reading said, "You bear an honoured name." Wasn't it nice of him? ...'

Washington, Nov. 21st, 1918

'My dear Maud,

Your last of November first was whisked away by Nellie before I had time to read and inwardly digest its contents. You made some remark indicating surprise that Wilson had appealed to his known supporters to send back Congressmen to work with him instead of against him. You would not wonder if you knew the bitterness of feeling against him shown by Roosevelt, Taft, Lodge and their like. They are in terror lest the people should elect him for a third term. Everything he has said or done has met with their criticism. He wants to finish the work he has done thus far so successfully and a President's work can be so terribly hampered by a Congress that wants him to fail.

[1] Lord Reading had succeeded Sir Cecil Spring-Rice as British Ambassador early in 1918.

'Roosevelt is beyond bearing. "E'en though beaten, he can argue still." He ignores all he said about the corruption of the leaders of his own party and cares not a jot how much they steal and bribe if only he can hinder Wilson.

'Some of the English Embassy here interest me. Two have told me that Wilson made a great mistake in intimating that he would make no terms with the Kaiser. "We don't know who to deal with," said Mrs. Seymour a week ago. "There wouldn't for instance have been this trouble about the Navy." But I said, "In Mr. Wilson's view the Kaiser is a criminal without truth or honour." "Oh, they all are the same in Germany. The people go with the Kaiser in everything." "Well," I said, "we know the Kaiser's 'scrap of paper' theory about treaties. Why not give the Reichstag a chance?"

'Today's paper says that the ships are all quietly sailing into Harwich, that the submarines to the number of twenty have been taken over by England, with more to follow, that the Americans are marching into Germany to occupy the Rhine forts, that they find no signs of "making desolate" by the German Army as it retreats. Everything is being honourably done on the battlefront. What better could the Emperor have done?

'The truth is Europe does not quite like the President's belief in the people, except France. She does. The English say "Government of the people, by the people, for the people" is a fine phrase, but they don't really want it. The class that has it now wish to continue class government.

'And really the earth was made for the human race to stand on. There seems something to be said against one man fencing in a hundred thousand acres and taking toll from everything produced on it. People can't go to another planet. They must accept terms they vaguely think unjust. When the crofters got too crowded up north, Arthur Balfour would not allow the younger portion to stay with their people. He *made* them emigrate. Now transportation used to be the punishment of criminals. I dare say it was good for them to go, but what if the earth had been too full everywhere?

'But my thoughts are running away with me, and boring you. I never did think leasing land an equitable principal. But mind, I am an individualist, not a socialist all the same.

'Now for personal news. There isn't any. I told you about Sir Henry Babington Smith in my last letter.[1] He is a real dear, kind and affectionate in his heart towards old friends. But he can't talk. Carrie and I went to luncheon with him, and it was uphill work. . . .'

'My dear Maud,   *Washington, Dec., 1918*

Your last letter wasn't marked "censor" but it was just as long in coming. You were as jubilant over the peace as we were here. A letter came from Sir Charles [Walpole] by the same post, wild with rejoicing. I can hardly realize it yet, but oh, won't the world be a delightful place without war? Yesterday was "British Day" in Washington and all the churches had good preachers and fine music and speeches and tableaux to celebrate with. . . . Louisa made us English badges of "Union Jack" pattern which we wore to show we loved England.

'I have been playing a hard game of chess with a young Mr. MacNeil from four to seven this afternoon and am in consequence almost too tired to write. I tried the King's Bishop opening and *won*! But only think of three hours to one game. Of course he wanted to come again. . . .

'It seems there is going to be great trouble before the nations settle down. Our paper is full of revolutions, present and to come, and endless bickerings about divisions and boundary lines. The Greeks want Constantinople! Very bold of them in my opinion. I think Roumania ought to get it if anyone should. It delights me that Serbia is to have Bosnia, Herzegovina, Montenegro and still more. What an awful collapse it is for Austria and Germany. Who could have imagined it?

'Do you know Napoleon's definition of a great man? He is praised, he is blamed, he does not care; he keeps going the way he set for himself. Foch and Pétain seem to me the *great* Generals of the War. I wonder what history will say. Haig twice had a gap made in his lines by want of coordination. Once the gap was eleven miles. General Townsend and General Allenby are big men,

[1] Sir Henry Babington Smith, 1863-1923. Trinity, 1882. Member of Financial Mission to U.S.A., 1915. Director of Bank of England. When at Cambridge he had been a friend and tennis partner of Cara and her nieces.

both. I hope I shall live long enough to read the history of the war as told without prejudice by some good writer. Germany had to yield to a greater commander than it was able to produce. Ludendorf was inferior in military maneuvers to Foch; and Pétain beat Folkenheim at Verdun.'

In April, 1919 she wrote to her brother-in-law, Will Spencer, 'She who writes to you has just set up a car of her own, and very pleased she is with it; and if she can learn to drive and keep off the curb, very pleased she will be with herself. Louisa at present is chauffeur in addition to her other duties. . . .'

Unfortunately Cara, at eighty, was unable to learn to drive. Nellie suddenly became seriously ill of sleeping sickness.

'My dear Maud,   *Washington, Oct. 18th, 1920*
. . . Nellie has had no pain for the last two days, nor is she in pain now. I think she will die tonight, go out into the great unknown. I cannot tell you what a difference her going first will make to me. I try to think of *her*. She need not fear. Hers was a stainless soul, a fine sweet nature. All of us loved and valued her. Never a cross word passed between her and me. . . .'

'My dearest niece [Maud]   *Washington, Nov. 15th, 1920*
(For that you are, now that Nellie is gone.) Carrie says she means to go on living here. . . . She is very much chastened but will always be unreasonable from our point of view. But behind her queerness, which she can't really help, being born with it, she is really a fine creature, generous and anxious to be kind. I think the praise that comes for Nellie from every quarter rather surprises her. She never saw how really able as well as sweet and gracious to everyone Nellie was. . . .'

'My dear Maud,   *Washington, Jan., 1921*
. . . You know, I think the League [of Nations] the craziest proposition man ever made, human nature being such as it is, even divine nature, for the matter of that. Wasn't there war

among the angles, and didn't Lucifer, son of the morning, fall almost as badly as our Wilson did?

'Yet, when a clergyman calling here with his wife, mentioned he had just seen the *poor old paralytic* out driving, it made me very angry. Physical weakness no man can help. It oughtn't to be made a slur. I shan't like that man though he does tell good stories. I do like his wife and I wish he weren't always there on her days at home, and didn't always talk to me! . . .'

Washington, Feb. 21st, 1921

'My dear Maud,

No matter whether you send short or long letters I always like to hear from you. It keeps me in touch with your life and with Cambridge which is more to me than any other home.

'Your list of books is always useful. I have already read two books you mentioned long ago. Miss Sedgely lent me *Mirrors from Downing Street* which gave a new opinion of some of my friends. Ever since that sensational message Arthur Balfour sent to *The Times* when the first news of the Battle of Jutland came in, I have been wondering if he is overestimated by his friends and brother politicians. Lately even his suavity seems to have failed him. For instance, when he told the meeting of the League Council at Geneva (?) that no matter what the majority settled, neither England nor France would pay the least attention to it. It is interesting to see what the writer says in the Mirror about him.

'Margot Asquith's book in two volumes Herbert DuPuy sent to me at Christmas. I am a useful circulating library about it, too. I have *no* room for more books, here, but shall try again to get *The Road from Endor* and your other recommendations. . . .

'Caroline is establishing herself slowly in her home, and I think will be content to live here. . . . She has given up her mission of being my good angel since I wrote, in answer to one of her enquiries about my state of health, "that my only fear now was that I might be the last survivor of my family".

'I am to go to a little luncheon party at which Lady Geddes will be the only other guest on Wednesday at Miss Litchfield's. I like that. You never get to know anybody when you go to his or her reception. Lady Geddes is really the nicest of women, pretty, kindly, forthcoming and fond of people. I shall ask her to my very next luncheon. . . . Last week I met Mrs. Marshal, wife of the Vice President, the very simplest and nicest of women. I wish she were not going away for we took to each other at once. So you see this ancient being has almost more society than is good for her! . . .'

'My dear Maud,   *Washington, Dec. 6th, 1921*

I went to Lady Geddes' big reception last week and my head is still in a whirl. I was introduced to Admiral Lord Beatty, to our Secretary of State Mr. Hughes, a splendid intellect, but one had no chance for a real talk with anyone.

'The pleasantest incident of the evening came first. After Lady Geddes and Sir Auckland[1] shook hands with me, a little in the rear at their side loomed up the tall figure of Arthur Balfour. He knew me at once and threw up his hands and head in astonished welcome and I held up mine in real surprise. He has, as you know, a most charming manner. Somebody impelled me on so one could only say a few words. He just got in, "How well you are looking," and my answer, "It is all from this climate," when the line parted us. . . .

'Mrs. Wetmore introduced me with a flourish to Prince —— of Japan, a solemn young man who may have expected me to go down on my knees, or bow with deep reverence before him; anyway he was very silent. . . .

'Who do you think I had a very nice letter from last week? Sir George Trevelyan! He was impelled to write to me because he had just been reading over again Dick's *Bentley*. The letter was really charming. . . .'

The last sheet has been preserved of this letter. In it he tells of a correspondence he had had with Mrs. Montagu Butler.[2] He wrote:

'. . . I was reminded of that delightful dinner-party at the Installation of Lord Rayleigh as Chancellor, when she did me the

[1] Sir Auckland Geddes, K.C.B., 1879–1954. British Ambassador to U.S.A., 1920–4.

[2] Mrs. Butler (Agnata Ramsay), a famous classical scholar and wife of the Master of Trinity.

kindness of sending me down with you. In her reply she told me a little story which I venture to tell you. "You would be amused to know," she writes, "that when we were considering a name for our Jim in 1889, Montagu suggested 'Richard' as a good scholarly name, associated with Bentley, Porson and Jebb."

'My wife sends you her love and a wish that we were nearer to each other.

'Ever yours, dear Lady Jebb,

GEORGE OTTO TREVELYAN'

In the spring of 1924, Carrie DuPuy died of cancer, quite suddenly.

Washington, May 14th, 1924

'My dear Maud,

. . . I saw a great deal of Carrie after she came back to put her house in running order. We became great friends. She seemed very well at first and to improve in beauty from day to day. . . . But she complained of pains, and Herbert told Mary Spencer to bring her on to New York in case an operation was required. . . . She gradually sank on Sunday morning. She knew that she was dying and was glad to go.

'It is strange that she and Nellie should go so prematurely [both aged 53], as if their mother had not given them the stamina you and Mary inherited, as if her own strength was wearing out. She had greatly sweetened in character this last year and was always loving to me. I miss her very much. . . .

'I seem not to care to live here any longer. You know I came here partly to be with Nellie and because my big house seemed to be so empty when I lost Dick. I thought I should get over this with the passage of time, but when Nellie asked me to come, I had a longing to make a complete change, though I hated leaving you. Now Carrie has gone, too, I feel I have had enough of Washington. . . .

'With dearest love to all. . . .'

And so Cara moved again, this time to live in Erie, Pennsylvania, with her niece, Mary Spencer, who looked after her devotedly to the end. Gradually she lost touch with the outer world, although never losing her gracious manner and smile. She died on July 11th, 1930, at the age of ninety. In her will she left directions that her body should be cremated and the ashes sent to Cambridge, to be buried under Richard's tombstone in St. Giles' Cemetery where they lie today.

The Times letter from a Cambridge friend, parts of which were mentioned at the beginning of this book, is given below. One feels no better epitaph could be written.

'Many who would have grieved deeply at the news of Lady Jebb's death (recorded in *The Times* earlier this month) are now no longer here to describe, as they would have done, a most brilliant and remarkable personality. Yet not a few remain on whom she made an ineffaceable impression. . . .

'To that strange Cambridge of the Seventies, about which a book has been written, still without telling all,[1] Mrs. Slemmer, as she then was, a young and most beautiful American widow, came on a visit. Cambridge was at that time a semi-monastic society, but it did not need this contributory circumstance for the future Lady Jebb to send a thrill through the social atmosphere. It was not only that she possessed a Titianesque beauty of eyes, dark auburn hair, and rich colouring, but there was colour also and beauty in the tones of the voice which reminded one of Ellen Terry.

'Soon followed her marriage to the distinguished and fastidious Greek scholar who ultimately became Professor Sir Richard Jebb, and Lady Jebb for many years reigned as a beloved queen of a delightful society, of which the Balfour, Butcher and Darwin brothers, together with their sisters, were members. Lady Jebb had not only beauty but a fine mental equipment; and her literary capacity showed itself when she came to write the memoir of her husband. Perhaps what was chiefly remarkable about her was her unusual vitality, a vitality of the mind as well as of the body. She was immensely interested in life, whether it was the life of nations and the achievements of statesmen, or the personal fortunes of her

[1] This may be the last article in *The Eighteen Seventies* by Harley Granville-Barker, Cambridge University Press, 1929, called 'Cambridge in the 'Seventies', by W. E. Heitland.

own friends, their hopes or disappointments, the mysteries of their successes or failures.

'As a hostess she radiated life and happiness. In her company the quick-witted appeared even more mentally agile; and the dull could convince themselves that when properly handled and appreciated they shone as brightly as the best. Her kindliness and warmth fused even the most refractory human elements into geniality. Some of us, young in those days, when we spoke about the American woman, thought always of Lady Jebb, and, springing in thought from the particular to the general, we declared the American woman to be incomparable.'

INDEX

Tyng, Dr. Stephen H., 178

Vanderbilt, Com. Cornelius, 62, 130
Vanderbilt, Frank (Mrs. Cornelius), 62
Vanderbilt, Sophia (Mrs. Cornelius), 62
Vanderlip, Mr., 253-4
Vantz, Mr. (found Slemmer's medal), 102
Veitch, Prof. John, 105, 200, 221
Veitch, Mrs. John, 200
Verrall, Dr. A. W., 250
Via Crucis, 244
Vicksburg, 48
Victoria, Queen, 74, 130, 132, 237
Vogdes, Capt., 42

Walpole, Mrs., of Cambridge, 99
Walpole, (Sir) Charles, 69, 72, 150, 258
Walpole, Spencer, 150
Walpole, Mrs. Spencer, 150
Walrond, Sir William, 244
Waring, Charlotte, 142
Warrington, Mrs., of Pensacola, 30, 32
Warrington, Fla., 21, 31, 34
Washburn, The Hon. Mr., 58
Waterhouse, Alfred, 215
Waterhouse, Mrs. Alfred, 215

Watson, Miss, 169
Welles, Mr. (artist), 72
Wellington, Mr., of Ireland, 98
Wesley, John, 60, 61n
West Point Military Academy, 18, 50
Wetmore, Mrs., of Washington, D.C., 261
Whistler, James A. McNeill, 168
White, Prof., of Harvard, 202
White, Harry (Ambassador), 253, 256
White, Mrs. Harry, 238, 253
Whitehead, Alfred North, 103-4, 104n
Wilcox, Richard, 42
Wilhelmina, Queen of Holland, 241
Williams (Confederate soldier), 43
Williams, Neville, 216
Williamson, R. P. G., 105
Wilson, John (*pseud.* Christopher North), 131, 138
Wilson, Pres. Woodrow, 256-7, 260
Winder, Capt. (Col., Brevet-Maj.) John H., 24, 24n-25n, 25, 26, 37
Woolf, Virginia, 230n
Worden, Lt., 24
Wordsworth, William, 105
Wright, Miss, of Ireland, 96
Wright, Walter, 52, 88-9
Wyandotte (ship), 35, 40, 41n
Wyman, Belle, 20-1
Wyman, Lt. Powell, 20-1